SNOWPIERCER

1: THE ESCAPE

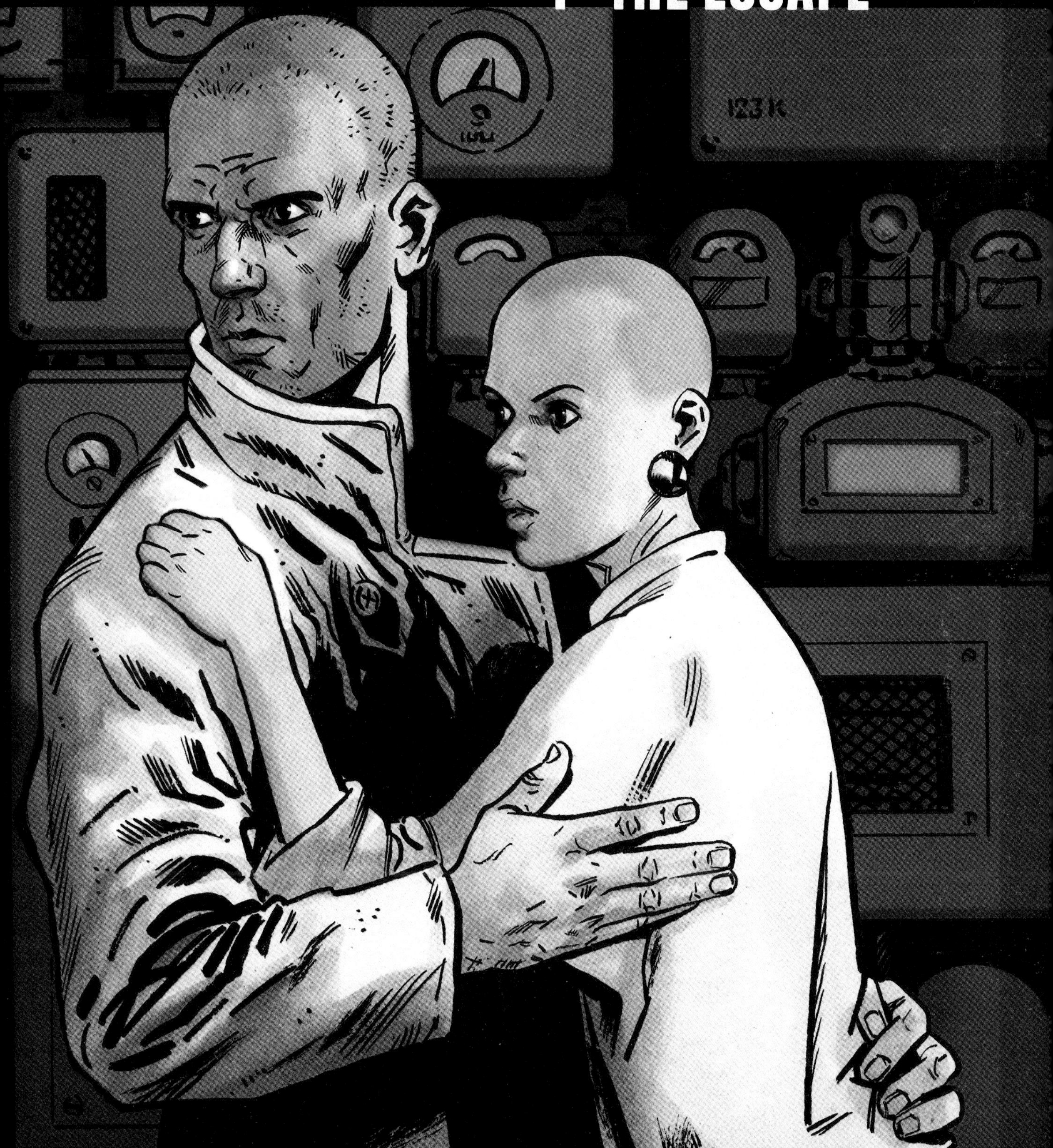
123 K

LOB / ROCHETTE

SNOWPIERCER

1: THE ESCAPE

WRITTEN BY

JACQUES LOB

ART BY

JEAN-MARC ROCHETTE

TRANSLATED BY

VIRGINIE SELAVY

LETTERING BY

GABRIELA HOUSTON

What did you think of this book?
We love to hear from our readers.
Please email us at: **readercomments@titanemail.com,**
or write to us at the address opposite.

To receive news, competitions, and exclusive offers online,
please sign up for the Titan Comics newsletter on our website:
www.titan-comics.com

Follow us on Twitter **@ComicsTitan**

Visit us at **facebook.com/comicstitan**

TitanCOMICS

Collection Editor
Gabriela Houston

Collection Designer
Sara Greasley

Senior Editor
Steve White

Titan Comics Editorial
Andrew James, Tom Williams

Production Supervisor
Jackie Flook

Production Assistant
Peter James

Art Director
Oz Browne

Studio Manager
Selina Juneja

Circulation Manager
Steve Tothill

Marketing Manager
Ricky Claydon

Senior Marketing and Press Executive
Owen Johnson

Publishing Manager
Darryl Tothill

Publishing Director
Chris Teather

Operations Director
Leigh Baulch

Executive Director
Vivian Cheung

Publisher
Nick Landau

SNOWPIERCER VOLUME 1: THE ESCAPE

ISBN: 9781782761433

Published by Titan Comics
A division of Titan Publishing Group Ltd.
144 Southwark St.
London
SE1 0UP

Transperceneige / Snowpiercer and all contents are trademark™
and copyright © 2013 Casterman.

A CIP catalogue record for this title is available
from the British Library.

First published in hardcover: February 2014
This sofcover edition: June 2014

Originally published in 1984 by
Casterman, France as *Transperceneige*,
and reissued as *Transperceneige: L'Échappé* in 1999.

10 9 8 7 6 5 4 3 2 1

Printed in The United States.
Titan Comics. TC0172

ACROSS THE WHITE IMMENSITY OF AN ETERNAL WINTER, FROM ONE END OF THE FROZEN PLANET TO THE OTHER, THERE TRAVELS A TRAIN THAT NEVER STOPS.

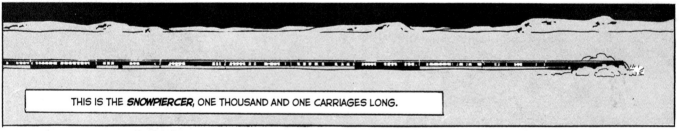

THIS IS THE **SNOWPIERCER**, ONE THOUSAND AND ONE CARRIAGES LONG.

YOU LOUSY **TAIL-FUCKER!** I'M GONNA BREAK YOU!!!

OUCH...

THIS IS THE LAST BASTION OF CIVILIZATION...

YOU'RE GONNA REGRET LEAVING YOUR SHITTY CARRIAGE!

TBAP

HEY, **EASY!** BETTER NOT MESS HIM UP TOO MUCH BEFORE THE CHIEF SEES HIM...

WHAT'S GOING ON? THE FUCK'S ALL THIS RACKET ABOUT?

WE CAUGHT A TAIL-FUCKER TRYING TO GET THROUGH, LIEUTENANT!

WHAT ABOUT THIS ONE, LIEUTENANT?

LOCK HIM UP AND MAKE SURE HE DOESN'T ESCAPE. I'LL INTERROGATE HIM TOMORROW.

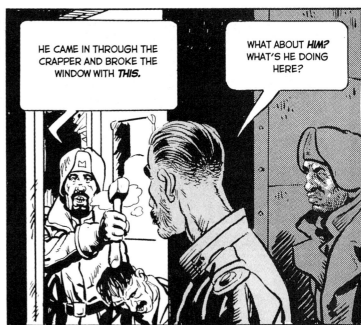

HE CAME IN THROUGH THE CRAPPER AND BROKE THE WINDOW WITH *THIS.*

WHAT ABOUT *HIM?* WHAT'S HE DOING HERE?

THAT'S *POITRINAUD*, SIR. HE WAS THERE WHEN THE GUY BURST IN -- MUST HAVE GOT KNOCKED OUT. I HEARD THE NOISE. GOOD THING THE DOOR WASN'T LOCKED.

SO WHY'S HE STILL HERE? YOU WAITING FOR HIS BOLLOCKS TO FREEZE?

OBVIOUSLY, NO ONE IS ALLOWED TO USE THIS... *CONVENIENCE* UNTIL FURTHER NOTICE. WE'LL HAVE TO REPLACE THE WINDOW QUICKLY...

AND STAY *VIGILANT.* THIS SHOULD BE A TIMELY REMINDER TO YOU ALL -- REMAIN WATCHFUL. KEEP YOUR EYES OPEN.

YES, LIEUTENANT, SIR!

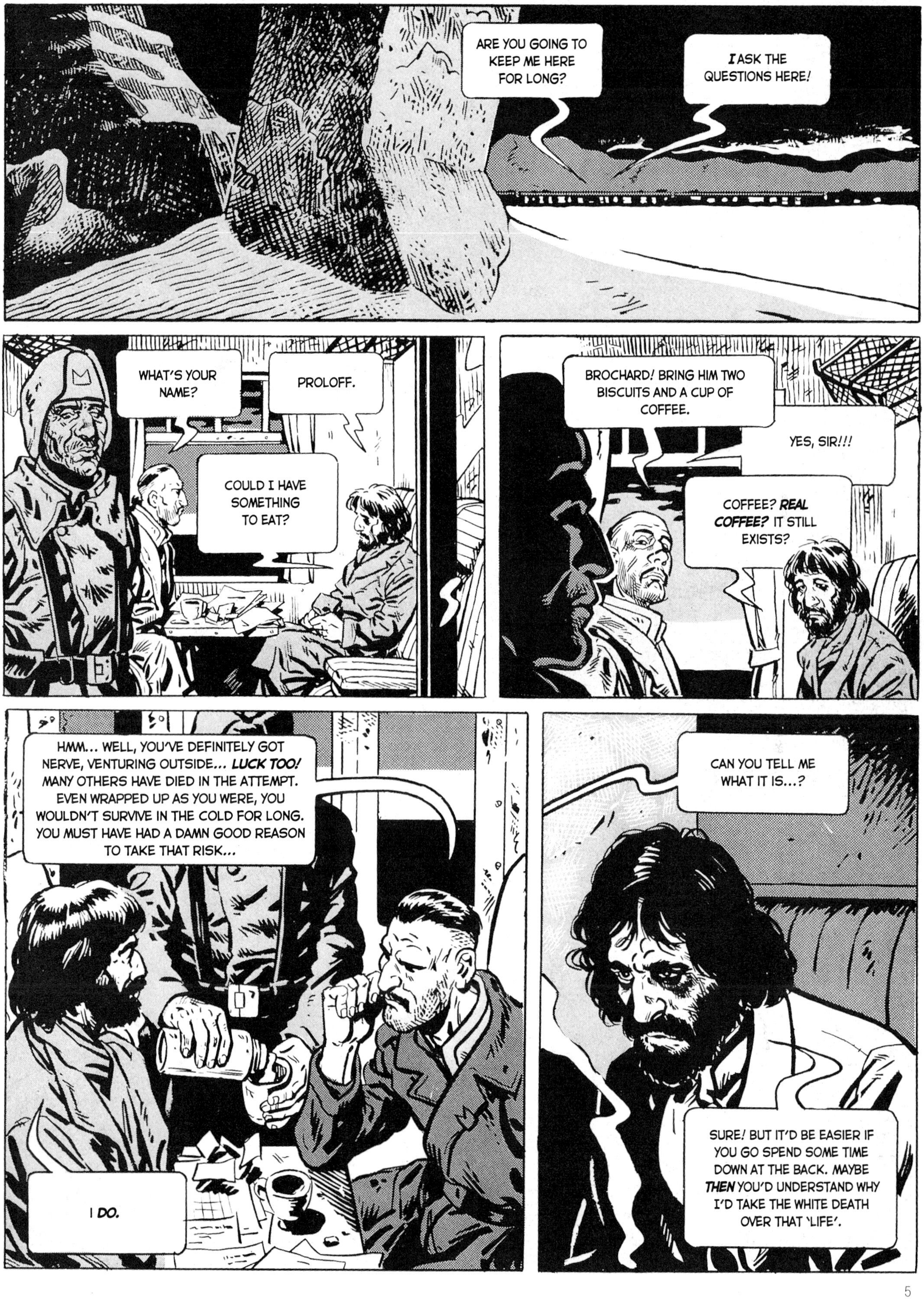
ARE YOU GOING TO KEEP ME HERE FOR LONG?
I ASK THE QUESTIONS HERE!
WHAT'S YOUR NAME?
PROLOFF.
COULD I HAVE SOMETHING TO EAT?
BROCHARD! BRING HIM TWO BISCUITS AND A CUP OF COFFEE.
YES, SIR!!!
COFFEE? REAL COFFEE? IT STILL EXISTS?
HMM... WELL, YOU'VE DEFINITELY GOT NERVE, VENTURING OUTSIDE... LUCK TOO! MANY OTHERS HAVE DIED IN THE ATTEMPT. EVEN WRAPPED UP AS YOU WERE, YOU WOULDN'T SURVIVE IN THE COLD FOR LONG. YOU MUST HAVE HAD A DAMN GOOD REASON TO TAKE THAT RISK...
I DO.
CAN YOU TELL ME WHAT IT IS...?
SURE! BUT IT'D BE EASIER IF YOU GO SPEND SOME TIME DOWN AT THE BACK. MAYBE THEN YOU'D UNDERSTAND WHY I'D TAKE THE WHITE DEATH OVER THAT 'LIFE'.

YES, COLONEL -- HE SEEMS SINCERE. HE APPEARS TO HAVE ACTED ALONE, ON HIS OWN INITIATIVE, NOT AS PART OF ANY PLANNED OPERATION.

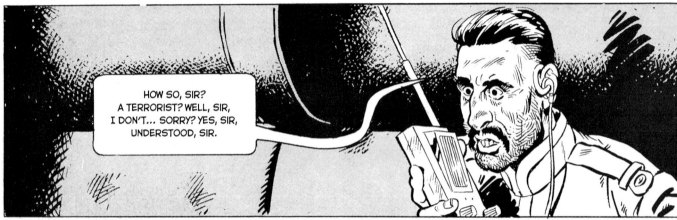

HOW SO, SIR? A TERRORIST? WELL, SIR, I DON'T... SORRY? YES, SIR, UNDERSTOOD, SIR.

KEEP YOUR HANDS ON YOUR HIPS AND YOUR CHEST BENT. CHIN UP, LEGS SPREAD WIDE!

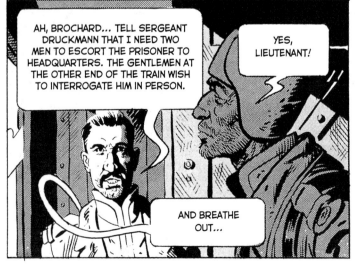

AH, BROCHARD... TELL SERGEANT DRUCKMANN THAT I NEED TWO MEN TO ESCORT THE PRISONER TO HEADQUARTERS. THE GENTLEMEN AT THE OTHER END OF THE TRAIN WISH TO INTERROGATE HIM IN PERSON.

YES, LIEUTENANT!

AND BREATHE OUT...

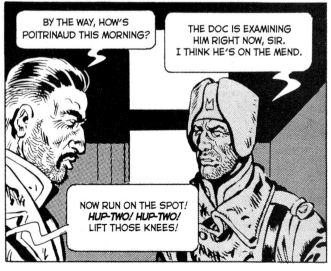

BY THE WAY, HOW'S POITRINAUD THIS MORNING?

THE DOC IS EXAMINING HIM RIGHT NOW, SIR. I THINK HE'S ON THE MEND.

NOW RUN ON THE SPOT! *HUP-TWO! HUP-TWO!* LIFT THOSE KNEES!

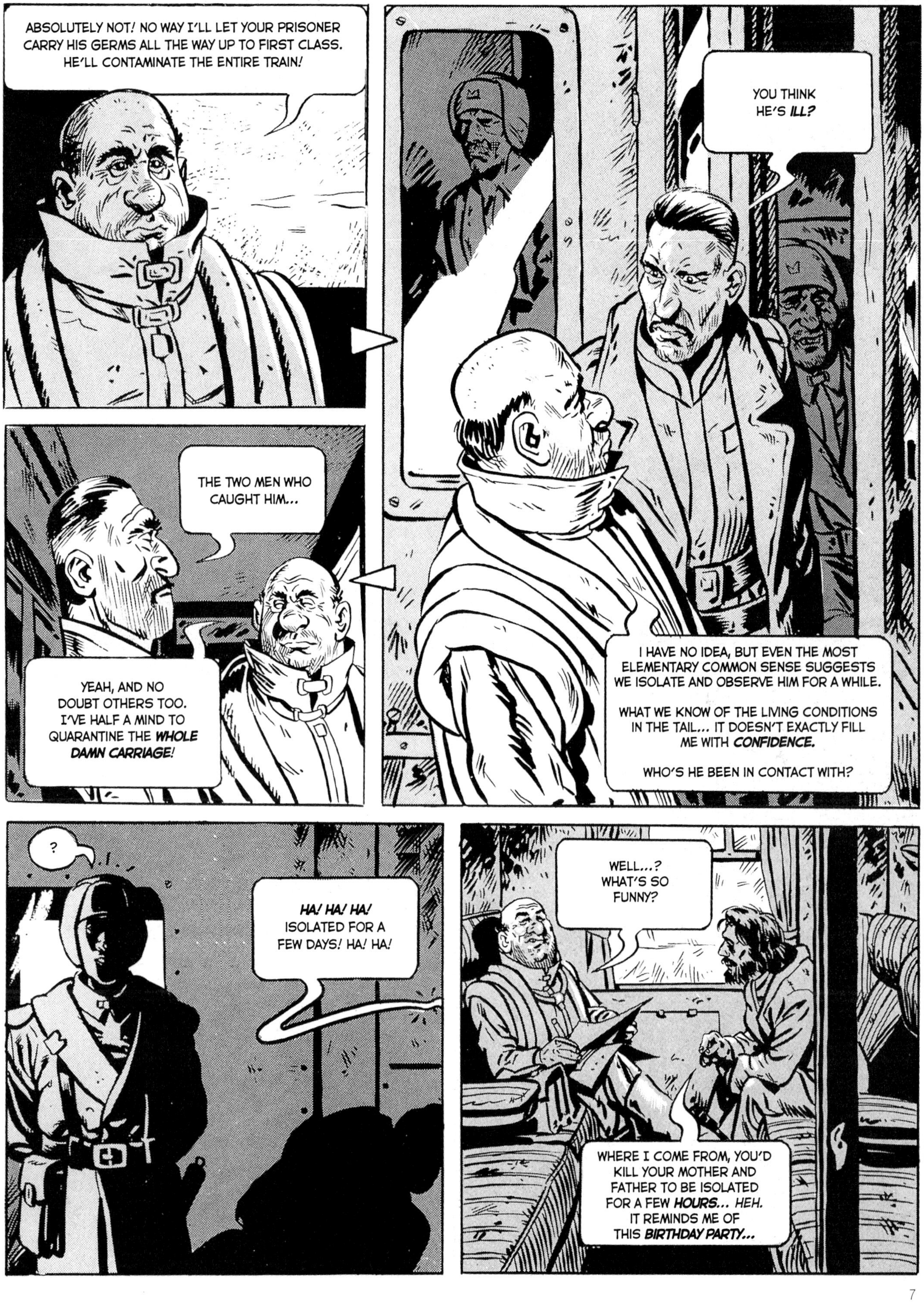
ABSOLUTELY NOT! NO WAY I'LL LET YOUR PRISONER CARRY HIS GERMS ALL THE WAY UP TO FIRST CLASS. HE'LL CONTAMINATE THE ENTIRE TRAIN!
YOU THINK HE'S ILL?
THE TWO MEN WHO CAUGHT HIM...
YEAH, AND NO DOUBT OTHERS TOO. I'VE HALF A MIND TO QUARANTINE THE WHOLE DAMN CARRIAGE!
I HAVE NO IDEA, BUT EVEN THE MOST ELEMENTARY COMMON SENSE SUGGESTS WE ISOLATE AND OBSERVE HIM FOR A WHILE.
WHAT WE KNOW OF THE LIVING CONDITIONS IN THE TAIL... IT DOESN'T EXACTLY FILL ME WITH CONFIDENCE.
WHO'S HE BEEN IN CONTACT WITH?
?
HA! HA! HA! ISOLATED FOR A FEW DAYS! HA! HA!
WELL...? WHAT'S SO FUNNY?
WHERE I COME FROM, YOU'D KILL YOUR MOTHER AND FATHER TO BE ISOLATED FOR A FEW HOURS... HEH. IT REMINDS ME OF THIS BIRTHDAY PARTY...

A BIRTHDAY PARTY?

IT WAS IN THE TAIL, BACK WHEN WE WERE STILL TRYING TO MAKE OUR LIVES MORE OR LESS BEARABLE...

DON'T GET ME WRONG, IT WASN'T *FUN.* THAT CONSTANT, STIFLING PROXIMITY TO EVERYONE ELSE: WHATEVER YOU DID, WHEREVER YOU WENT...

IN MY CARRIAGE, THERE WAS THIS LITTLE OLD MAN, SWEET AND QUIET. EVERYBODY LOVED HIM. ONE DAY, SOMEONE DECIDED TO CELEBRATE HIS BIRTHDAY...

HEY, GRANDDAD, WHAT KIND OF PRESENT WOULD REALLY MAKE YOU HAPPY?

WHAT WOULD MAKE ME *HAPPY?*

YES, WHAT WOULD YOU LIKE?

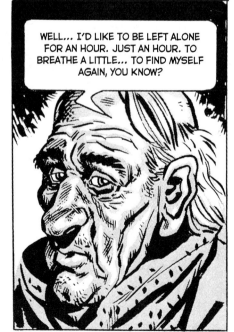

WELL... I'D LIKE TO BE LEFT ALONE FOR AN HOUR. JUST AN HOUR. TO BREATHE A LITTLE... TO FIND MYSELF AGAIN, YOU KNOW?

AN HOUR OF SOLITUDE! A BLISSFUL SIXTY MINUTES!

IT WASN'T EASY TO CONVINCE EVERYBODY TO LEAVE THE CARRIAGE, EVEN FOR AN HOUR -- EVEN HARDER TO GET THE NEIGHBOURING CARRIAGES TO TAKE US, EVEN TEMPORARILY...

FINALLY, IT WAS ALL SORTED OUT. WHILE WE WERE WAITING, I TRIED TO IMAGINE THE LITTLE OLD MAN IN THE BIG CARRIAGE HE HAD ALL TO HIMSELF...

MAYBE HE'S JERKING OFF?

HA! HA!

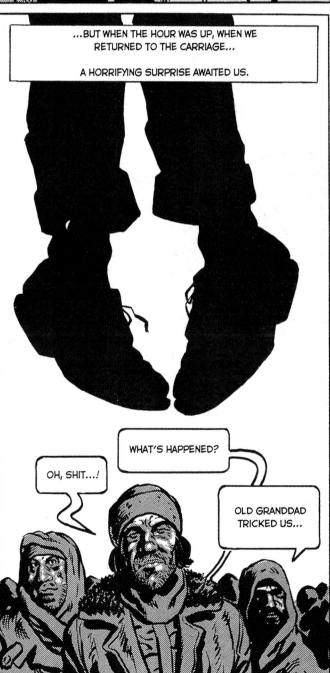

...BUT WHEN THE HOUR WAS UP, WHEN WE RETURNED TO THE CARRIAGE...

A HORRIFYING SURPRISE AWAITED US.

WHAT'S HAPPENED?

OH, SHIT...!

OLD GRANDDAD TRICKED US...

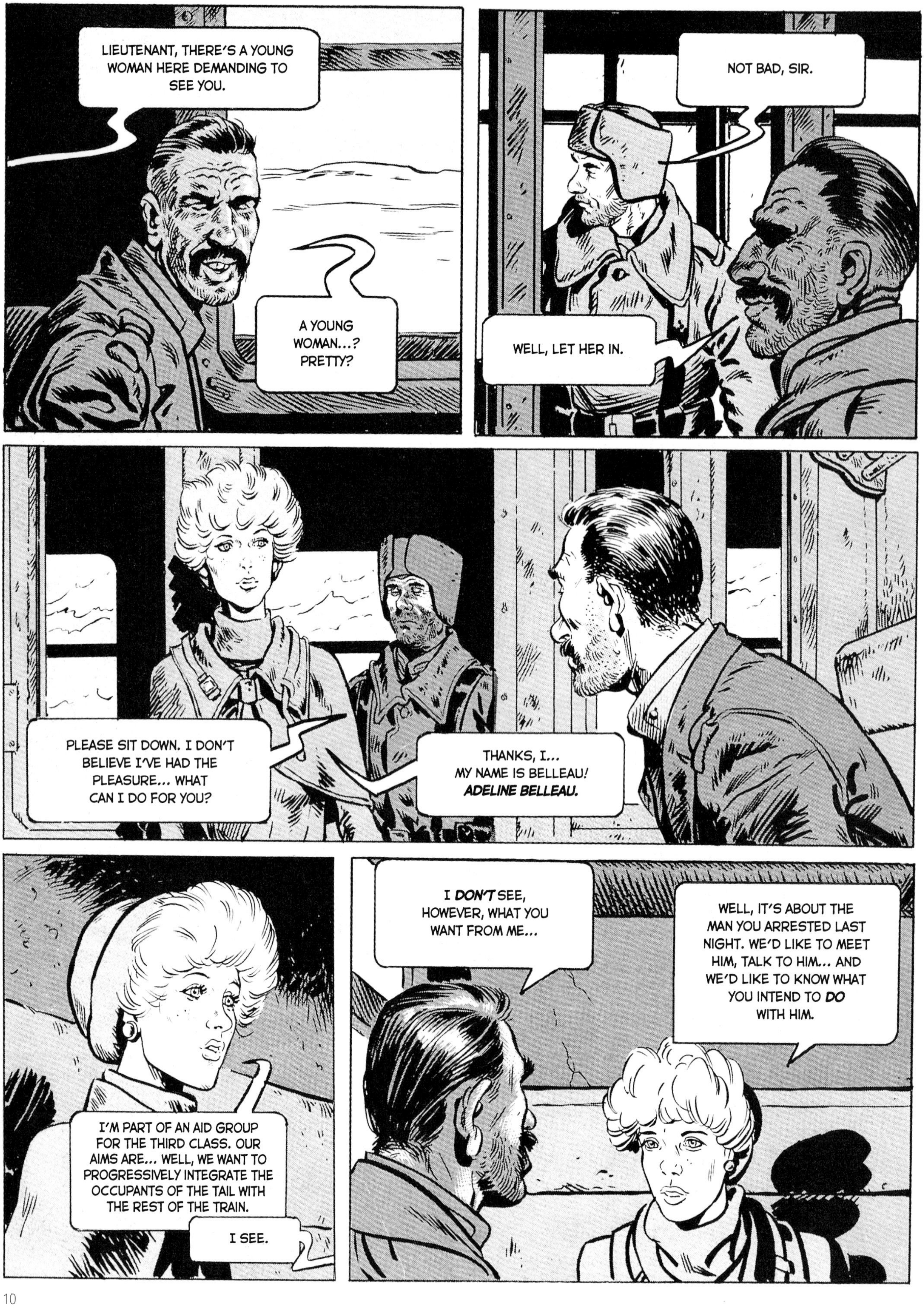
LIEUTENANT, THERE'S A YOUNG WOMAN HERE DEMANDING TO SEE YOU.
A YOUNG WOMAN...? PRETTY?
NOT BAD, SIR.
WELL, LET HER IN.
PLEASE SIT DOWN. I DON'T BELIEVE I'VE HAD THE PLEASURE... WHAT CAN I DO FOR YOU?
THANKS, I... MY NAME IS BELLEAU! ***ADELINE BELLEAU.***
I'M PART OF AN AID GROUP FOR THE THIRD CLASS. OUR AIMS ARE... WELL, WE WANT TO PROGRESSIVELY INTEGRATE THE OCCUPANTS OF THE TAIL WITH THE REST OF THE TRAIN.
I SEE.
I ***DON'T*** SEE, HOWEVER, WHAT YOU WANT FROM ME...
WELL, IT'S ABOUT THE MAN YOU ARRESTED LAST NIGHT. WE'D LIKE TO MEET HIM, TALK TO HIM... AND WE'D LIKE TO KNOW WHAT YOU INTEND TO ***DO*** WITH HIM.

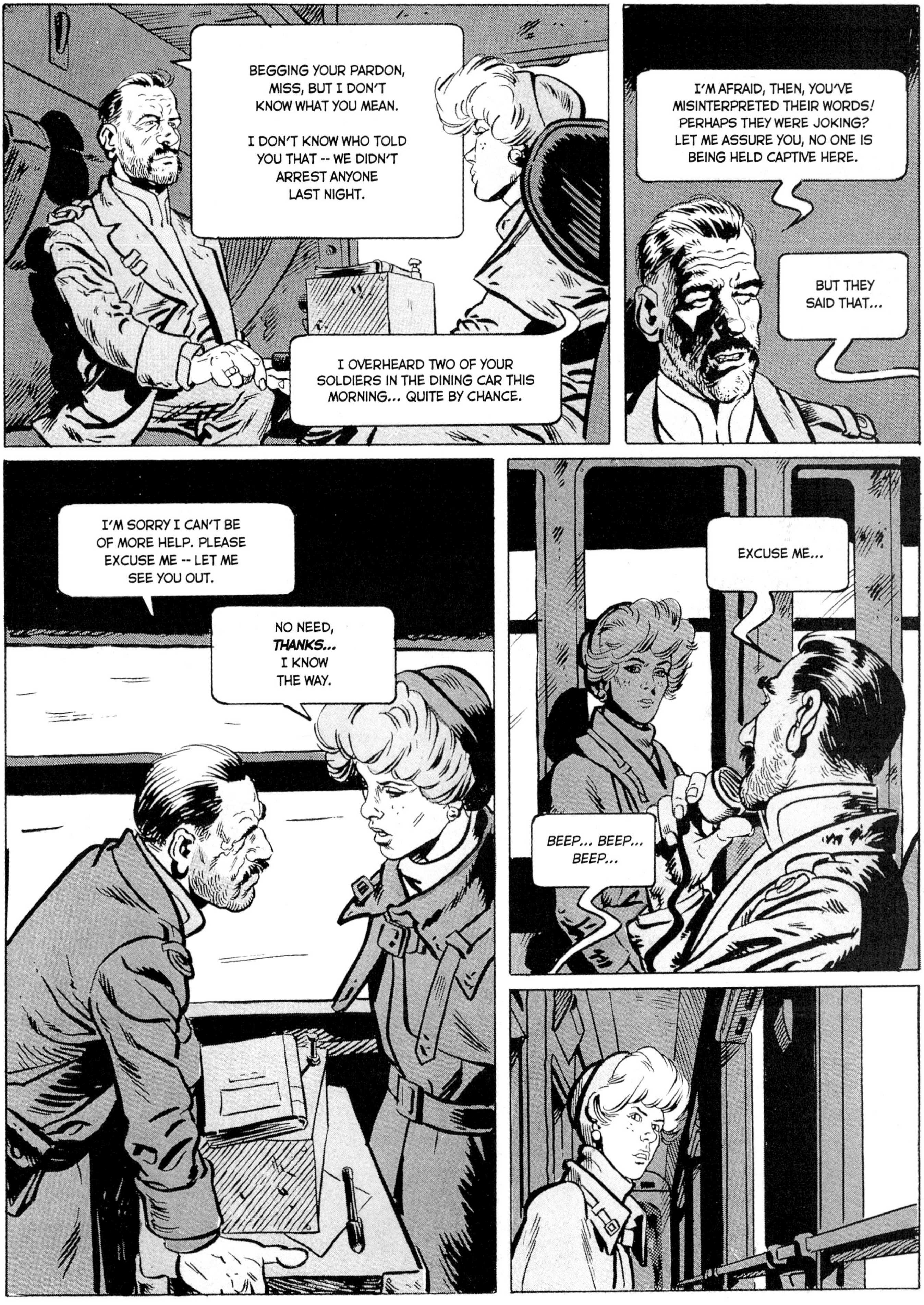
BEGGING YOUR PARDON, MISS, BUT I DON'T KNOW WHAT YOU MEAN.
I DON'T KNOW WHO TOLD YOU THAT -- WE DIDN'T ARREST ANYONE LAST NIGHT.
I OVERHEARD TWO OF YOUR SOLDIERS IN THE DINING CAR THIS MORNING... QUITE BY CHANCE.
I'M AFRAID, THEN, YOU'VE MISINTERPRETED THEIR WORDS! PERHAPS THEY WERE JOKING? LET ME ASSURE YOU, NO ONE IS BEING HELD CAPTIVE HERE.
BUT THEY SAID THAT...
I'M SORRY I CAN'T BE OF MORE HELP. PLEASE EXCUSE ME -- LET ME SEE YOU OUT.
NO NEED, *THANKS...* I KNOW THE WAY.
EXCUSE ME...
BEEP... BEEP... BEEP...

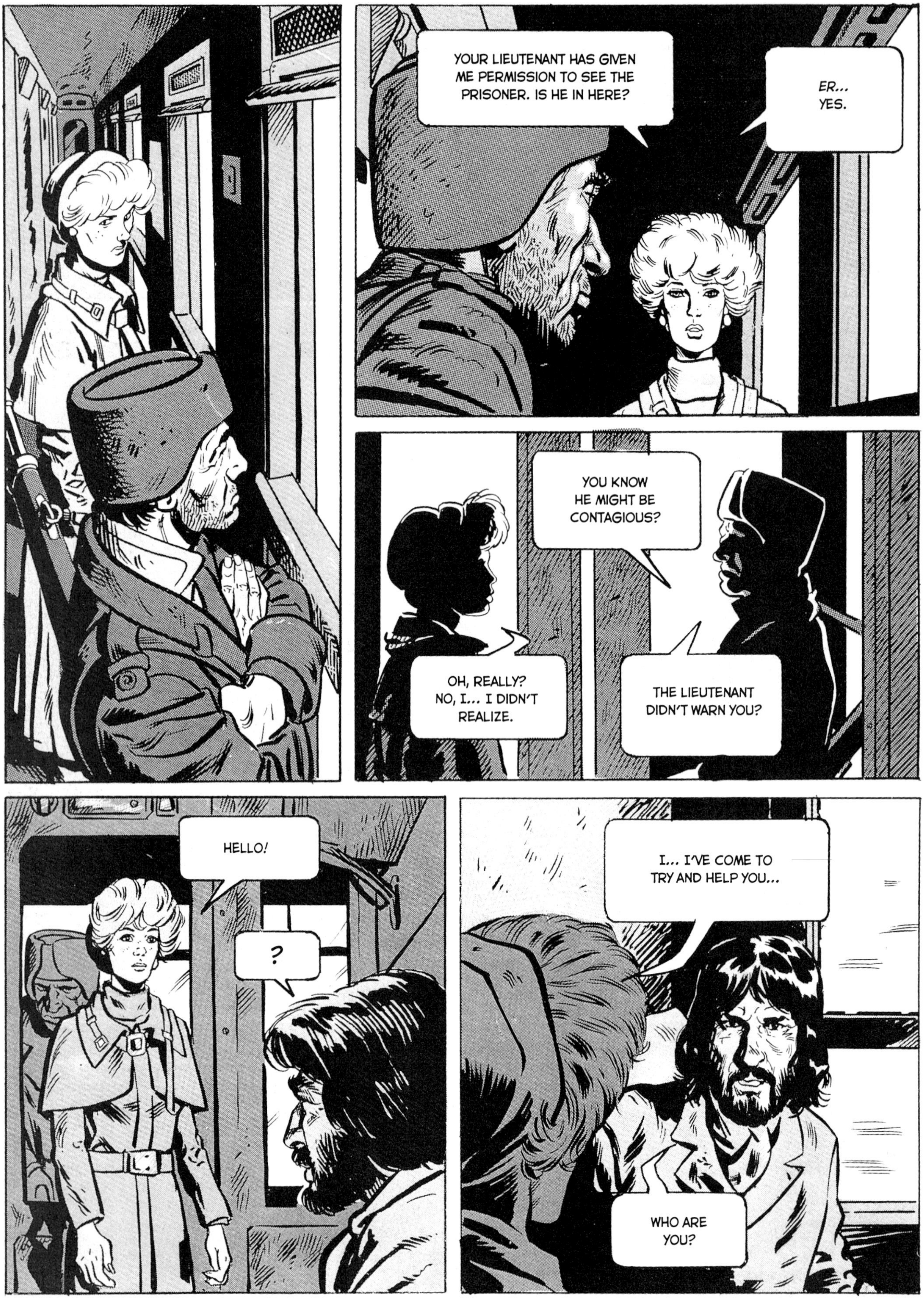
YOUR LIEUTENANT HAS GIVEN ME PERMISSION TO SEE THE PRISONER. IS HE IN HERE?
ER... YES.
YOU KNOW HE MIGHT BE CONTAGIOUS?
OH, REALLY? NO, I... I DIDN'T REALIZE.
THE LIEUTENANT DIDN'T WARN YOU?
HELLO!
?
I... I'VE COME TO TRY AND HELP YOU...
WHO ARE YOU?

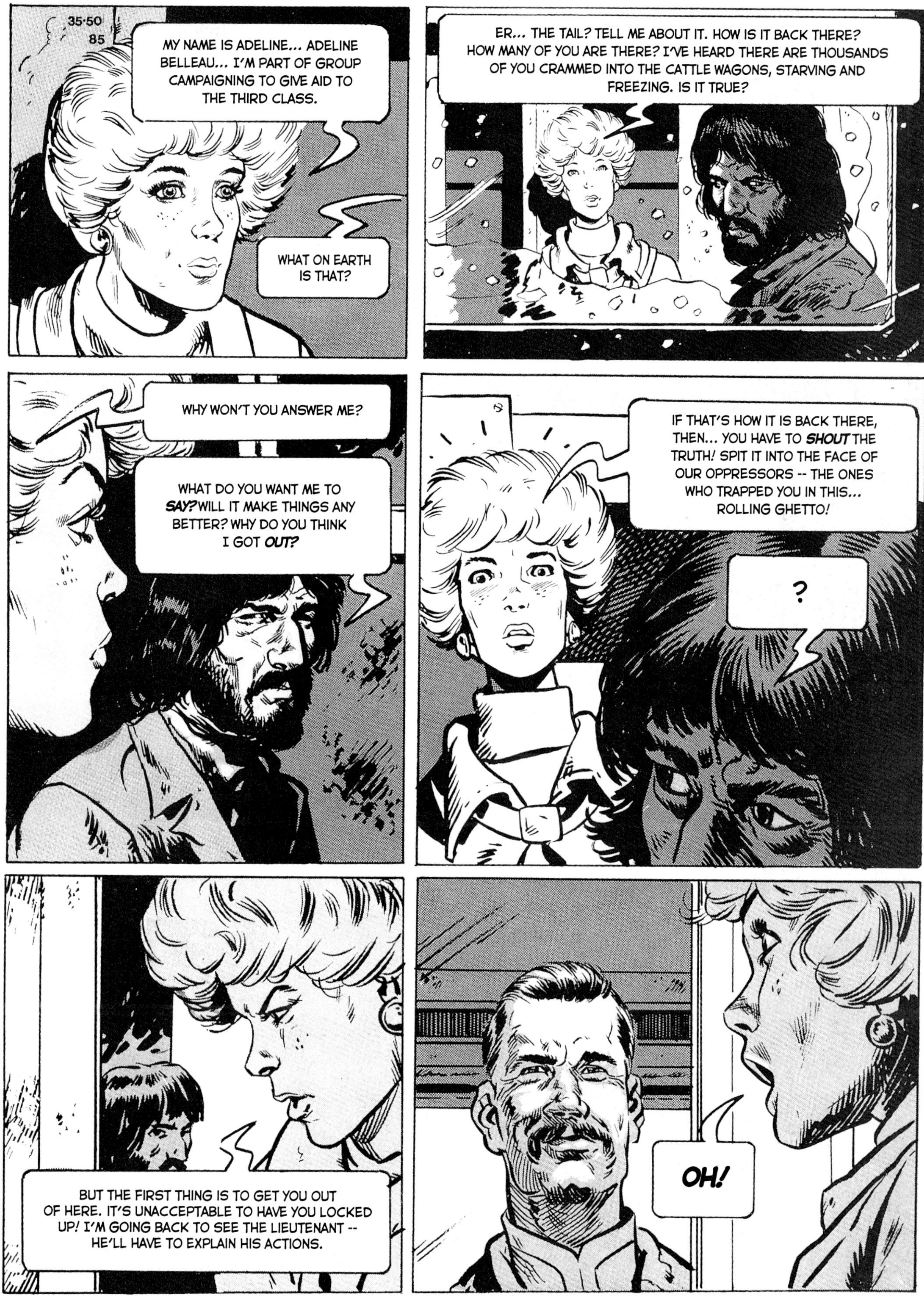
MY NAME IS ADELINE... ADELINE BELLEAU... I'M PART OF GROUP CAMPAIGNING TO GIVE AID TO THE THIRD CLASS.
WHAT ON EARTH IS THAT?
ER... THE TAIL? TELL ME ABOUT IT. HOW IS IT BACK THERE? HOW MANY OF YOU ARE THERE? I'VE HEARD THERE ARE THOUSANDS OF YOU CRAMMED INTO THE CATTLE WAGONS, STARVING AND FREEZING. IS IT TRUE?
WHY WON'T YOU ANSWER ME?
WHAT DO YOU WANT ME TO **SAY?** WILL IT MAKE THINGS ANY BETTER? WHY DO YOU THINK I GOT **OUT?**
IF THAT'S HOW IT IS BACK THERE, THEN... YOU HAVE TO **SHOUT** THE TRUTH! SPIT IT INTO THE FACE OF OUR OPPRESSORS -- THE ONES WHO TRAPPED YOU IN THIS... ROLLING GHETTO!
?
BUT THE FIRST THING IS TO GET YOU OUT OF HERE. IT'S UNACCEPTABLE TO HAVE YOU LOCKED UP! I'M GOING BACK TO SEE THE LIEUTENANT -- HE'LL HAVE TO EXPLAIN HIS ACTIONS.
OH!

NO NEED TO GET ALL WORKED UP. YOU'LL HAVE PLENTY OF TIME TO FIGURE IT OUT.
YOU LOCKED THE DOOR?!
LET ME OUT! YOU'VE NO RIGHT!
SORRY, BUT IT'S YOUR OWN FAULT! YOU WERE ***WARNED*** YOUR FRIEND WAS IN QUARANTINE, MS. BELLEAU... SO YOU MUST UNDERSTAND THAT I CAN'T RISK LETTING YOU GO. NOT WITHOUT MEDICAL ADVICE.
WELL, WHAT ARE YOU WAITING FOR?! CALL THE DOCTOR!
I WILL -- AS SOON AS WE'VE FOUND HIM, I PROMISE! BUT IT COULD TAKE A WHILE, I'M AFRAID! YOU KNOW HOW DOCTORS ARE. THEY TEND TO BE VERY BUSY.
SMUG BASTARD! HE'S ENJOYING THIS...
COOL IT. JUST COME AND SIT DOWN. IT'S NOT TOO BAD IN HERE. AT LEAST IT'S WARM.
LISTEN...
WHAT?
ARE YOU ***REALLY*** CONTAGIOUS?

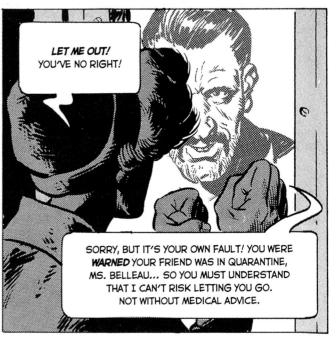

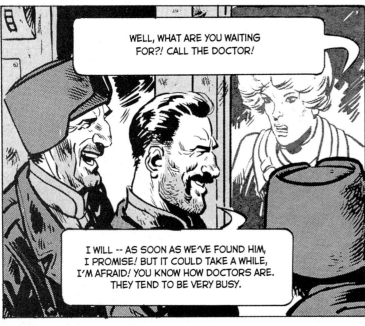

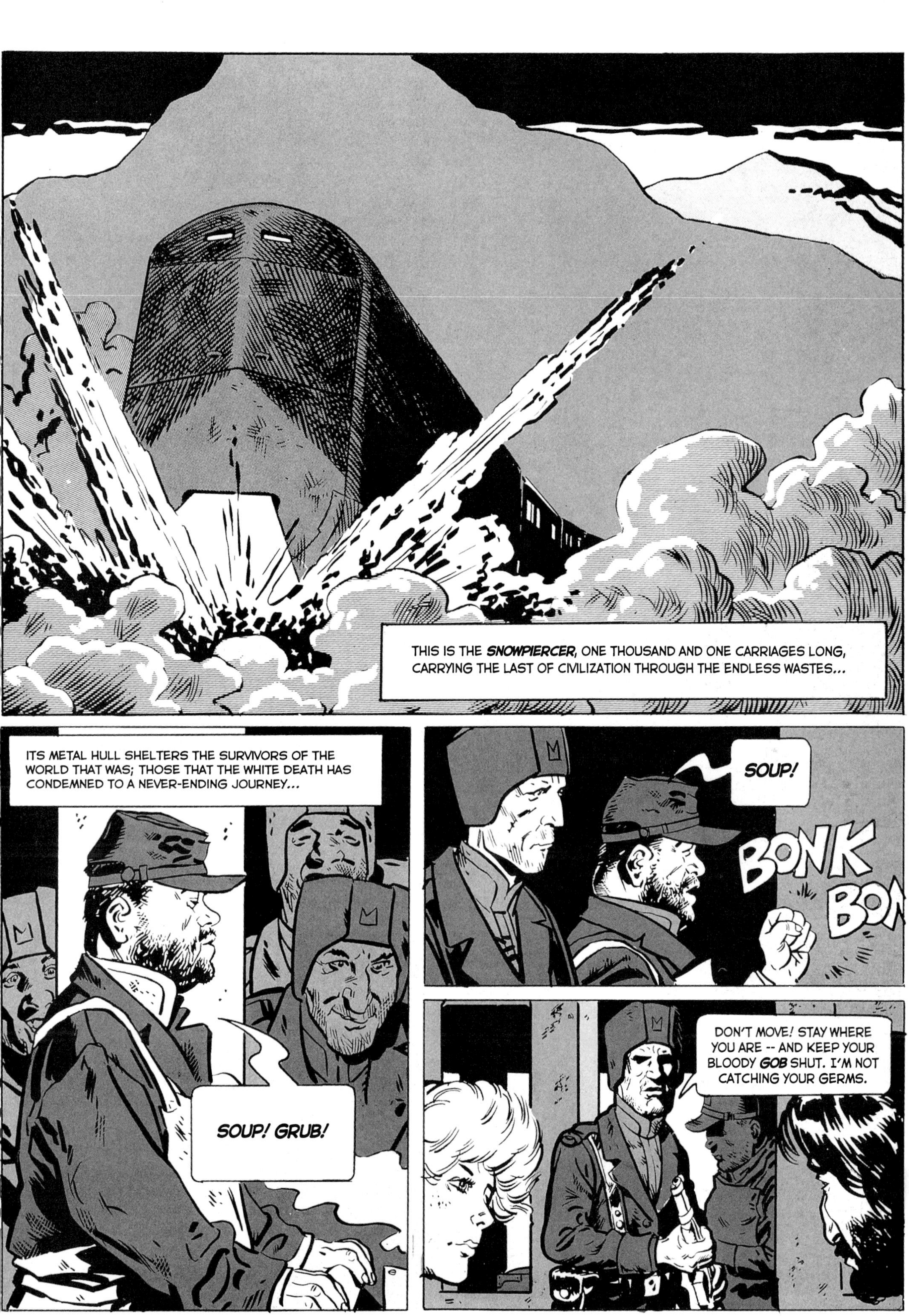
THIS IS THE SNOWPIERCER, ONE THOUSAND AND ONE CARRIAGES LONG, CARRYING THE LAST OF CIVILIZATION THROUGH THE ENDLESS WASTES...
ITS METAL HULL SHELTERS THE SURVIVORS OF THE WORLD THAT WAS; THOSE THAT THE WHITE DEATH HAS CONDEMNED TO A NEVER-ENDING JOURNEY...
SOUP! GRUB!
SOUP!
BONK
BON
DON'T MOVE! STAY WHERE YOU ARE -- AND KEEP YOUR BLOODY GOB SHUT. I'M NOT CATCHING YOUR GERMS.

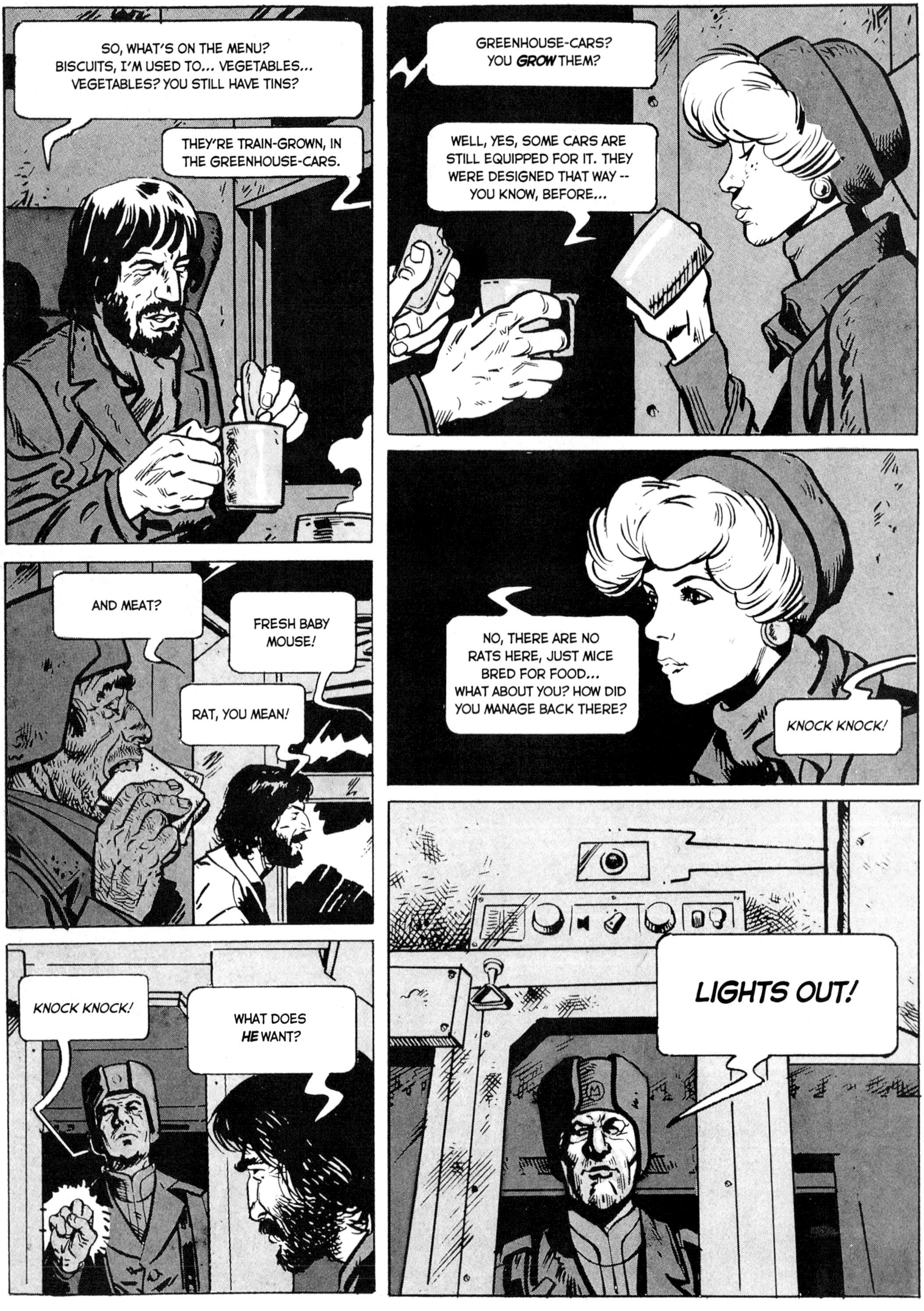
SO, WHAT'S ON THE MENU? BISCUITS, I'M USED TO... VEGETABLES... VEGETABLES? YOU STILL HAVE TINS?
THEY'RE TRAIN-GROWN, IN THE GREENHOUSE-CARS.
GREENHOUSE-CARS? YOU GROW THEM?
WELL, YES, SOME CARS ARE STILL EQUIPPED FOR IT. THEY WERE DESIGNED THAT WAY -- YOU KNOW, BEFORE...
AND MEAT?
FRESH BABY MOUSE!
RAT, YOU MEAN!
NO, THERE ARE NO RATS HERE, JUST MICE BRED FOR FOOD... WHAT ABOUT YOU? HOW DID YOU MANAGE BACK THERE?
KNOCK KNOCK!
KNOCK KNOCK!
WHAT DOES HE WANT?
LIGHTS OUT!

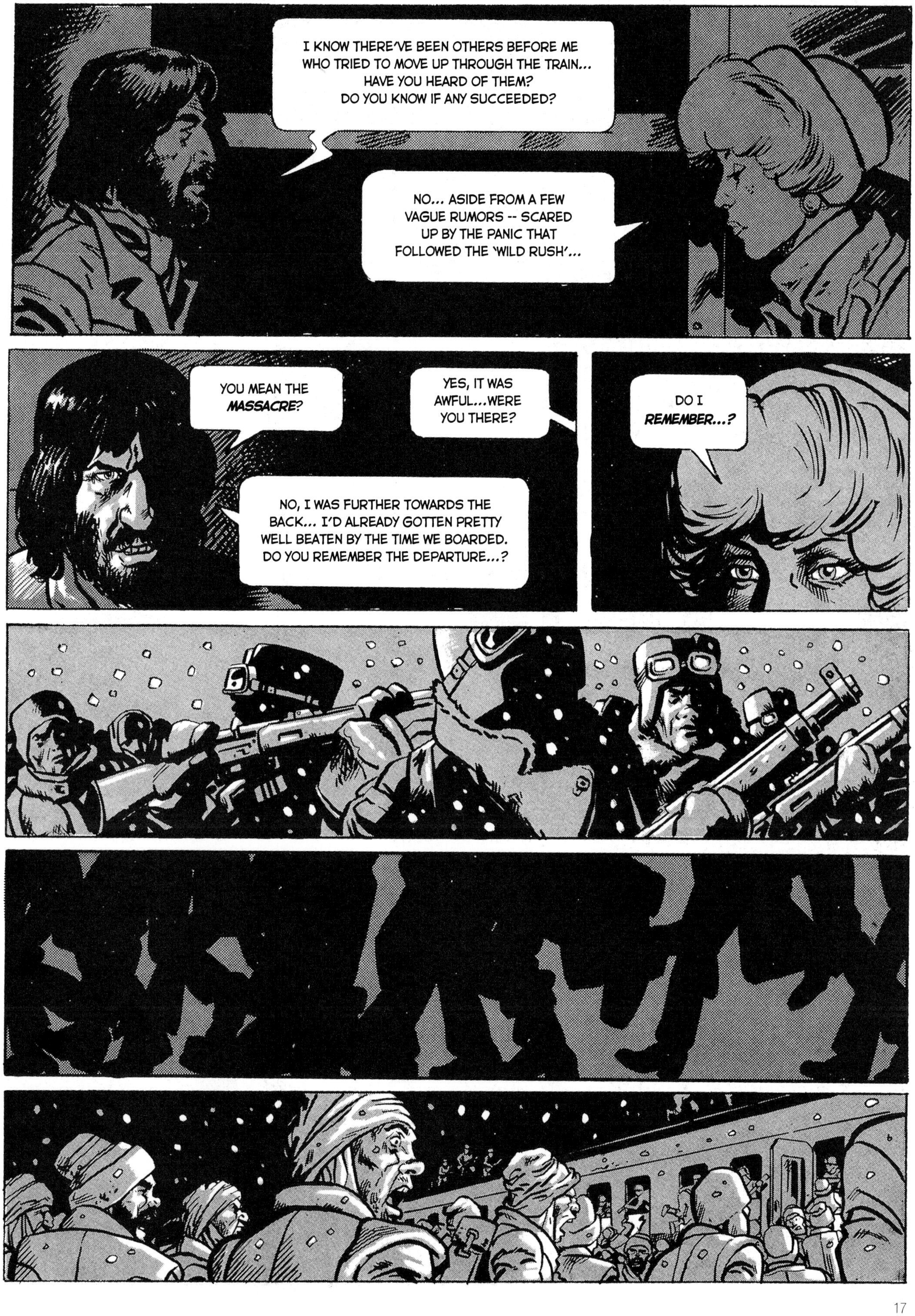
I KNOW THERE'VE BEEN OTHERS BEFORE ME WHO TRIED TO MOVE UP THROUGH THE TRAIN... HAVE YOU HEARD OF THEM? DO YOU KNOW IF ANY SUCCEEDED?
NO... ASIDE FROM A FEW VAGUE RUMORS -- SCARED UP BY THE PANIC THAT FOLLOWED THE 'WILD RUSH'...
YOU MEAN THE *MASSACRE?*
YES, IT WAS AWFUL...WERE YOU THERE?
NO, I WAS FURTHER TOWARDS THE BACK... I'D ALREADY GOTTEN PRETTY WELL BEATEN BY THE TIME WE BOARDED. DO YOU REMEMBER THE DEPARTURE...?
DO I *REMEMBER...?*

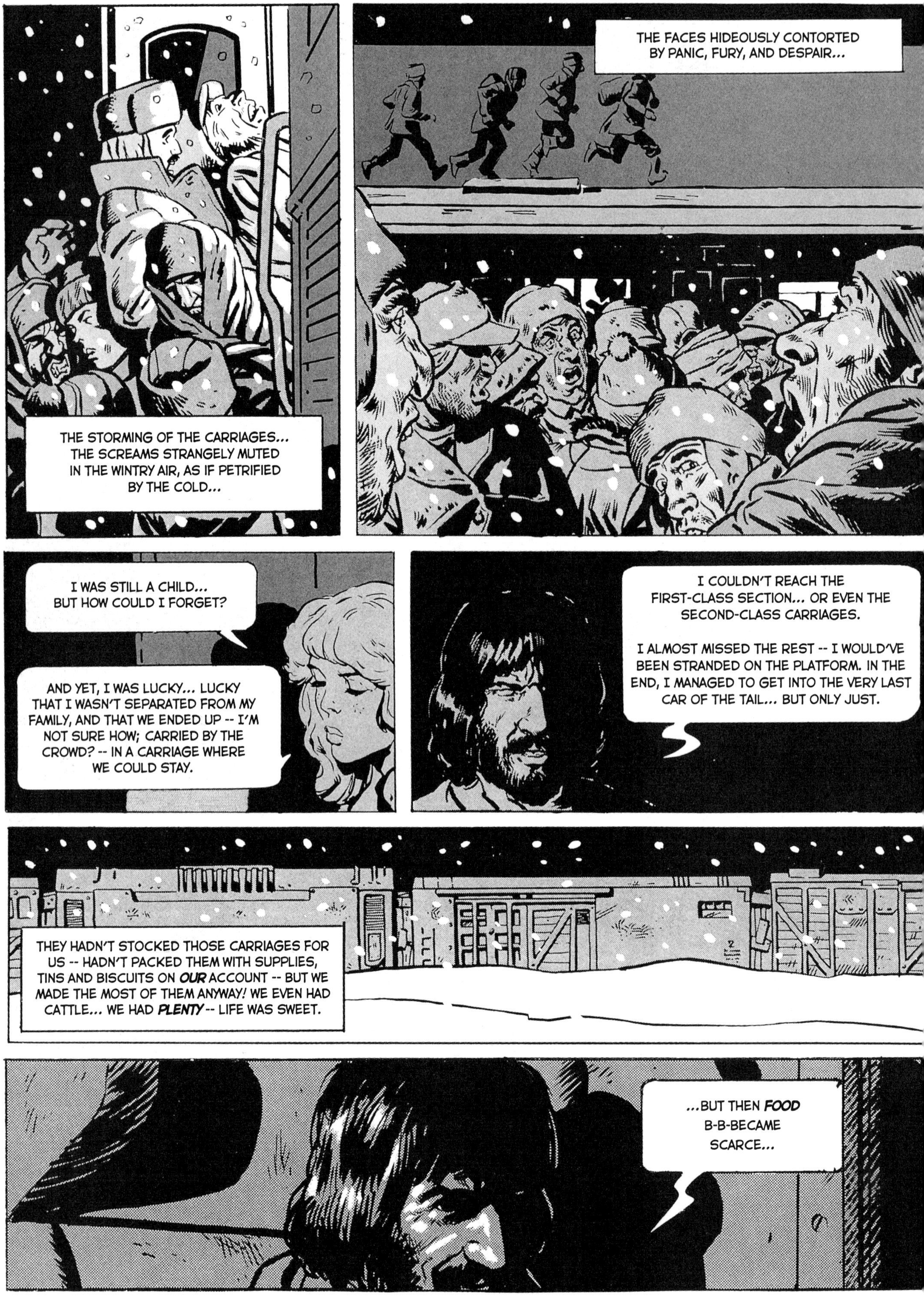
THE STORMING OF THE CARRIAGES... THE SCREAMS STRANGELY MUTED IN THE WINTRY AIR, AS IF PETRIFIED BY THE COLD...
THE FACES HIDEOUSLY CONTORTED BY PANIC, FURY, AND DESPAIR...
I WAS STILL A CHILD... BUT HOW COULD I FORGET?
AND YET, I WAS LUCKY... LUCKY THAT I WASN'T SEPARATED FROM MY FAMILY, AND THAT WE ENDED UP -- I'M NOT SURE HOW; CARRIED BY THE CROWD? -- IN A CARRIAGE WHERE WE COULD STAY.
I COULDN'T REACH THE FIRST-CLASS SECTION... OR EVEN THE SECOND-CLASS CARRIAGES.
I ALMOST MISSED THE REST -- I WOULD'VE BEEN STRANDED ON THE PLATFORM. IN THE END, I MANAGED TO GET INTO THE VERY LAST CAR OF THE TAIL... BUT ONLY JUST.
THEY HADN'T STOCKED THOSE CARRIAGES FOR US -- HADN'T PACKED THEM WITH SUPPLIES, TINS AND BISCUITS ON OUR ACCOUNT -- BUT WE MADE THE MOST OF THEM ANYWAY! WE EVEN HAD CATTLE... WE HAD PLENTY -- LIFE WAS SWEET.
...BUT THEN FOOD B-B-BECAME SCARCE...

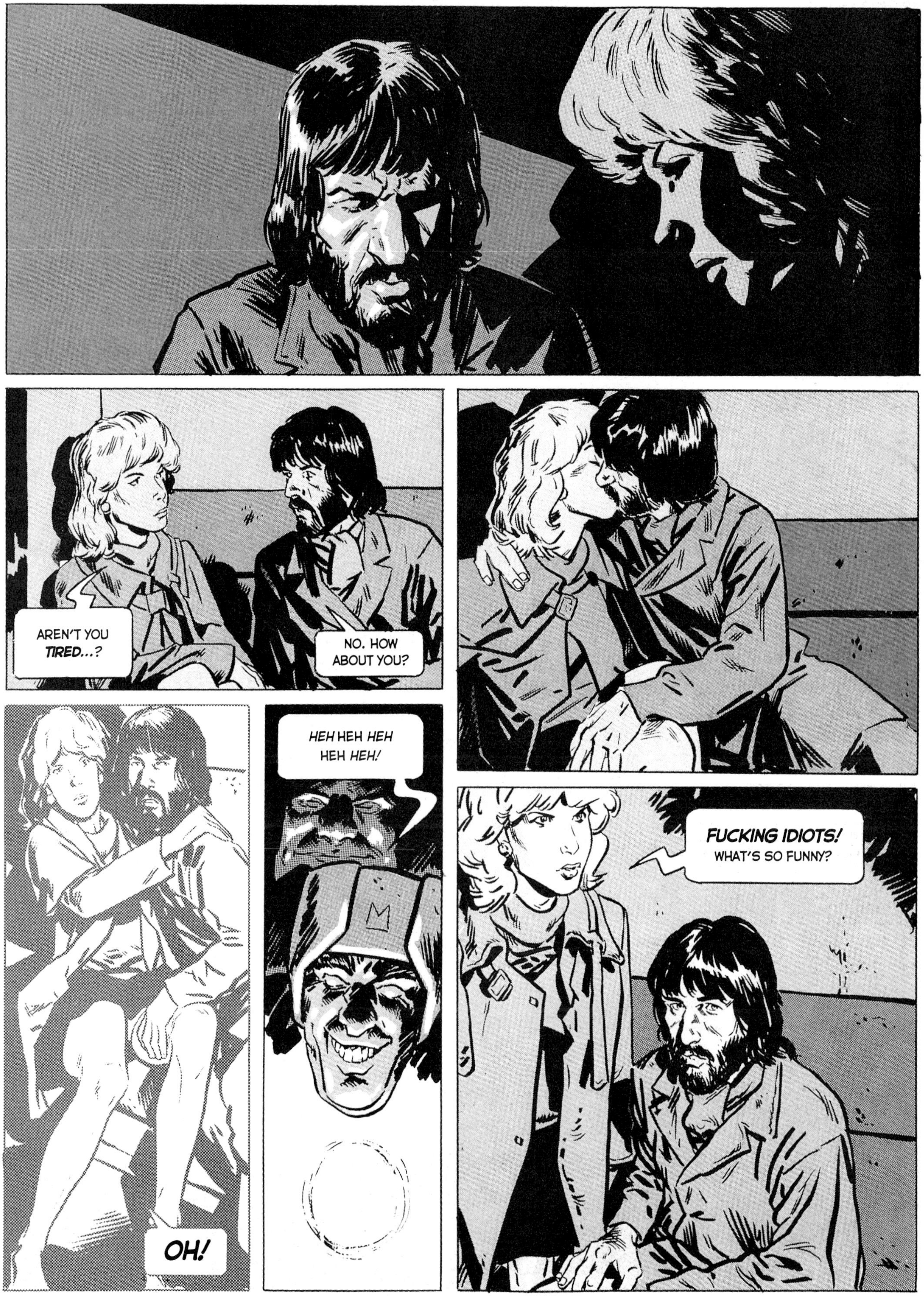
ARE'NT YOU TIRED...?
NO. HOW ABOUT YOU?
OH!
HEH HEH HEH HEH HEH!
FUCKING IDIOTS! WHAT'S SO FUNNY?

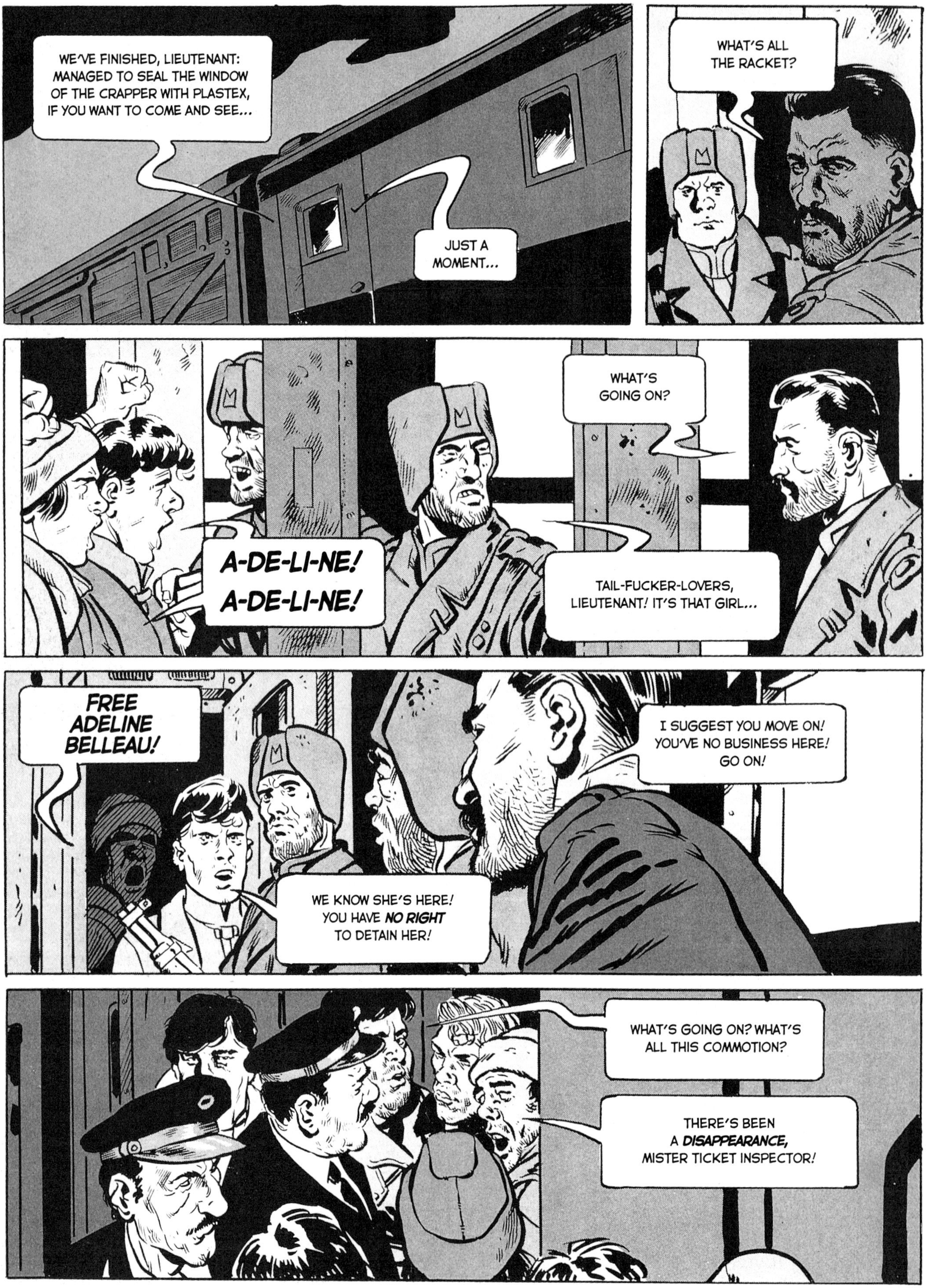
WE'VE FINISHED, LIEUTENANT: MANAGED TO SEAL THE WINDOW OF THE CRAPPER WITH PLASTEX, IF YOU WANT TO COME AND SEE...
JUST A MOMENT...
WHAT'S ALL THE RACKET?
WHAT'S GOING ON?
A-DE-LI-NE! A-DE-LI-NE!
TAIL-FUCKER-LOVERS, LIEUTENANT! IT'S THAT GIRL...
FREE ADELINE BELLEAU!
I SUGGEST YOU MOVE ON! YOU'VE NO BUSINESS HERE! GO ON!
WE KNOW SHE'S HERE! YOU HAVE NO RIGHT TO DETAIN HER!
WHAT'S GOING ON? WHAT'S ALL THIS COMMOTION?
THERE'S BEEN A DISAPPEARANCE, MISTER TICKET INSPECTOR!

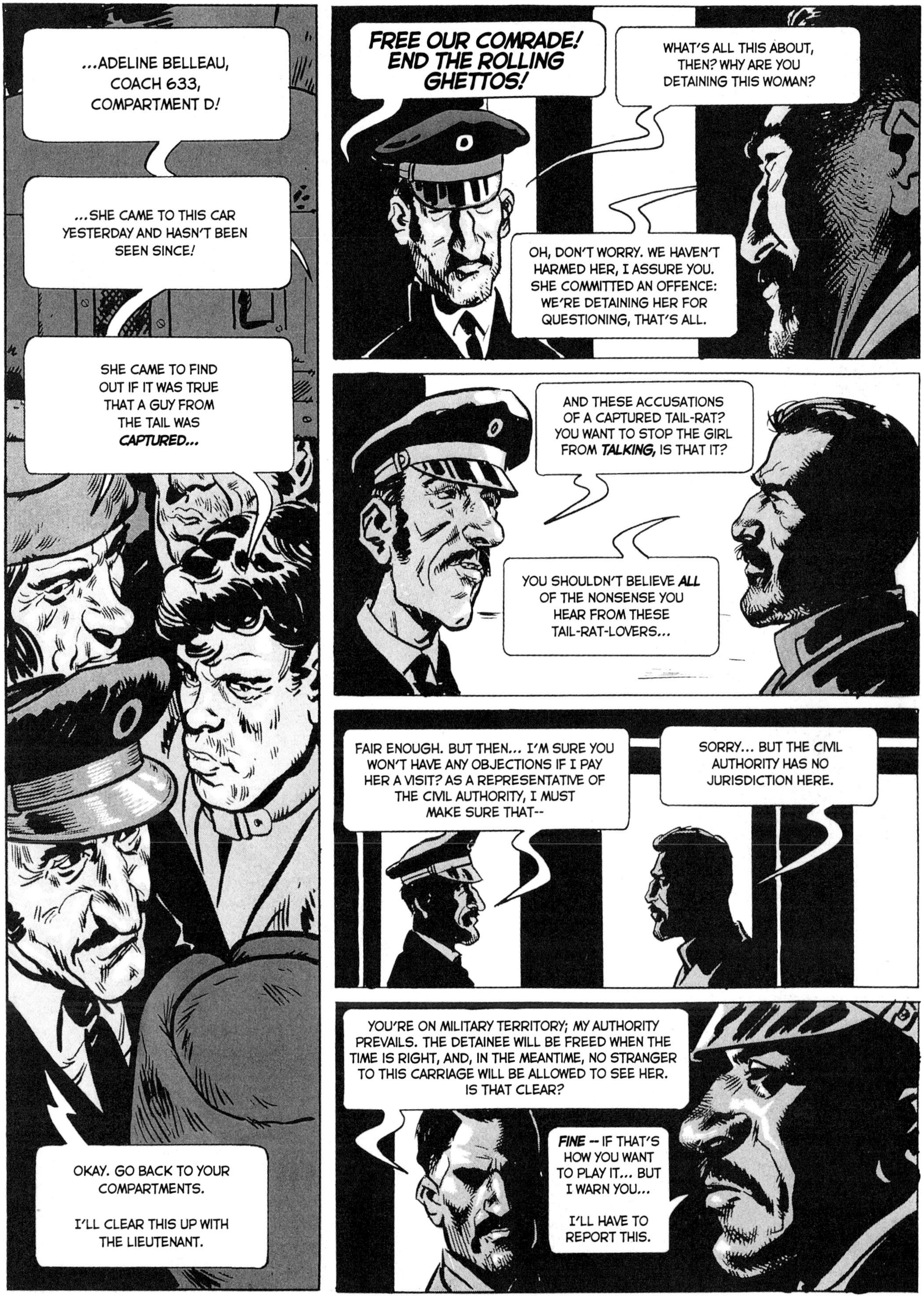
...ADELINE BELLEAU, COACH 633, COMPARTMENT D!
...SHE CAME TO THIS CAR YESTERDAY AND HASN'T BEEN SEEN SINCE!
SHE CAME TO FIND OUT IF IT WAS TRUE THAT A GUY FROM THE TAIL WAS *CAPTURED...*
OKAY. GO BACK TO YOUR COMPARTMENTS.
I'LL CLEAR THIS UP WITH THE LIEUTENANT.
FREE OUR COMRADE! END THE ROLLING GHETTOS!
WHAT'S ALL THIS ABOUT, THEN? WHY ARE YOU DETAINING THIS WOMAN?
OH, DON'T WORRY. WE HAVEN'T HARMED HER, I ASSURE YOU. SHE COMMITTED AN OFFENCE: WE'RE DETAINING HER FOR QUESTIONING, THAT'S ALL.
AND THESE ACCUSATIONS OF A CAPTURED TAIL-RAT? YOU WANT TO STOP THE GIRL FROM *TALKING,* IS THAT IT?
YOU SHOULDN'T BELIEVE *ALL* OF THE NONSENSE YOU HEAR FROM THESE TAIL-RAT-LOVERS...
FAIR ENOUGH. BUT THEN... I'M SURE YOU WON'T HAVE ANY OBJECTIONS IF I PAY HER A VISIT? AS A REPRESENTATIVE OF THE CIVIL AUTHORITY, I MUST MAKE SURE THAT--
SORRY... BUT THE CIVIL AUTHORITY HAS NO JURISDICTION HERE.
YOU'RE ON MILITARY TERRITORY; MY AUTHORITY PREVAILS. THE DETAINEE WILL BE FREED WHEN THE TIME IS RIGHT, AND, IN THE MEANTIME, NO STRANGER TO THIS CARRIAGE WILL BE ALLOWED TO SEE HER. IS THAT CLEAR?
FINE -- IF THAT'S HOW YOU WANT TO PLAY IT... BUT I WARN YOU...
I'LL HAVE TO REPORT THIS.

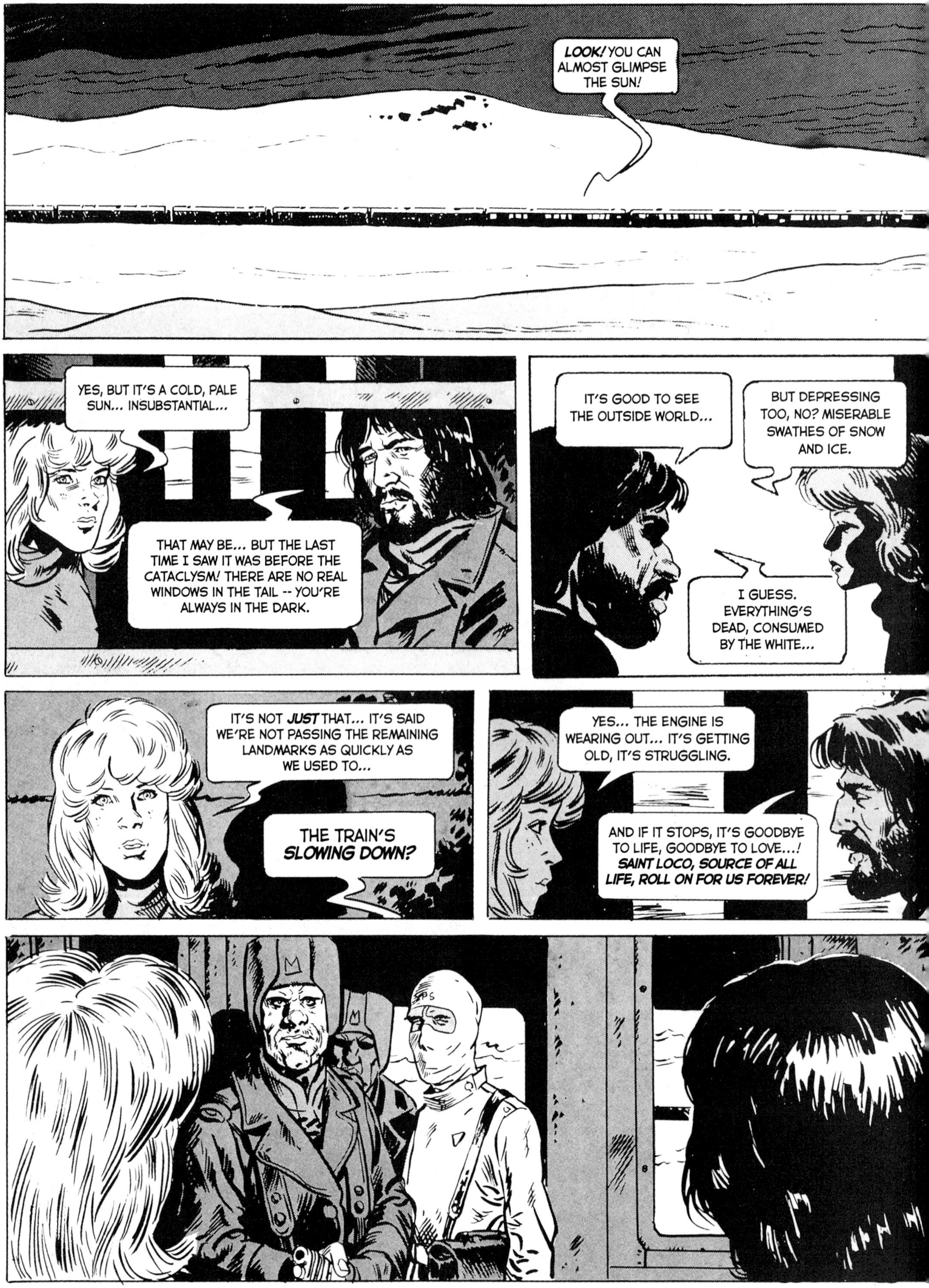
LOOK! YOU CAN ALMOST GLIMPSE THE SUN!
YES, BUT IT'S A COLD, PALE SUN... INSUBSTANTIAL...
THAT MAY BE... BUT THE LAST TIME I SAW IT WAS BEFORE THE CATACLYSM! THERE ARE NO REAL WINDOWS IN THE TAIL -- YOU'RE ALWAYS IN THE DARK.
IT'S GOOD TO SEE THE OUTSIDE WORLD...
BUT DEPRESSING TOO, NO? MISERABLE SWATHES OF SNOW AND ICE.
I GUESS. EVERYTHING'S DEAD, CONSUMED BY THE WHITE...
IT'S NOT JUST THAT... IT'S SAID WE'RE NOT PASSING THE REMAINING LANDMARKS AS QUICKLY AS WE USED TO...
THE TRAIN'S SLOWING DOWN?
YES... THE ENGINE IS WEARING OUT... IT'S GETTING OLD, IT'S STRUGGLING.
AND IF IT STOPS, IT'S GOODBYE TO LIFE, GOODBYE TO LOVE...! SAINT LOCO, SOURCE OF ALL LIFE, ROLL ON FOR US FOREVER!

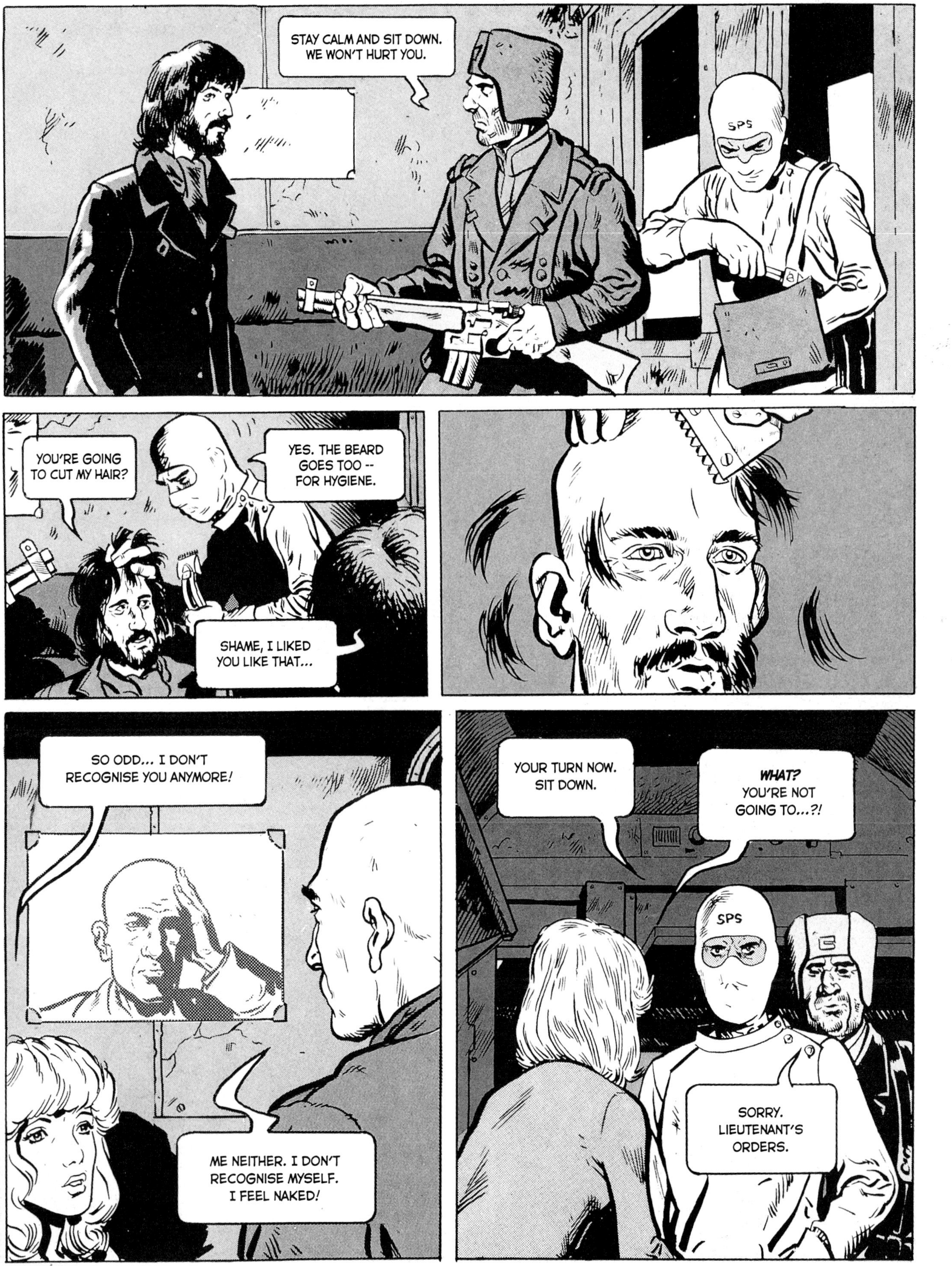
STAY CALM AND SIT DOWN. WE WON'T HURT YOU.
SPS
YOU'RE GOING TO CUT MY HAIR?
YES. THE BEARD GOES TOO -- FOR HYGIENE.
SHAME, I LIKED YOU LIKE THAT...
SO ODD... I DON'T RECOGNISE YOU ANYMORE!
ME NEITHER. I DON'T RECOGNISE MYSELF. I FEEL NAKED!
YOUR TURN NOW. SIT DOWN.
WHAT? YOU'RE NOT GOING TO...?!
SPS
SORRY. LIEUTENANT'S ORDERS.

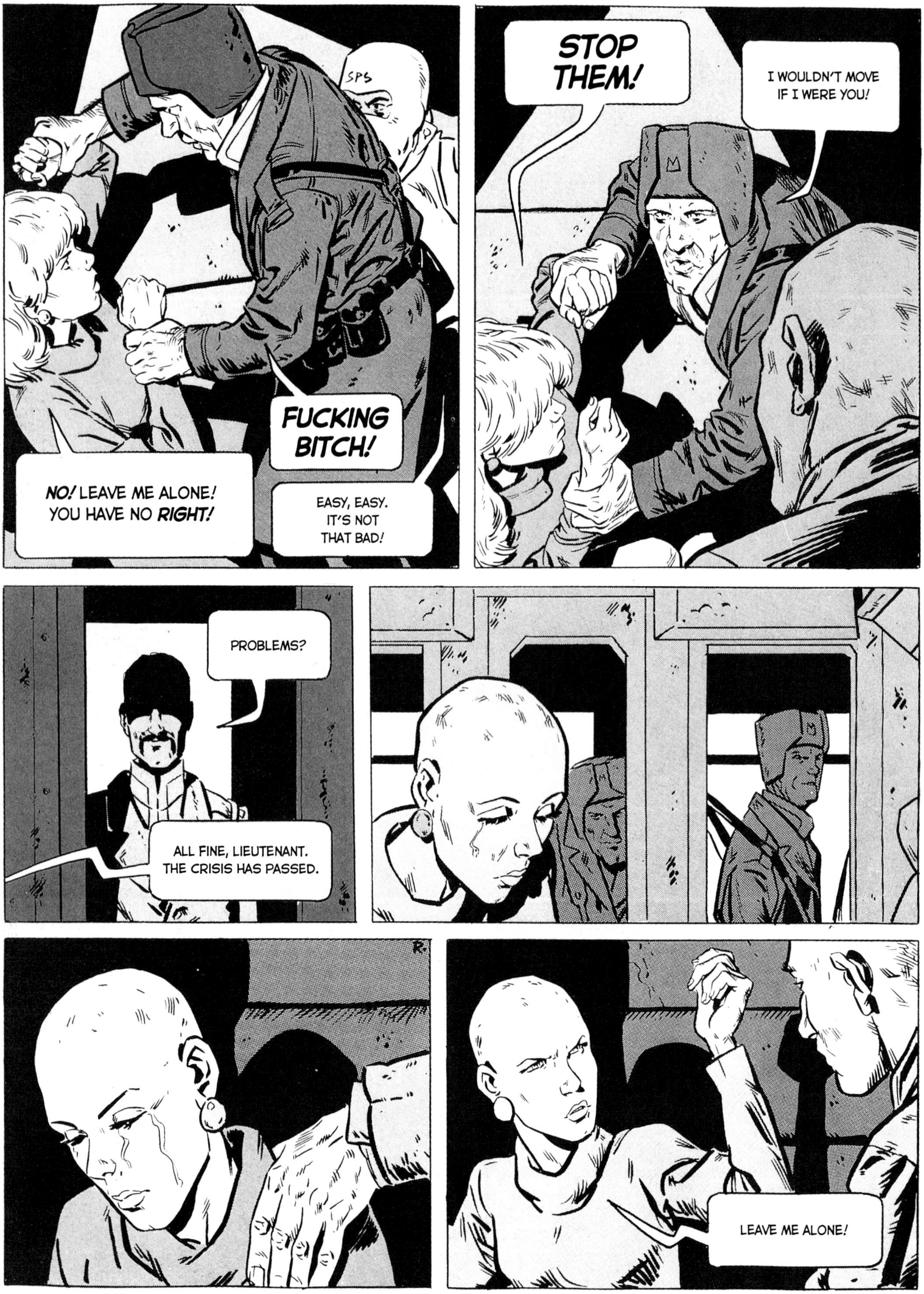
FUCKING BITCH!
NO! LEAVE ME ALONE! YOU HAVE NO RIGHT!
EASY, EASY. IT'S NOT THAT BAD!
STOP THEM!
I WOULDN'T MOVE IF I WERE YOU!
PROBLEMS?
ALL FINE, LIEUTENANT. THE CRISIS HAS PASSED.
LEAVE ME ALONE!

YES, THE LIEUTENANT TOLD ME, COLONEL, BUT IT'S A BIT SHORT NOTICE. WE NEED EIGHT DAYS AT LEAST.

SORRY? YES, I UNDERSTAND. BUT... FINE. AS YOU WISH, COLONEL -- BUT *YOU'RE* TAKING THE RESPONSIBILITY, NOT ME.

SHIRT OFF, MISTER PROLOFF! AND THE LADY TOO.

ANOTHER EXAMINATION?

THE *LAST* -- TO SEE IF YOU CAN LEAVE. BUT...

SAY, HAVE YOU DONE SOMETHING *DIFFERENT* WITH YOUR HAIR?

LEAVE...? THEY'RE GOING TO FREE US?

LIE DOWN, SWEETIE, AND DON'T LOOK AT ME LIKE THAT.

UNHAPPY WITH YOUR BARBER? *BAH!* YOURS WILL GROW BACK -- YOU'RE LUCKY! NOT LIKE MINE!

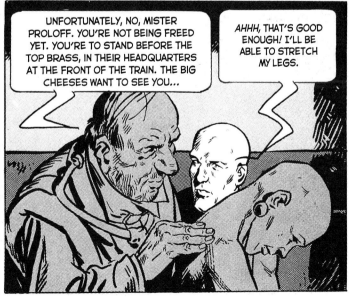

UNFORTUNATELY, NO, MISTER PROLOFF. YOU'RE NOT BEING FREED YET. YOU'RE TO STAND BEFORE THE TOP BRASS, IN THEIR HEADQUARTERS AT THE FRONT OF THE TRAIN. THE BIG CHEESES WANT TO SEE YOU...

AHHH, THAT'S GOOD ENOUGH! I'LL BE ABLE TO STRETCH MY LEGS.

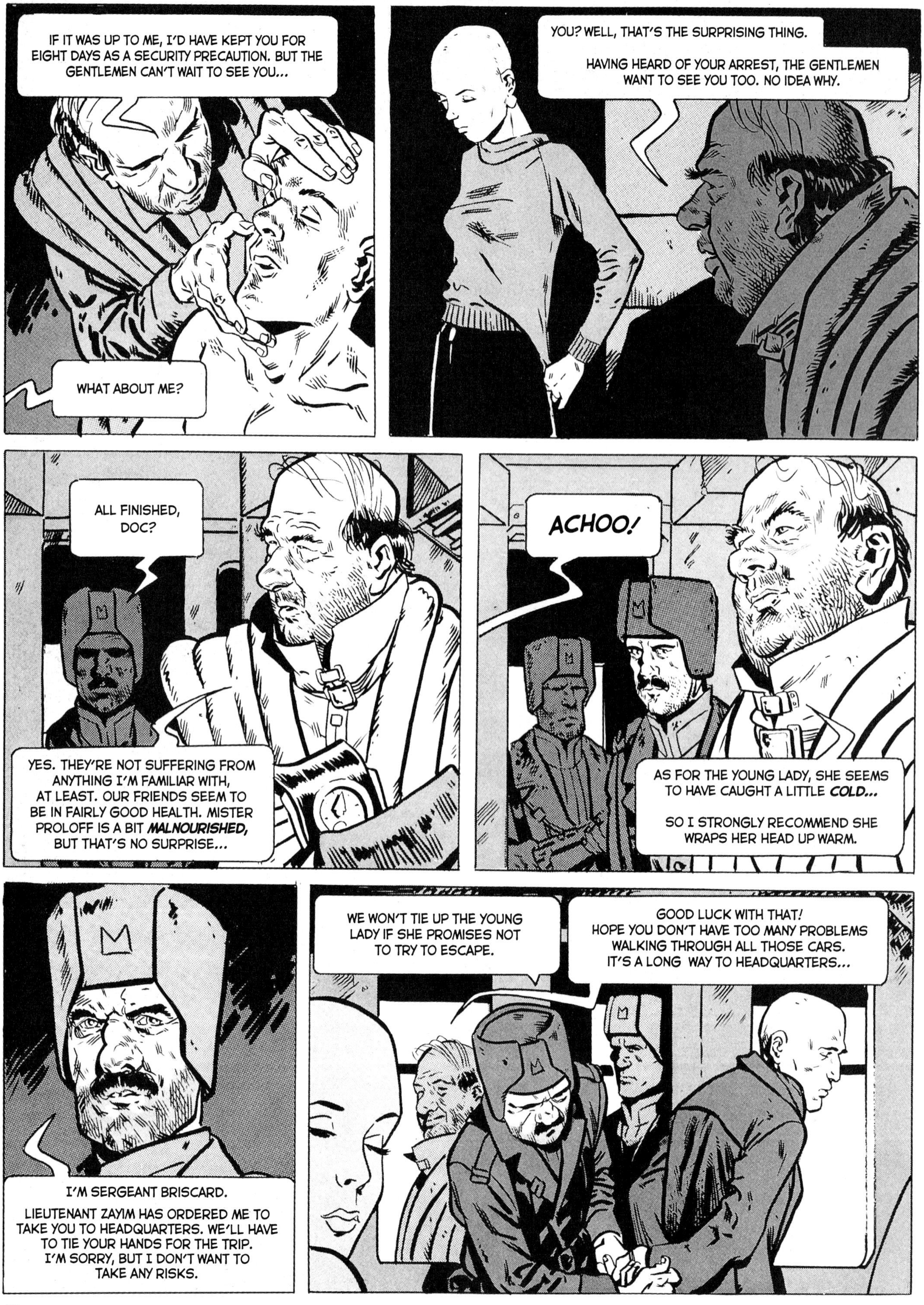
IF IT WAS UP TO ME, I'D HAVE KEPT YOU FOR EIGHT DAYS AS A SECURITY PRECAUTION. BUT THE GENTLEMEN CAN'T WAIT TO SEE YOU...
WHAT ABOUT ME?
YOU? WELL, THAT'S THE SURPRISING THING.
HAVING HEARD OF YOUR ARREST, THE GENTLEMEN WANT TO SEE YOU TOO. NO IDEA WHY.
ALL FINISHED, DOC?
YES. THEY'RE NOT SUFFERING FROM ANYTHING I'M FAMILIAR WITH, AT LEAST. OUR FRIENDS SEEM TO BE IN FAIRLY GOOD HEALTH. MISTER PROLOFF IS A BIT ***MALNOURISHED,*** BUT THAT'S NO SURPRISE...
ACHOO!
AS FOR THE YOUNG LADY, SHE SEEMS TO HAVE CAUGHT A LITTLE ***COLD...***
SO I STRONGLY RECOMMEND SHE WRAPS HER HEAD UP WARM.
I'M SERGEANT BRISCARD.
LIEUTENANT ZAYIM HAS ORDERED ME TO TAKE YOU TO HEADQUARTERS. WE'LL HAVE TO TIE YOUR HANDS FOR THE TRIP. I'M SORRY, BUT I DON'T WANT TO TAKE ANY RISKS.
WE WON'T TIE UP THE YOUNG LADY IF SHE PROMISES NOT TO TRY TO ESCAPE.
GOOD LUCK WITH THAT! HOPE YOU DON'T HAVE TOO MANY PROBLEMS WALKING THROUGH ALL THOSE CARS. IT'S A LONG WAY TO HEADQUARTERS...

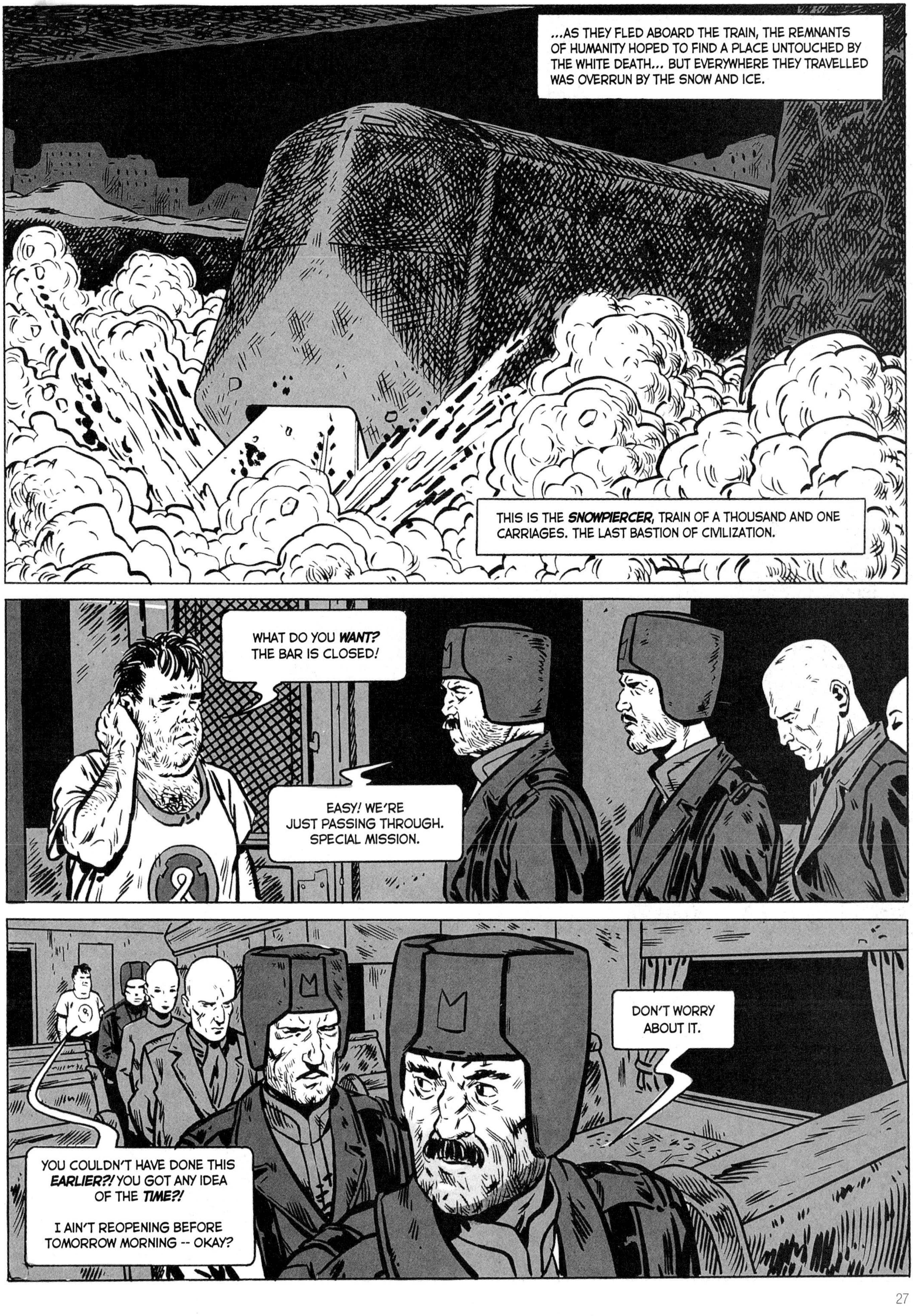
...AS THEY FLED ABOARD THE TRAIN, THE REMNANTS OF HUMANITY HOPED TO FIND A PLACE UNTOUCHED BY THE WHITE DEATH... BUT EVERYWHERE THEY TRAVELLED WAS OVERRUN BY THE SNOW AND ICE.
THIS IS THE ***SNOWPIERCER***, TRAIN OF A THOUSAND AND ONE CARRIAGES. THE LAST BASTION OF CIVILIZATION.
WHAT DO YOU ***WANT?*** THE BAR IS CLOSED!
EASY! WE'RE JUST PASSING THROUGH. SPECIAL MISSION.
YOU COULDN'T HAVE DONE THIS ***EARLIER?!*** YOU GOT ANY IDEA OF THE ***TIME?!***
I AIN'T REOPENING BEFORE TOMORROW MORNING -- OKAY?
DON'T WORRY ABOUT IT.

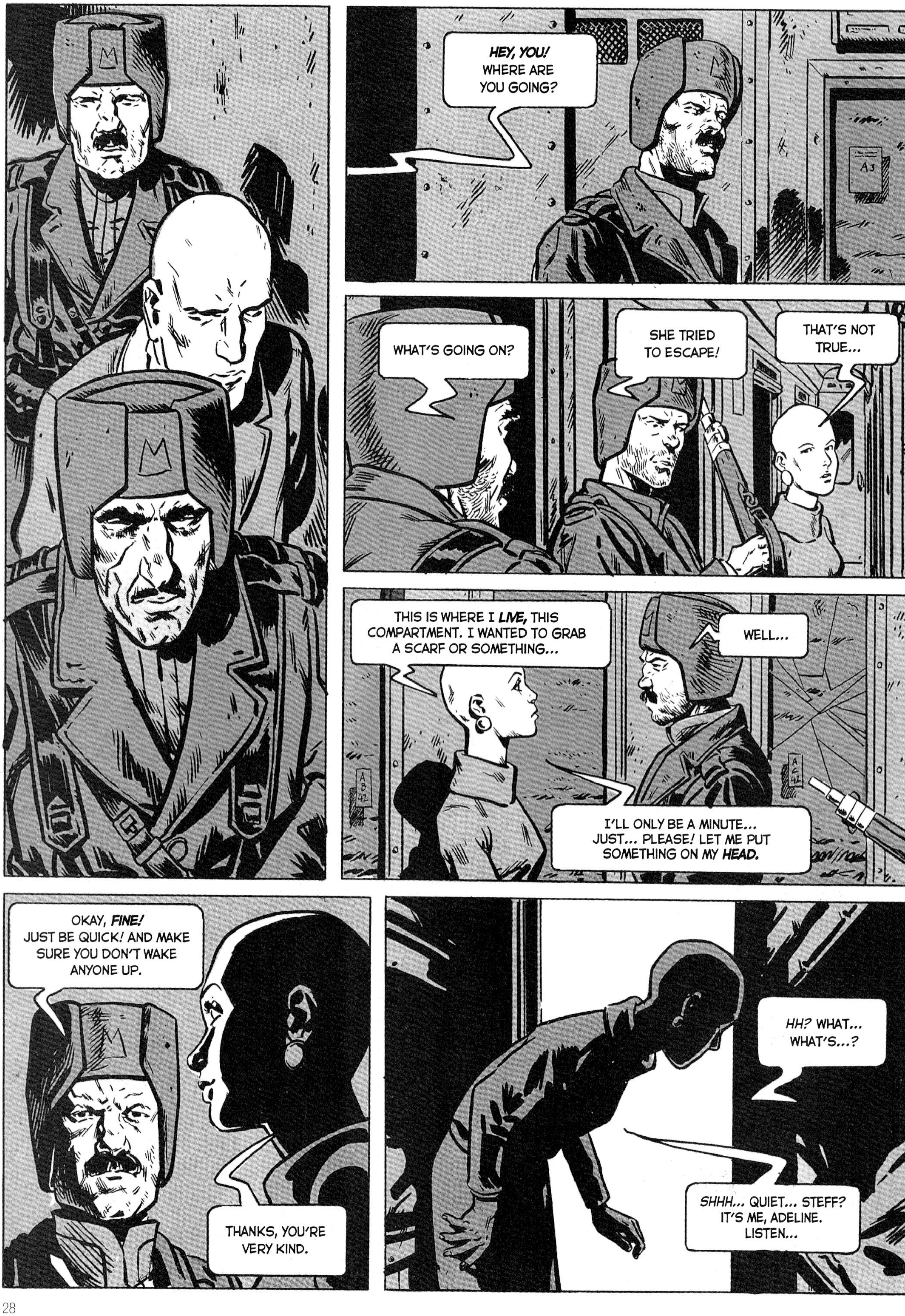
HEY, YOU! WHERE ARE YOU GOING?
A3
WHAT'S GOING ON?
SHE TRIED TO ESCAPE!
THAT'S NOT TRUE...
THIS IS WHERE I LIVE, THIS COMPARTMENT. I WANTED TO GRAB A SCARF OR SOMETHING...
WELL...
AB 42
AC 42
I'LL ONLY BE A MINUTE... JUST... PLEASE! LET ME PUT SOMETHING ON MY HEAD.
OKAY, FINE! JUST BE QUICK! AND MAKE SURE YOU DON'T WAKE ANYONE UP.
THANKS, YOU'RE VERY KIND.
HH? WHAT... WHAT'S...?
SHHH... QUIET... STEFF? IT'S ME, ADELINE. LISTEN...

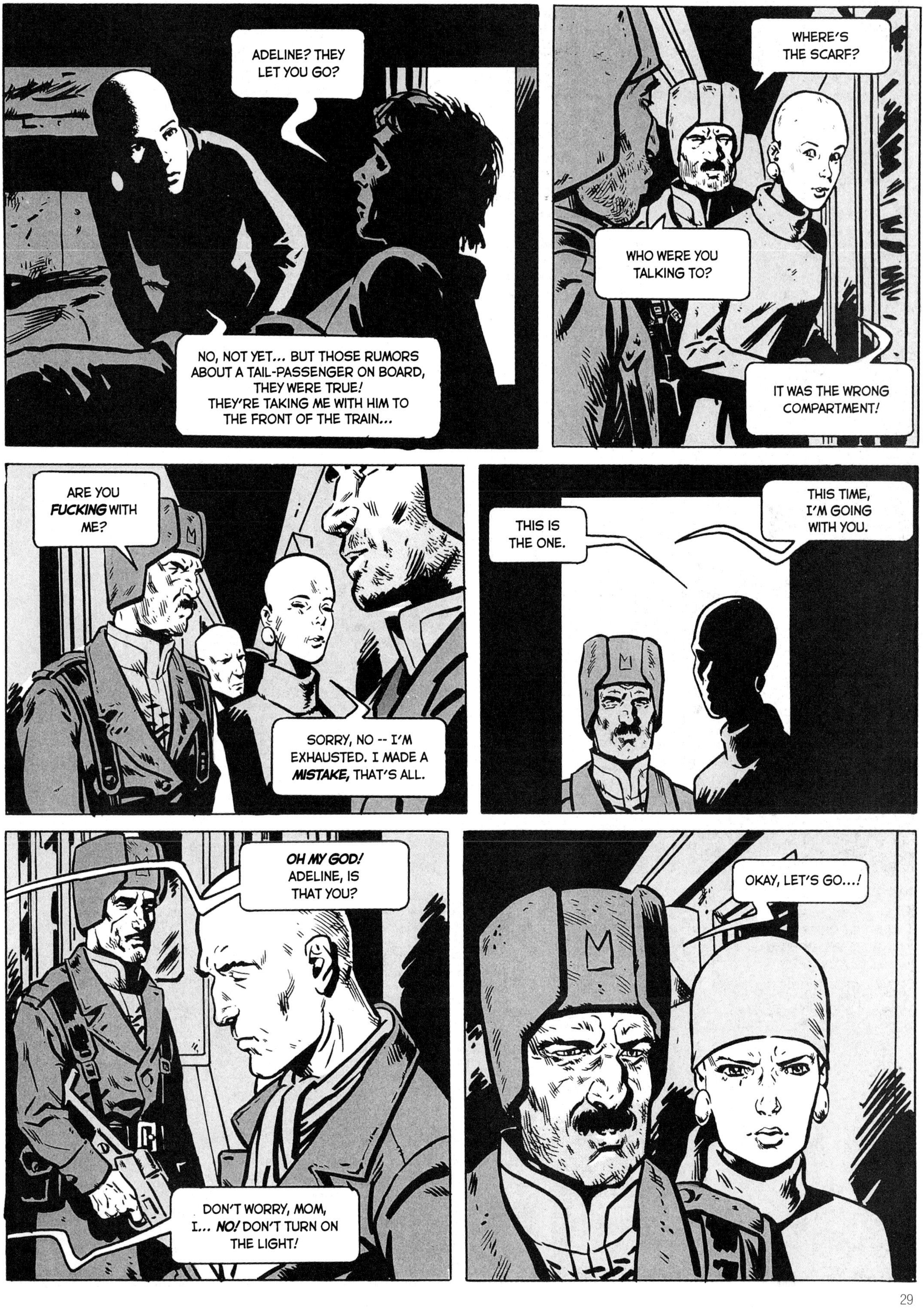
ADELINE? THEY LET YOU GO?
NO, NOT YET... BUT THOSE RUMORS ABOUT A TAIL-PASSENGER ON BOARD, THEY WERE TRUE! THEY'RE TAKING ME WITH HIM TO THE FRONT OF THE TRAIN...
WHERE'S THE SCARF?
WHO WERE YOU TALKING TO?
IT WAS THE WRONG COMPARTMENT!
ARE YOU FUCKING WITH ME?
SORRY, NO -- I'M EXHAUSTED. I MADE A MISTAKE, THAT'S ALL.
THIS IS THE ONE.
THIS TIME, I'M GOING WITH YOU.
OH MY GOD! ADELINE, IS THAT YOU?
DON'T WORRY, MOM, I... NO! DON'T TURN ON THE LIGHT!
OKAY, LET'S GO...!

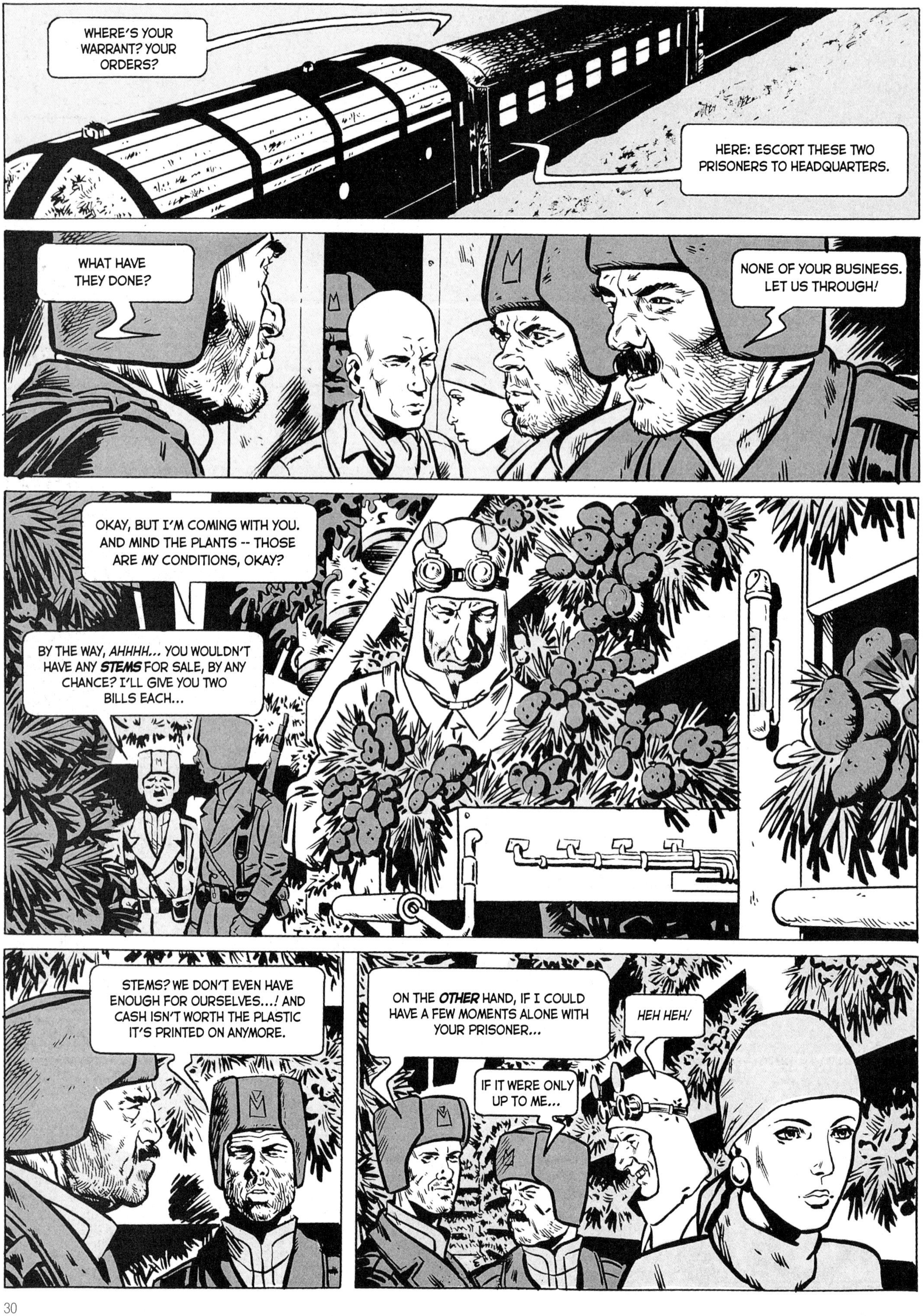
WHERE'S YOUR WARRANT? YOUR ORDERS?
HERE: ESCORT THESE TWO PRISONERS TO HEADQUARTERS.
WHAT HAVE THEY DONE?
NONE OF YOUR BUSINESS. LET US THROUGH!
OKAY, BUT I'M COMING WITH YOU. AND MIND THE PLANTS -- THOSE ARE MY CONDITIONS, OKAY?
BY THE WAY, *AHHHH...* YOU WOULDN'T HAVE ANY ***STEMS*** FOR SALE, BY ANY CHANCE? I'LL GIVE YOU TWO BILLS EACH...
STEMS? WE DON'T EVEN HAVE ENOUGH FOR OURSELVES...! AND CASH ISN'T WORTH THE PLASTIC IT'S PRINTED ON ANYMORE.
ON THE ***OTHER*** HAND, IF I COULD HAVE A FEW MOMENTS ALONE WITH YOUR PRISONER...
HEH HEH!
IF IT WERE ONLY UP TO ME...

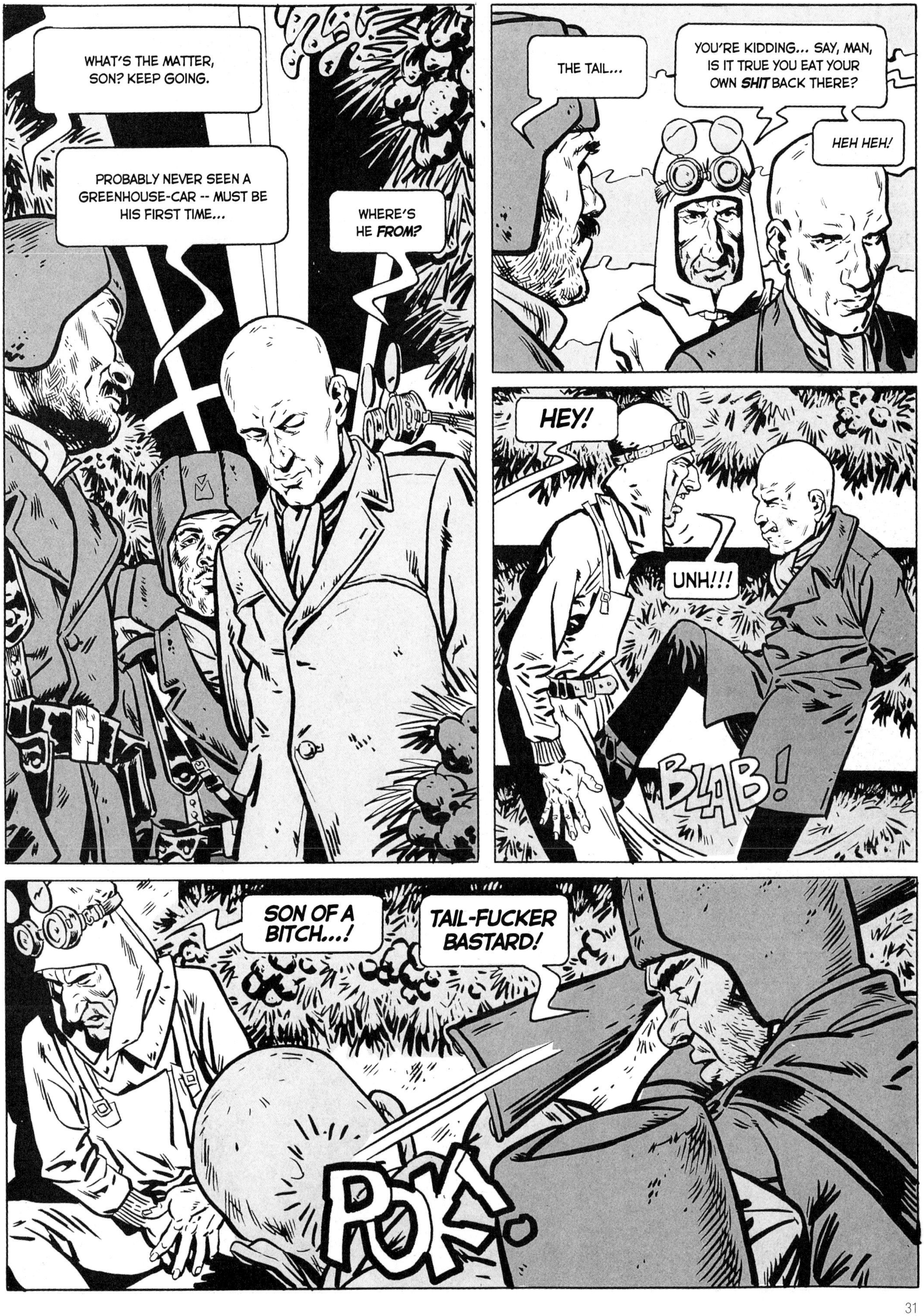
WHAT'S THE MATTER, SON? KEEP GOING.
PROBABLY NEVER SEEN A GREENHOUSE-CAR -- MUST BE HIS FIRST TIME...
WHERE'S HE *FROM?*
THE TAIL...
YOU'RE KIDDING... SAY, MAN, IS IT TRUE YOU EAT YOUR OWN *SHIT* BACK THERE?
HEH HEH!
HEY!
UNH!!!
BLAB!
SON OF A BITCH...!
TAIL-FUCKER BASTARD!
POK!

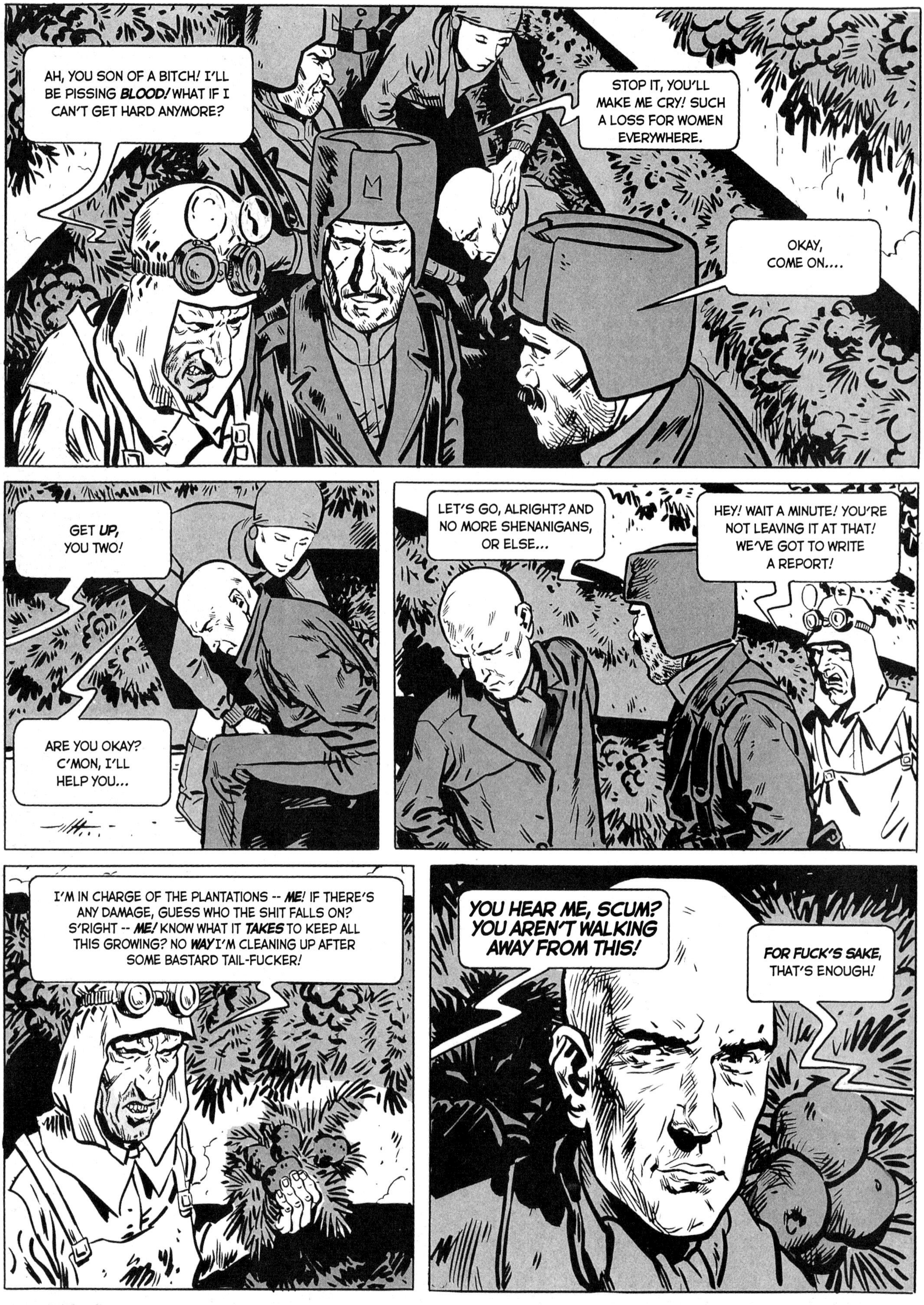
AH, YOU SON OF A BITCH! I'LL BE PISSING BLOOD! WHAT IF I CAN'T GET HARD ANYMORE?
STOP IT, YOU'LL MAKE ME CRY! SUCH A LOSS FOR WOMEN EVERYWHERE.
OKAY, COME ON....
GET UP, YOU TWO!
ARE YOU OKAY? C'MON, I'LL HELP YOU...
LET'S GO, ALRIGHT? AND NO MORE SHENANIGANS, OR ELSE...
HEY! WAIT A MINUTE! YOU'RE NOT LEAVING IT AT THAT! WE'VE GOT TO WRITE A REPORT!
I'M IN CHARGE OF THE PLANTATIONS -- ME! IF THERE'S ANY DAMAGE, GUESS WHO THE SHIT FALLS ON? S'RIGHT -- ME! KNOW WHAT IT TAKES TO KEEP ALL THIS GROWING? NO WAY I'M CLEANING UP AFTER SOME BASTARD TAIL-FUCKER!
YOU HEAR ME, SCUM? YOU AREN'T WALKING AWAY FROM THIS!
FOR FUCK'S SAKE, THAT'S ENOUGH!

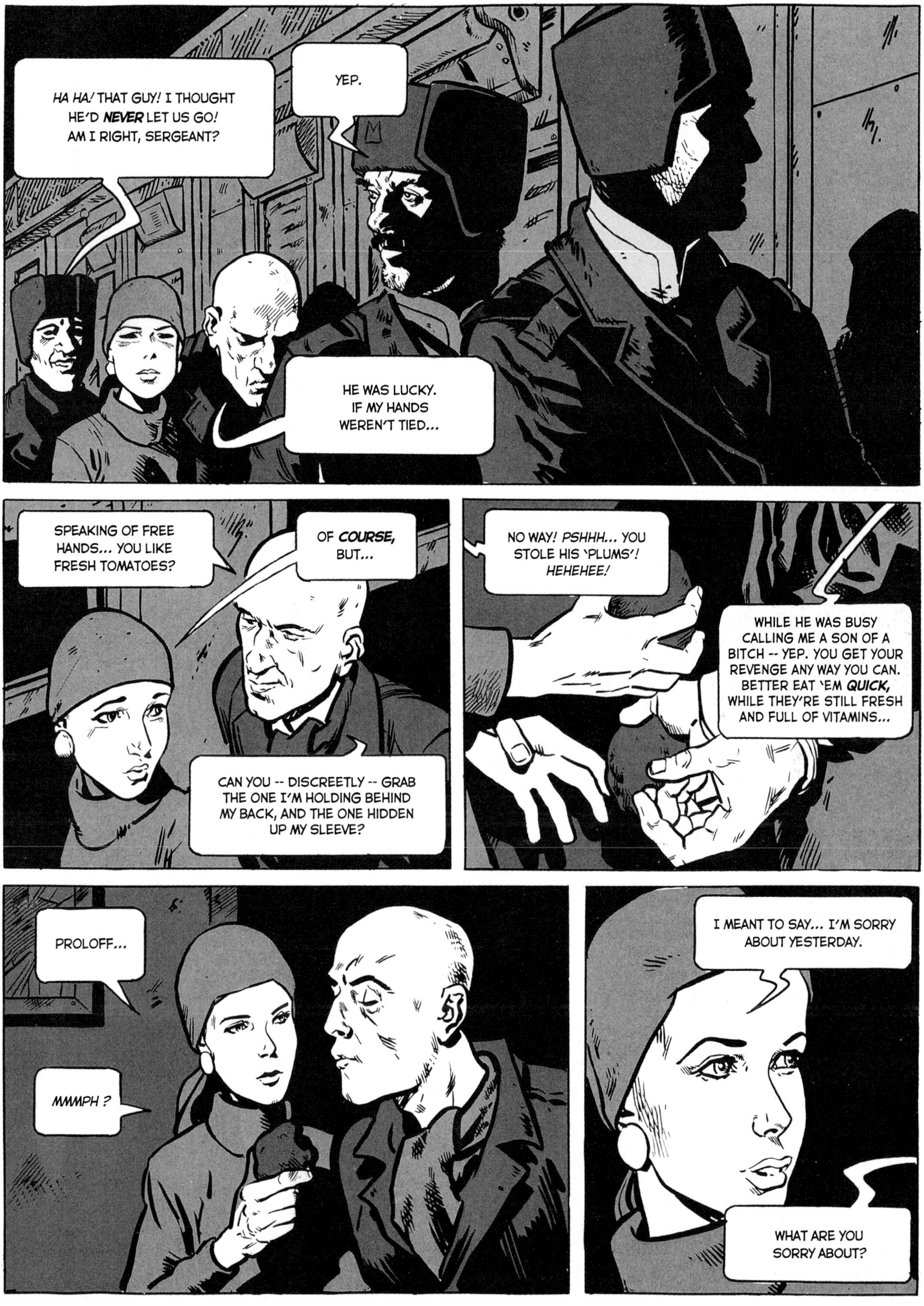
HA HA! THAT GUY! I THOUGHT HE'D ***NEVER*** LET US GO! AM I RIGHT, SERGEANT?
YEP.
HE WAS LUCKY. IF MY HANDS WEREN'T TIED...
SPEAKING OF FREE HANDS... YOU LIKE FRESH TOMATOES?
OF ***COURSE,*** BUT...
CAN YOU -- DISCREETLY -- GRAB THE ONE I'M HOLDING BEHIND MY BACK, AND THE ONE HIDDEN UP MY SLEEVE?
NO WAY! *PSHHH...* YOU STOLE HIS 'PLUMS'! *HEHEHEE!*
WHILE HE WAS BUSY CALLING ME A SON OF A BITCH -- YEP. YOU GET YOUR REVENGE ANY WAY YOU CAN. BETTER EAT 'EM ***QUICK,*** WHILE THEY'RE STILL FRESH AND FULL OF VITAMINS...
PROLOFF...
MMMPH ?
I MEANT TO SAY... I'M SORRY ABOUT YESTERDAY.
WHAT ARE YOU SORRY ABOUT?

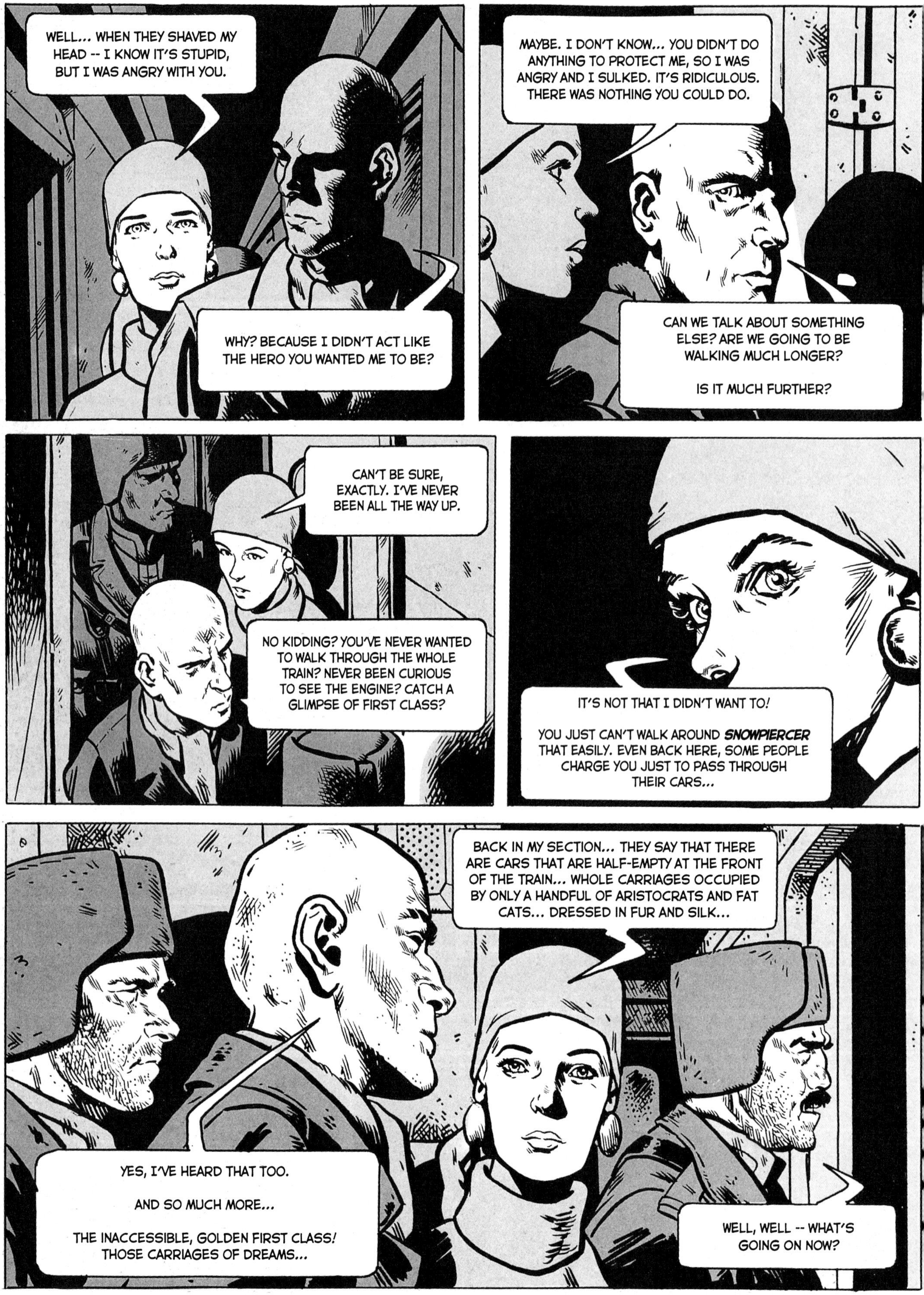
WELL... WHEN THEY SHAVED MY HEAD -- I KNOW IT'S STUPID, BUT I WAS ANGRY WITH YOU.
WHY? BECAUSE I DIDN'T ACT LIKE THE HERO YOU WANTED ME TO BE?
MAYBE. I DON'T KNOW... YOU DIDN'T DO ANYTHING TO PROTECT ME, SO I WAS ANGRY AND I SULKED. IT'S RIDICULOUS. THERE WAS NOTHING YOU COULD DO.
CAN WE TALK ABOUT SOMETHING ELSE? ARE WE GOING TO BE WALKING MUCH LONGER?
IS IT MUCH FURTHER?
CAN'T BE SURE, EXACTLY. I'VE NEVER BEEN ALL THE WAY UP.
NO KIDDING? YOU'VE NEVER WANTED TO WALK THROUGH THE WHOLE TRAIN? NEVER BEEN CURIOUS TO SEE THE ENGINE? CATCH A GLIMPSE OF FIRST CLASS?
IT'S NOT THAT I DIDN'T WANT TO!
YOU JUST CAN'T WALK AROUND ***SNOWPIERCER*** THAT EASILY. EVEN BACK HERE, SOME PEOPLE CHARGE YOU JUST TO PASS THROUGH THEIR CARS...
BACK IN MY SECTION... THEY SAY THAT THERE ARE CARS THAT ARE HALF-EMPTY AT THE FRONT OF THE TRAIN... WHOLE CARRIAGES OCCUPIED BY ONLY A HANDFUL OF ARISTOCRATS AND FAT CATS... DRESSED IN FUR AND SILK...
YES, I'VE HEARD THAT TOO.
AND SO MUCH MORE...
THE INACCESSIBLE, GOLDEN FIRST CLASS! THOSE CARRIAGES OF DREAMS...
WELL, WELL -- WHAT'S GOING ON NOW?

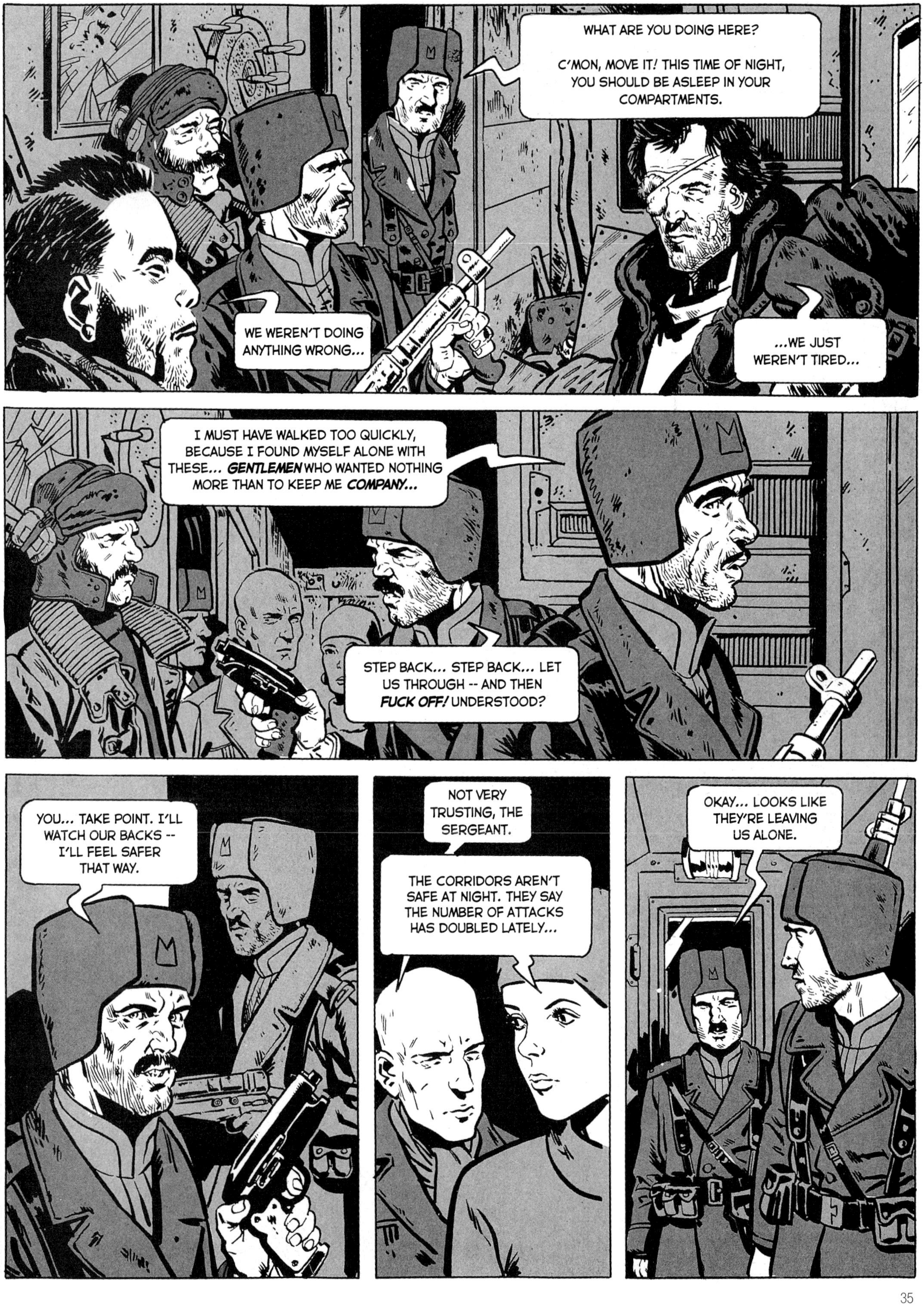
WHAT ARE YOU DOING HERE?
C'MON, MOVE IT! THIS TIME OF NIGHT, YOU SHOULD BE ASLEEP IN YOUR COMPARTMENTS.
WE WEREN'T DOING ANYTHING WRONG...
...WE JUST WEREN'T TIRED...
I MUST HAVE WALKED TOO QUICKLY, BECAUSE I FOUND MYSELF ALONE WITH THESE... GENTLEMEN WHO WANTED NOTHING MORE THAN TO KEEP ME COMPANY...
STEP BACK... STEP BACK... LET US THROUGH -- AND THEN FUCK OFF! UNDERSTOOD?
YOU... TAKE POINT. I'LL WATCH OUR BACKS -- I'LL FEEL SAFER THAT WAY.
NOT VERY TRUSTING, THE SERGEANT.
THE CORRIDORS AREN'T SAFE AT NIGHT. THEY SAY THE NUMBER OF ATTACKS HAS DOUBLED LATELY...
OKAY... LOOKS LIKE THEY'RE LEAVING US ALONE.

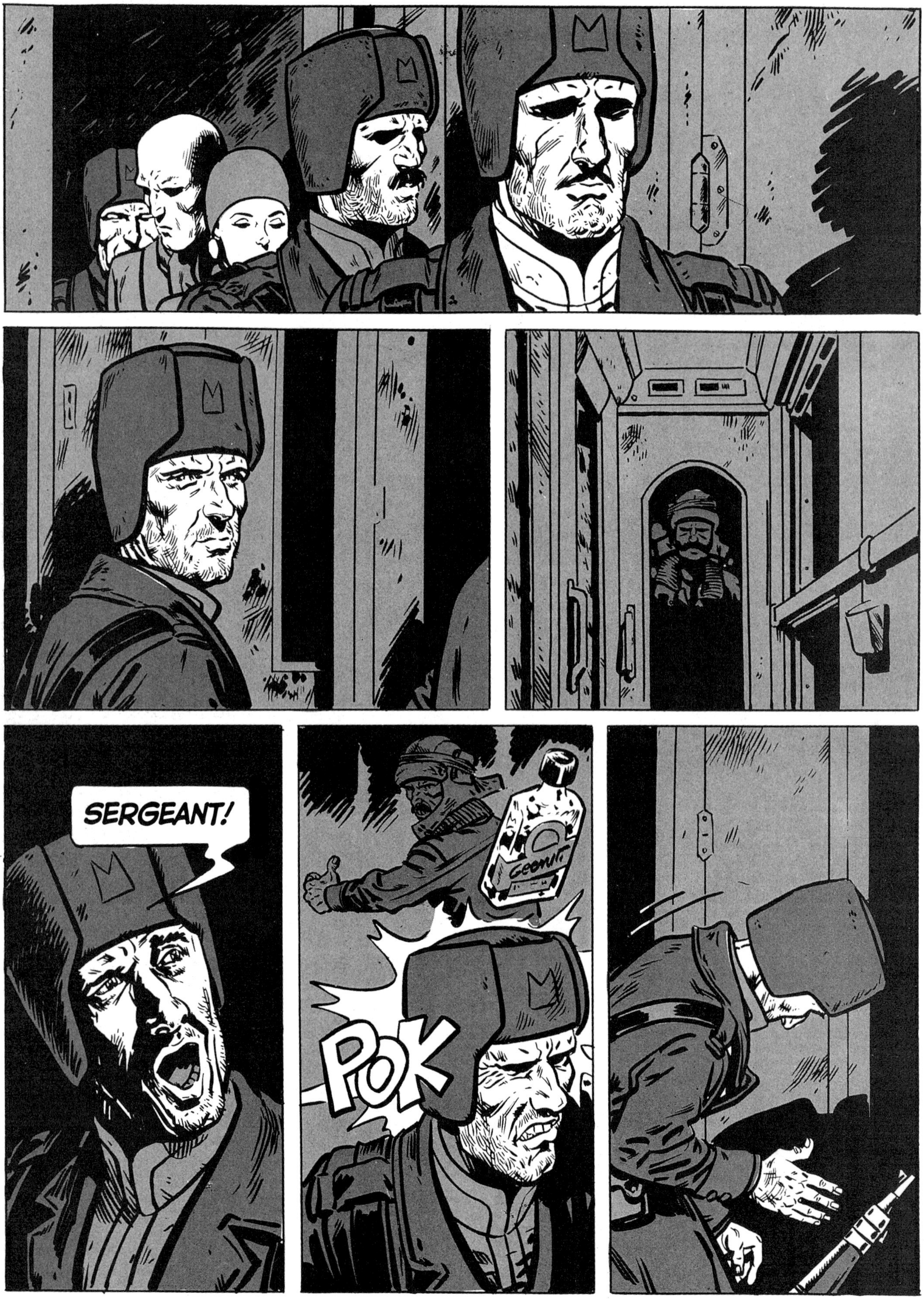
SERGEANT!
POK

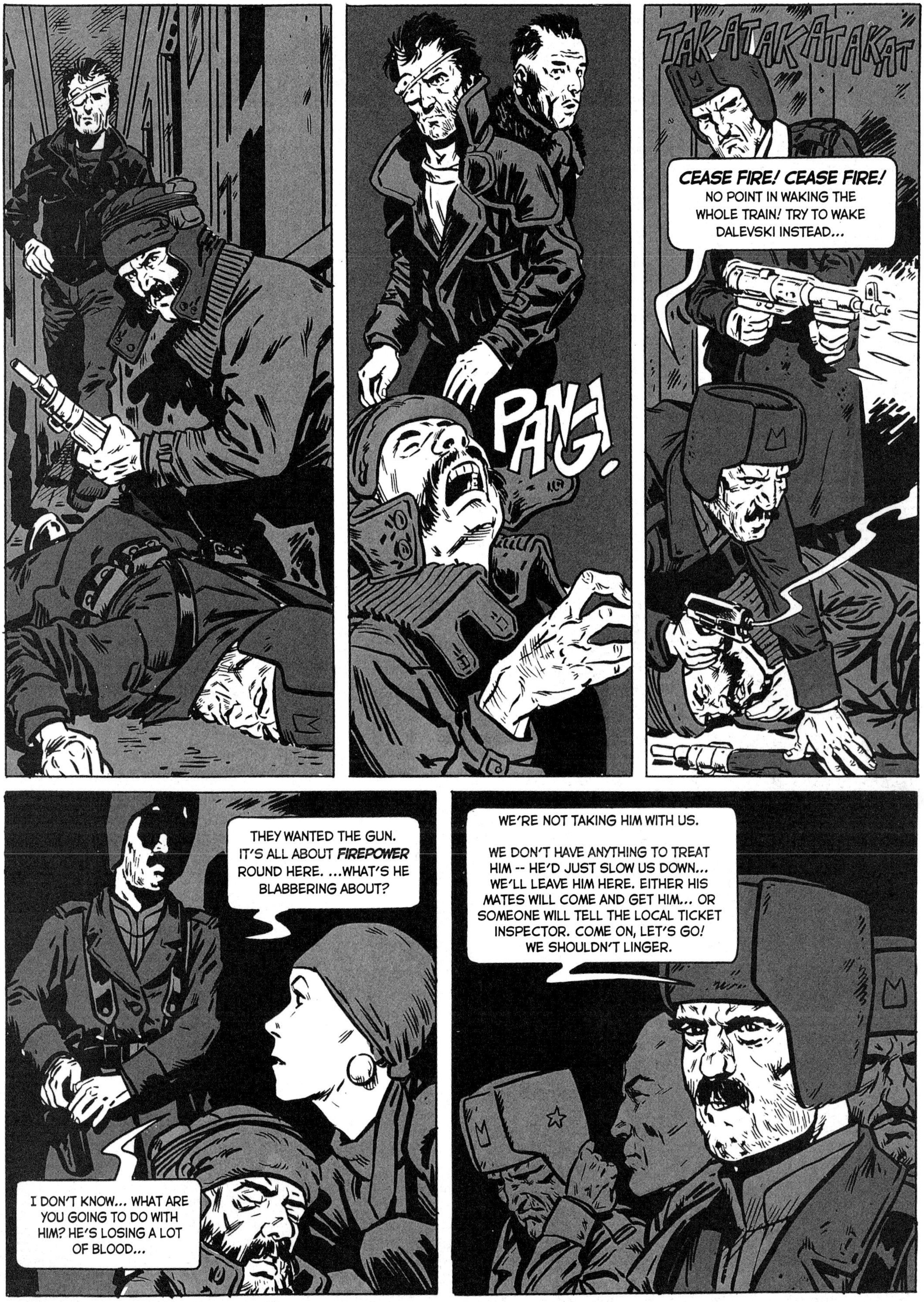
PANG!
TAKATAKATAKAT
CEASE FIRE! CEASE FIRE! NO POINT IN WAKING THE WHOLE TRAIN! TRY TO WAKE DALEVSKI INSTEAD...
THEY WANTED THE GUN. IT'S ALL ABOUT FIREPOWER ROUND HERE. ...WHAT'S HE BLABBERING ABOUT?
I DON'T KNOW... WHAT ARE YOU GOING TO DO WITH HIM? HE'S LOSING A LOT OF BLOOD...
WE'RE NOT TAKING HIM WITH US.
WE DON'T HAVE ANYTHING TO TREAT HIM -- HE'D JUST SLOW US DOWN... WE'LL LEAVE HIM HERE. EITHER HIS MATES WILL COME AND GET HIM... OR SOMEONE WILL TELL THE LOCAL TICKET INSPECTOR. COME ON, LET'S GO! WE SHOULDN'T LINGER.

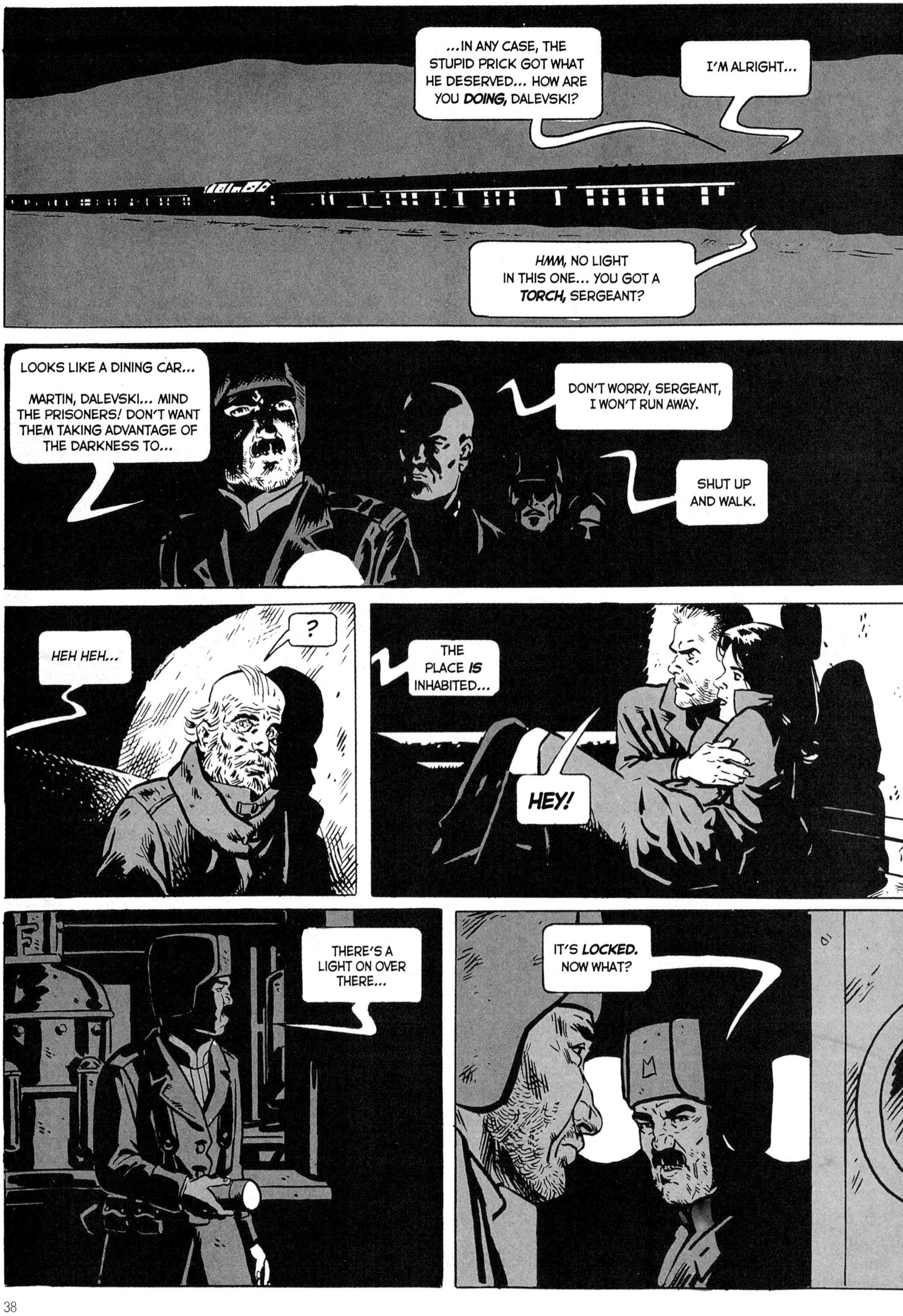
...IN ANY CASE, THE STUPID PRICK GOT WHAT HE DESERVED... HOW ARE YOU DOING, DALEVSKI?
I'M ALRIGHT...
HMM, NO LIGHT IN THIS ONE... YOU GOT A TORCH, SERGEANT?
LOOKS LIKE A DINING CAR...
MARTIN, DALEVSKI... MIND THE PRISONERS! DON'T WANT THEM TAKING ADVANTAGE OF THE DARKNESS TO...
DON'T WORRY, SERGEANT, I WON'T RUN AWAY.
SHUT UP AND WALK.
HEH HEH...
?
THE PLACE IS INHABITED...
HEY!
THERE'S A LIGHT ON OVER THERE...
IT'S LOCKED. NOW WHAT?

I CAN'T SEE ANYONE... AND NO WAY OF GETTING THROUGH!

STRANGE. THERE SHOULD BE A GUARD HERE. THERE'S ALWAYS A GUARD AT THE BUTCHERS'...

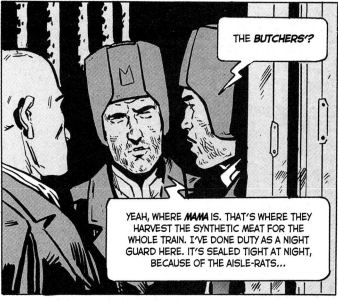

THE *BUTCHERS'*?

YEAH, WHERE *MAMA* IS. THAT'S WHERE THEY HARVEST THE SYNTHETIC MEAT FOR THE WHOLE TRAIN. I'VE DONE DUTY AS A NIGHT GUARD HERE. IT'S SEALED TIGHT AT NIGHT, BECAUSE OF THE AISLE-RATS...

WE COULD ASK A TICKET INSPECTOR TO OPEN THE DOOR...

THIS TIME OF NIGHT?

LET'S *DO* SOMETHING, ALREADY! I'M FREEZING MY BALLS OFF JUST STANDING AROUND.

WHAT'S THE PLAN?

LOCO, WILL YOU GIVE IT A REST...

HEY! HAVE YOU LOST YOUR MIND? I HAVEN'T DONE ANYTHING!

GO FIND A *TICKET INSPECTOR* AND GET HIM TO OPEN THE DOOR FOR US. *NOW!*

HOW?! I DON'T KNOW WHERE HE IS!

JUST BLOODY WELL *DO* IT! *MOVE!* OR I'LL BEAT THE SHIT OUT OF YOU WITH MY FLASHLIGHT!

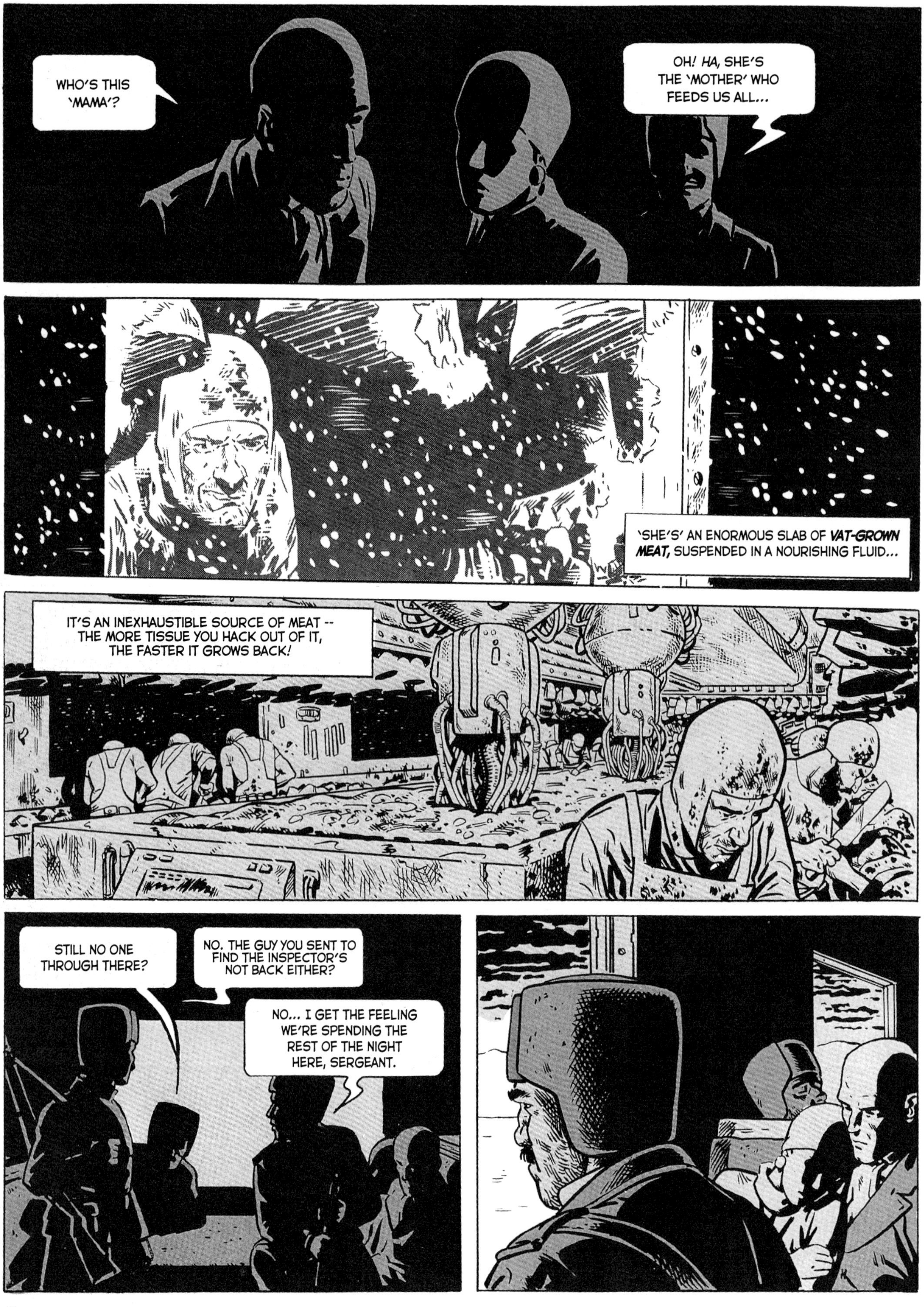
WHO'S THIS 'MAMA'?
OH! HA, SHE'S THE 'MOTHER' WHO FEEDS US ALL...
'SHE'S' AN ENORMOUS SLAB OF VAT-GROWN MEAT, SUSPENDED IN A NOURISHING FLUID...
IT'S AN INEXHAUSTIBLE SOURCE OF MEAT -- THE MORE TISSUE YOU HACK OUT OF IT, THE FASTER IT GROWS BACK!
STILL NO ONE THROUGH THERE?
NO. THE GUY YOU SENT TO FIND THE INSPECTOR'S NOT BACK EITHER?
NO... I GET THE FEELING WE'RE SPENDING THE REST OF THE NIGHT HERE, SERGEANT.

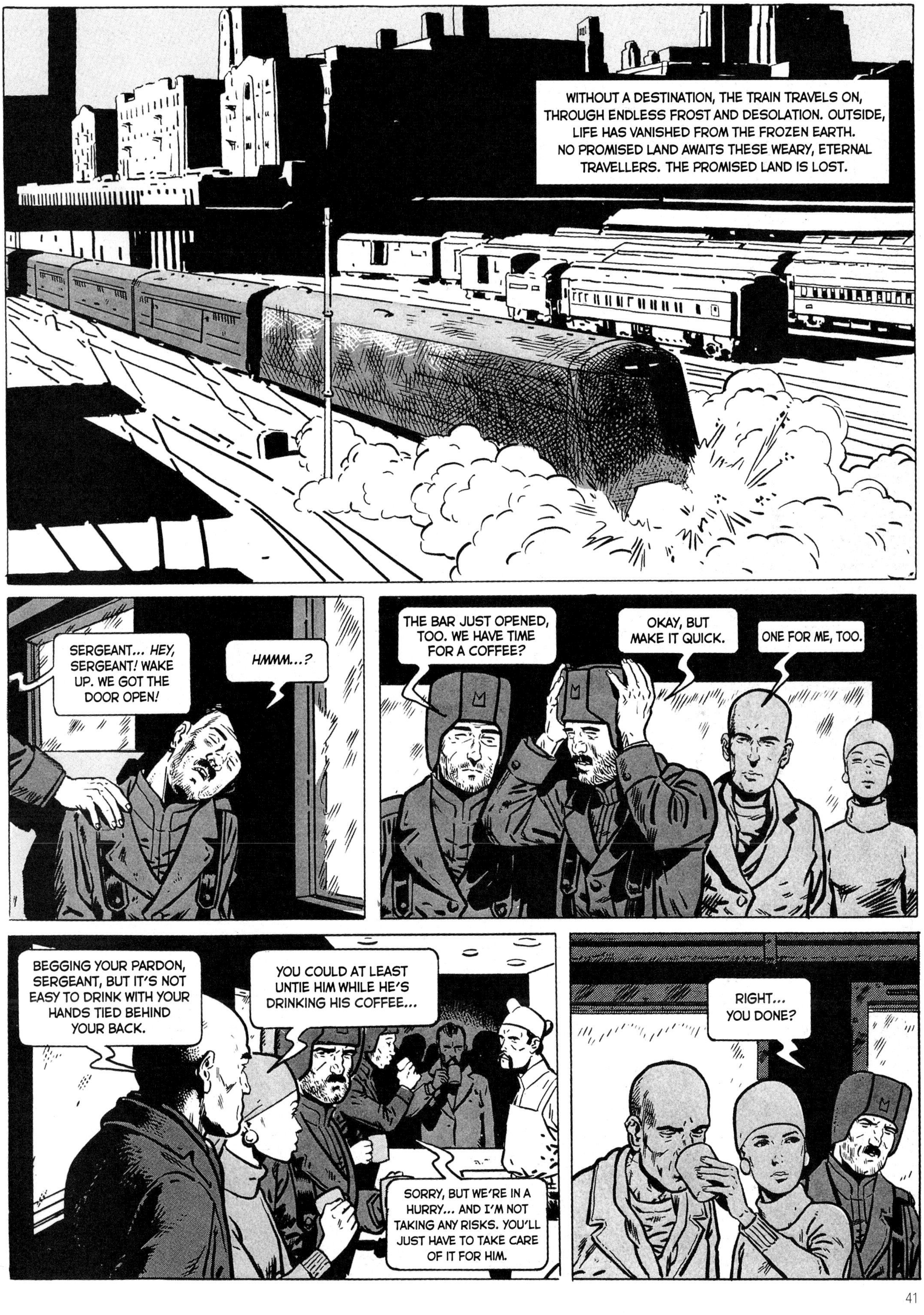
WITHOUT A DESTINATION, THE TRAIN TRAVELS ON, THROUGH ENDLESS FROST AND DESOLATION. OUTSIDE, LIFE HAS VANISHED FROM THE FROZEN EARTH. NO PROMISED LAND AWAITS THESE WEARY, ETERNAL TRAVELLERS. THE PROMISED LAND IS LOST.
SERGEANT... *HEY,* SERGEANT! WAKE UP. WE GOT THE DOOR OPEN!
HMMM...?
THE BAR JUST OPENED, TOO. WE HAVE TIME FOR A COFFEE?
OKAY, BUT MAKE IT QUICK.
ONE FOR ME, TOO.
BEGGING YOUR PARDON, SERGEANT, BUT IT'S NOT EASY TO DRINK WITH YOUR HANDS TIED BEHIND YOUR BACK.
YOU COULD AT LEAST UNTIE HIM WHILE HE'S DRINKING HIS COFFEE...
SORRY, BUT WE'RE IN A HURRY... AND I'M NOT TAKING ANY RISKS. YOU'LL JUST HAVE TO TAKE CARE OF IT FOR HIM.
RIGHT... YOU DONE?

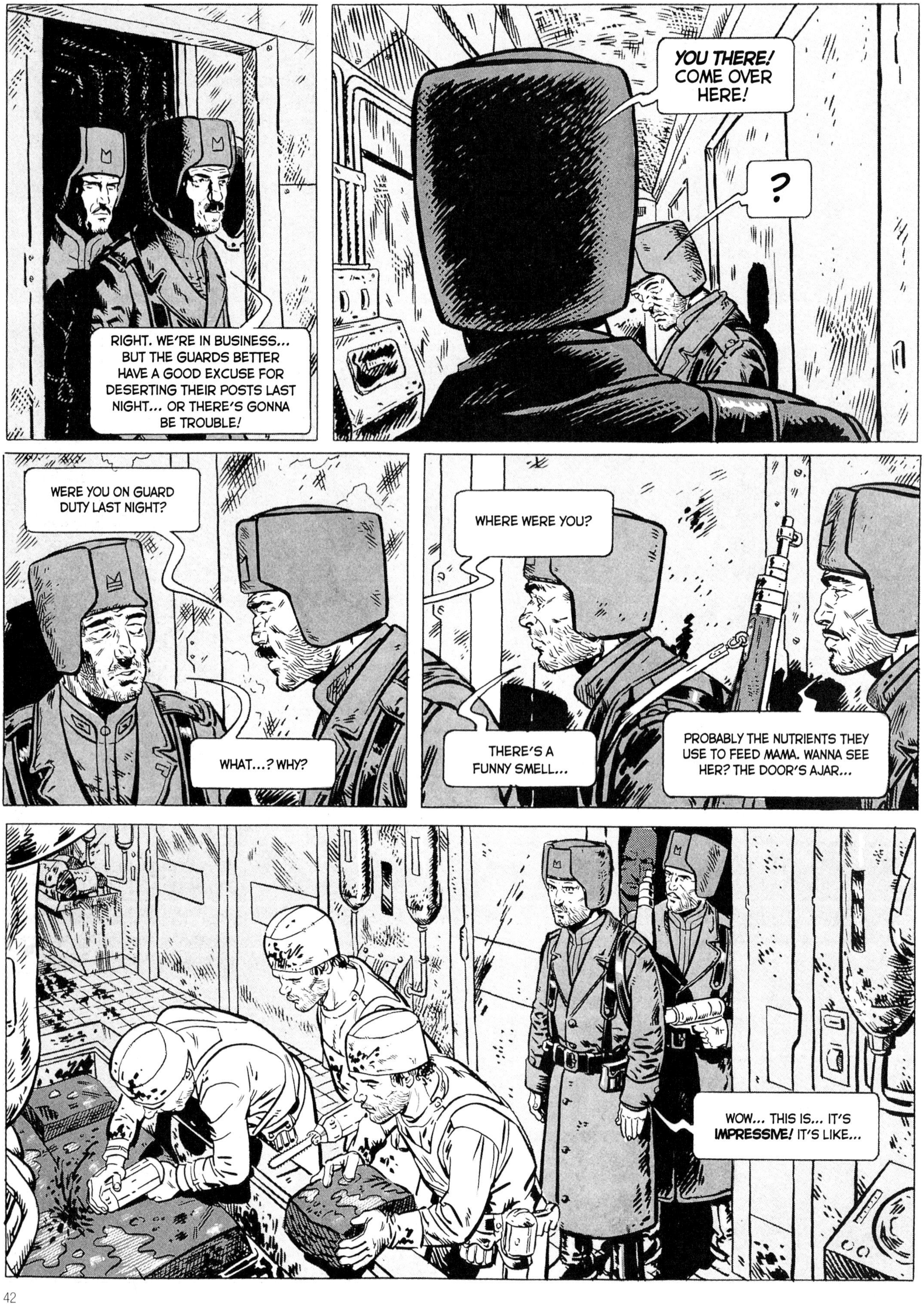
RIGHT. WE'RE IN BUSINESS... BUT THE GUARDS BETTER HAVE A GOOD EXCUSE FOR DESERTING THEIR POSTS LAST NIGHT... OR THERE'S GONNA BE TROUBLE!
YOU THERE! COME OVER HERE!
?
WERE YOU ON GUARD DUTY LAST NIGHT?
WHAT...? WHY?
WHERE WERE YOU?
THERE'S A FUNNY SMELL...
PROBABLY THE NUTRIENTS THEY USE TO FEED MAMA. WANNA SEE HER? THE DOOR'S AJAR...
WOW... THIS IS... IT'S IMPRESSIVE! IT'S LIKE...

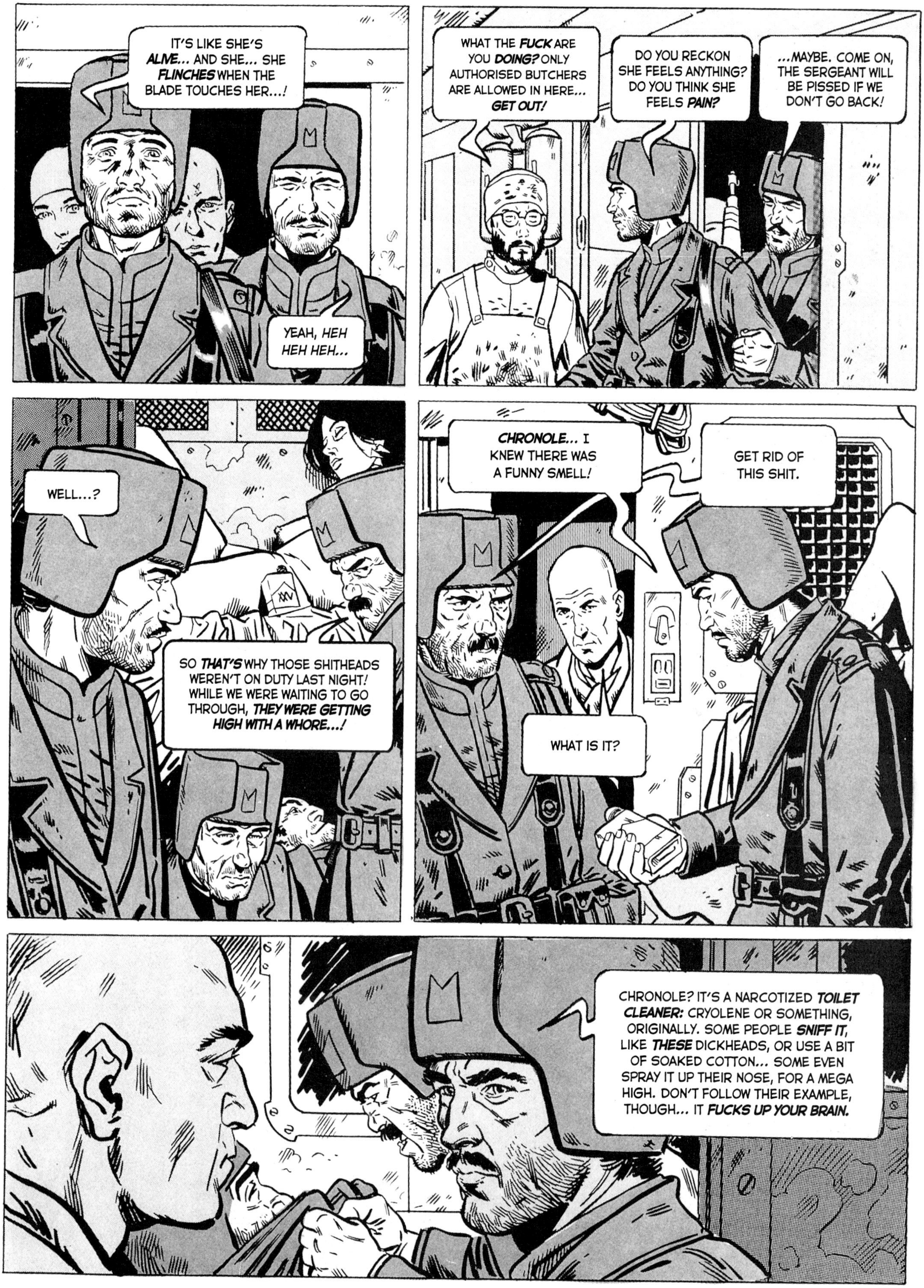
IT'S LIKE SHE'S ALIVE... AND SHE... SHE FLINCHES WHEN THE BLADE TOUCHES HER...!
YEAH, HEH HEH HEH...
WHAT THE FUCK ARE YOU DOING? ONLY AUTHORISED BUTCHERS ARE ALLOWED IN HERE... GET OUT!
DO YOU RECKON SHE FEELS ANYTHING? DO YOU THINK SHE FEELS PAIN?
...MAYBE. COME ON, THE SERGEANT WILL BE PISSED IF WE DON'T GO BACK!
WELL...?
SO THAT'S WHY THOSE SHITHEADS WEREN'T ON DUTY LAST NIGHT! WHILE WE WERE WAITING TO GO THROUGH, THEY WERE GETTING HIGH WITH A WHORE...!
CHRONOLE... I KNEW THERE WAS A FUNNY SMELL!
GET RID OF THIS SHIT.
WHAT IS IT?
CHRONOLE? IT'S A NARCOTIZED TOILET CLEANER: CRYOLENE OR SOMETHING, ORIGINALLY. SOME PEOPLE SNIFF IT, LIKE THESE DICKHEADS, OR USE A BIT OF SOAKED COTTON... SOME EVEN SPRAY IT UP THEIR NOSE, FOR A MEGA HIGH. DON'T FOLLOW THEIR EXAMPLE, THOUGH... IT FUCKS UP YOUR BRAIN.

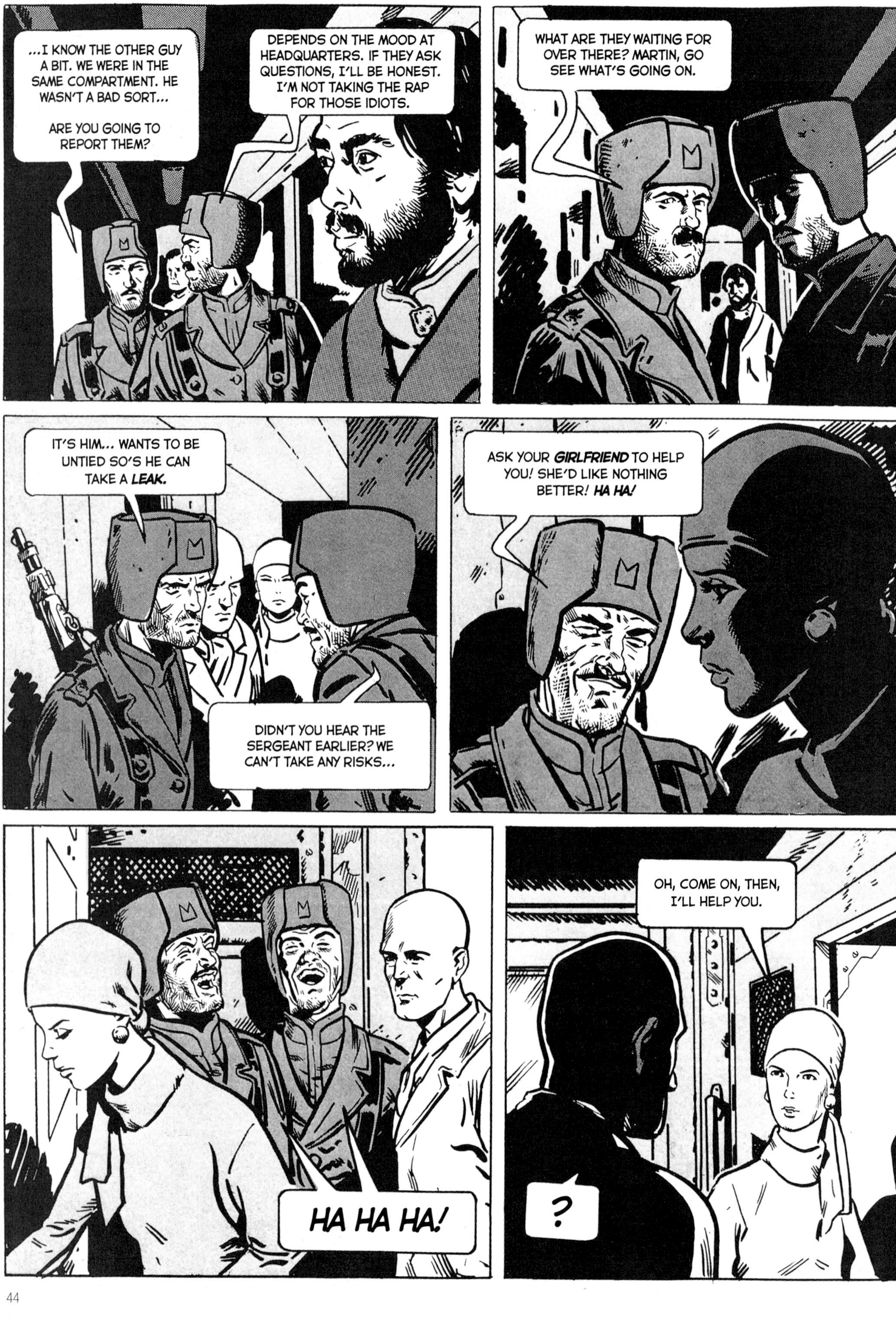
...I KNOW THE OTHER GUY A BIT. WE WERE IN THE SAME COMPARTMENT. HE WASN'T A BAD SORT...
ARE YOU GOING TO REPORT THEM?
DEPENDS ON THE MOOD AT HEADQUARTERS. IF THEY ASK QUESTIONS, I'LL BE HONEST. I'M NOT TAKING THE RAP FOR THOSE IDIOTS.
WHAT ARE THEY WAITING FOR OVER THERE? MARTIN, GO SEE WHAT'S GOING ON.
IT'S HIM... WANTS TO BE UNTIED SO'S HE CAN TAKE A **LEAK.**
DIDN'T YOU HEAR THE SERGEANT EARLIER? WE CAN'T TAKE ANY RISKS...
ASK YOUR **GIRLFRIEND** TO HELP YOU! SHE'D LIKE NOTHING BETTER! **HA HA!**
HA HA HA!
?
OH, COME ON, THEN, I'LL HELP YOU.

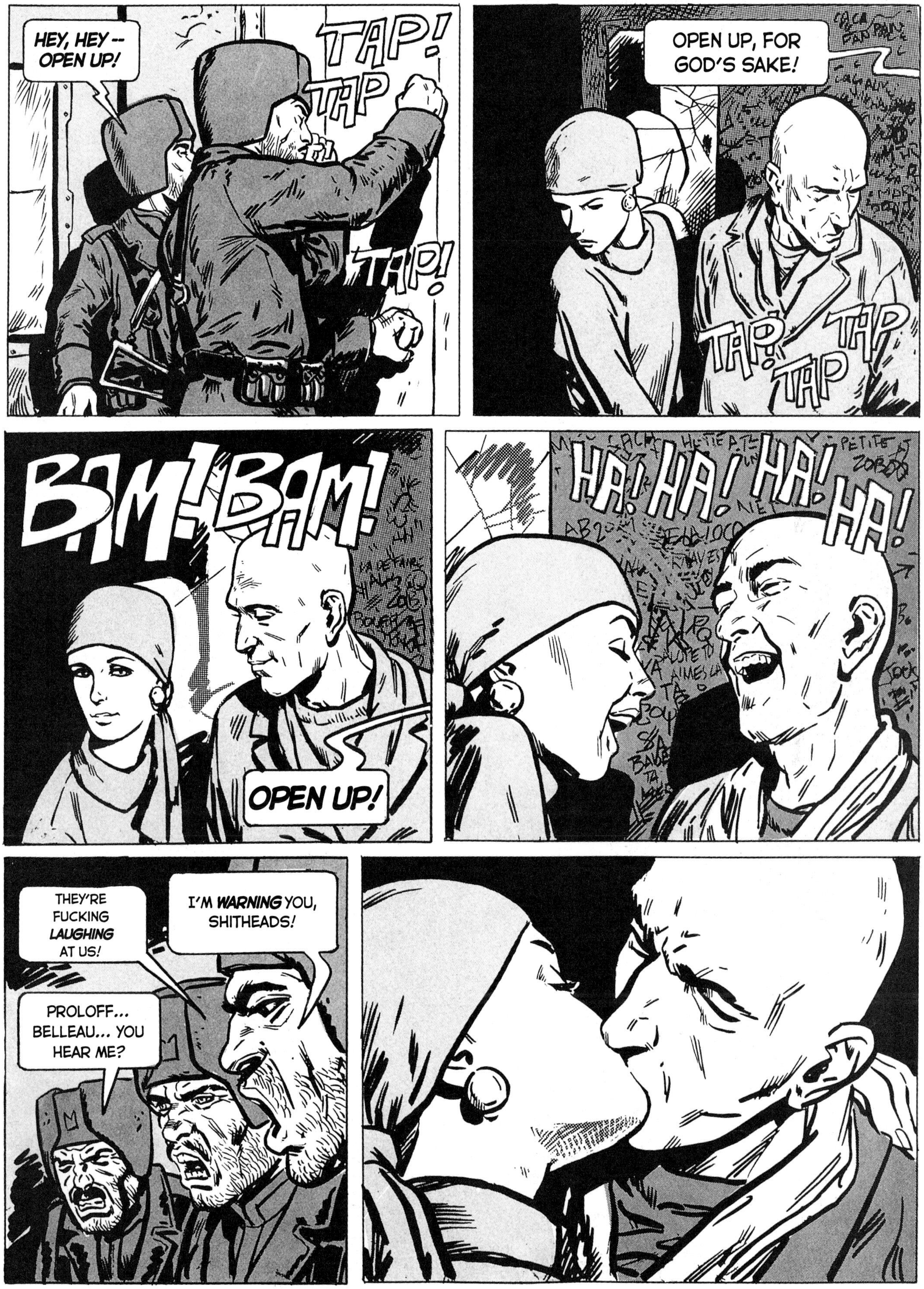
HEY, HEY -- OPEN UP!
TAP! TAP
TAP!
OPEN UP, FOR GOD'S SAKE!
TAP! TAP TAP
BAM! BAM!
OPEN UP!
HA! HA! HA! HA!
THEY'RE FUCKING LAUGHING AT US!
I'M WARNING YOU, SHITHEADS!
PROLOFF... BELLEAU... YOU HEAR ME?

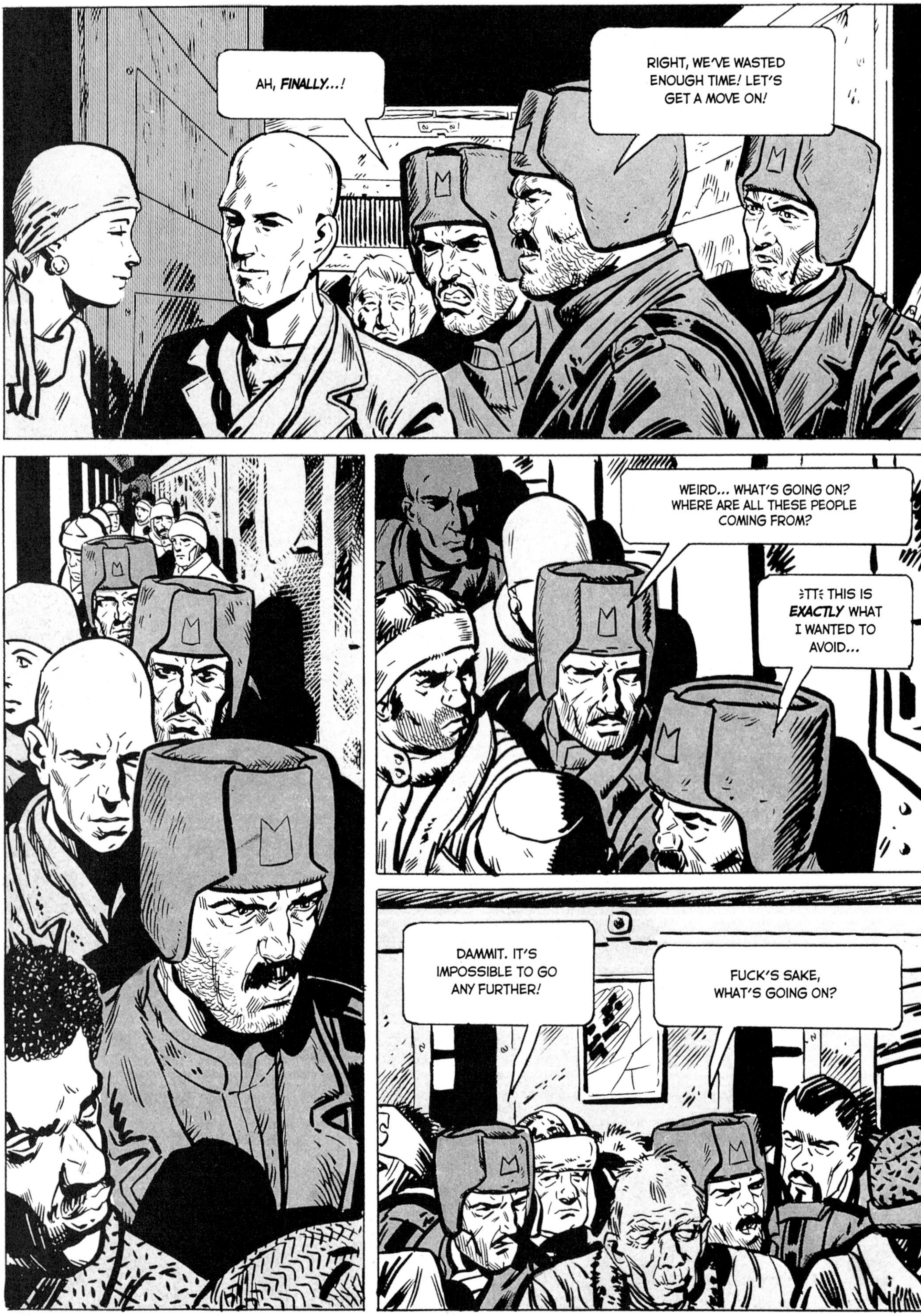
AH, FINALLY...!
RIGHT, WE'VE WASTED ENOUGH TIME! LET'S GET A MOVE ON!
WEIRD... WHAT'S GOING ON? WHERE ARE ALL THESE PEOPLE COMING FROM?
TT THIS IS EXACTLY WHAT I WANTED TO AVOID...
DAMMIT. IT'S IMPOSSIBLE TO GO ANY FURTHER!
FUCK'S SAKE, WHAT'S GOING ON?

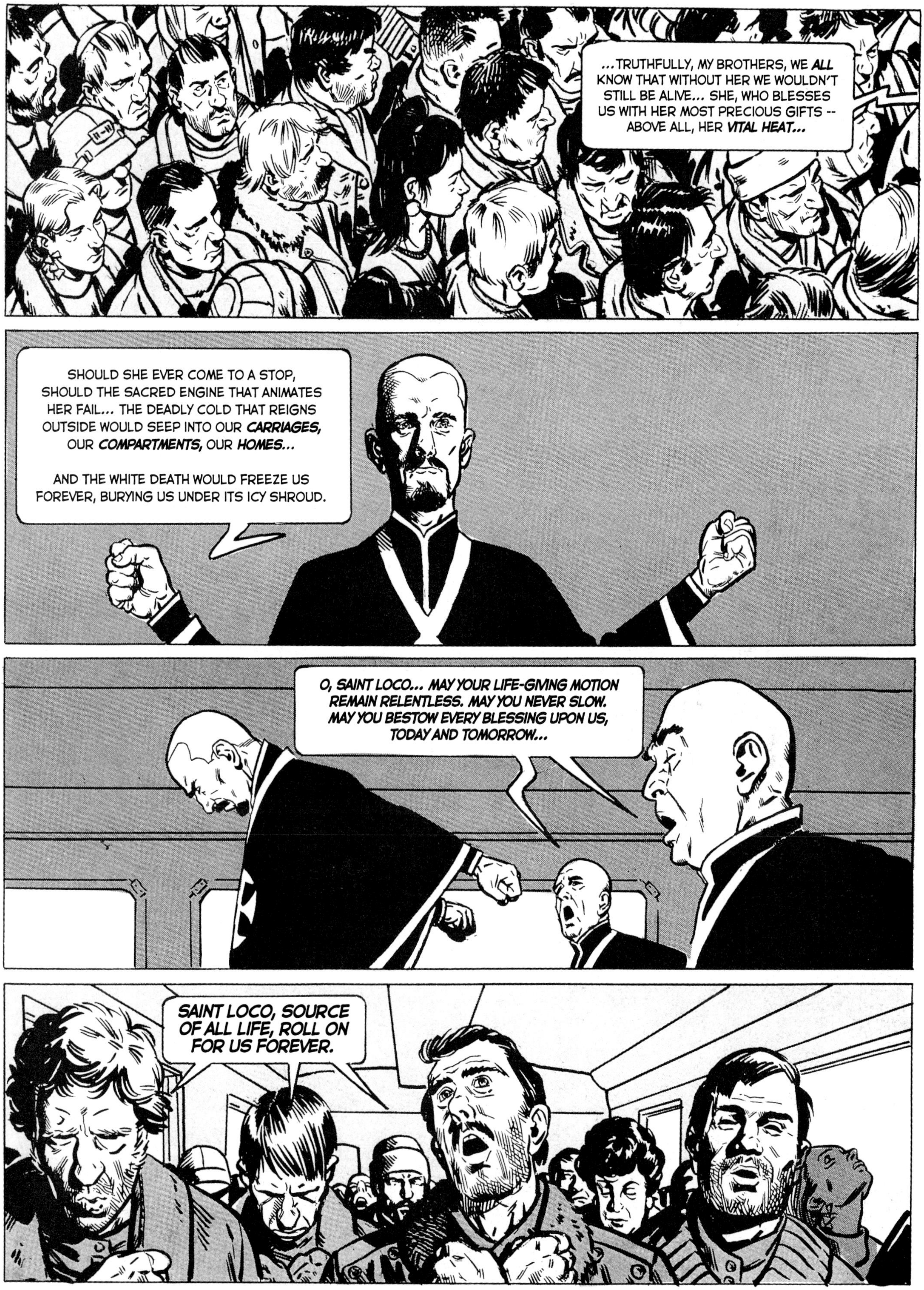
...TRUTHFULLY, MY BROTHERS, WE ALL KNOW THAT WITHOUT HER WE WOULDN'T STILL BE ALIVE... SHE, WHO BLESSES US WITH HER MOST PRECIOUS GIFTS -- ABOVE ALL, HER VITAL HEAT...
SHOULD SHE EVER COME TO A STOP, SHOULD THE SACRED ENGINE THAT ANIMATES HER FAIL... THE DEADLY COLD THAT REIGNS OUTSIDE WOULD SEEP INTO OUR CARRIAGES, OUR COMPARTMENTS, OUR HOMES...
AND THE WHITE DEATH WOULD FREEZE US FOREVER, BURYING US UNDER ITS ICY SHROUD.
O, SAINT LOCO... MAY YOUR LIFE-GIVING MOTION REMAIN RELENTLESS. MAY YOU NEVER SLOW. MAY YOU BESTOW EVERY BLESSING UPON US, TODAY AND TOMORROW...
SAINT LOCO, SOURCE OF ALL LIFE, ROLL ON FOR US FOREVER.

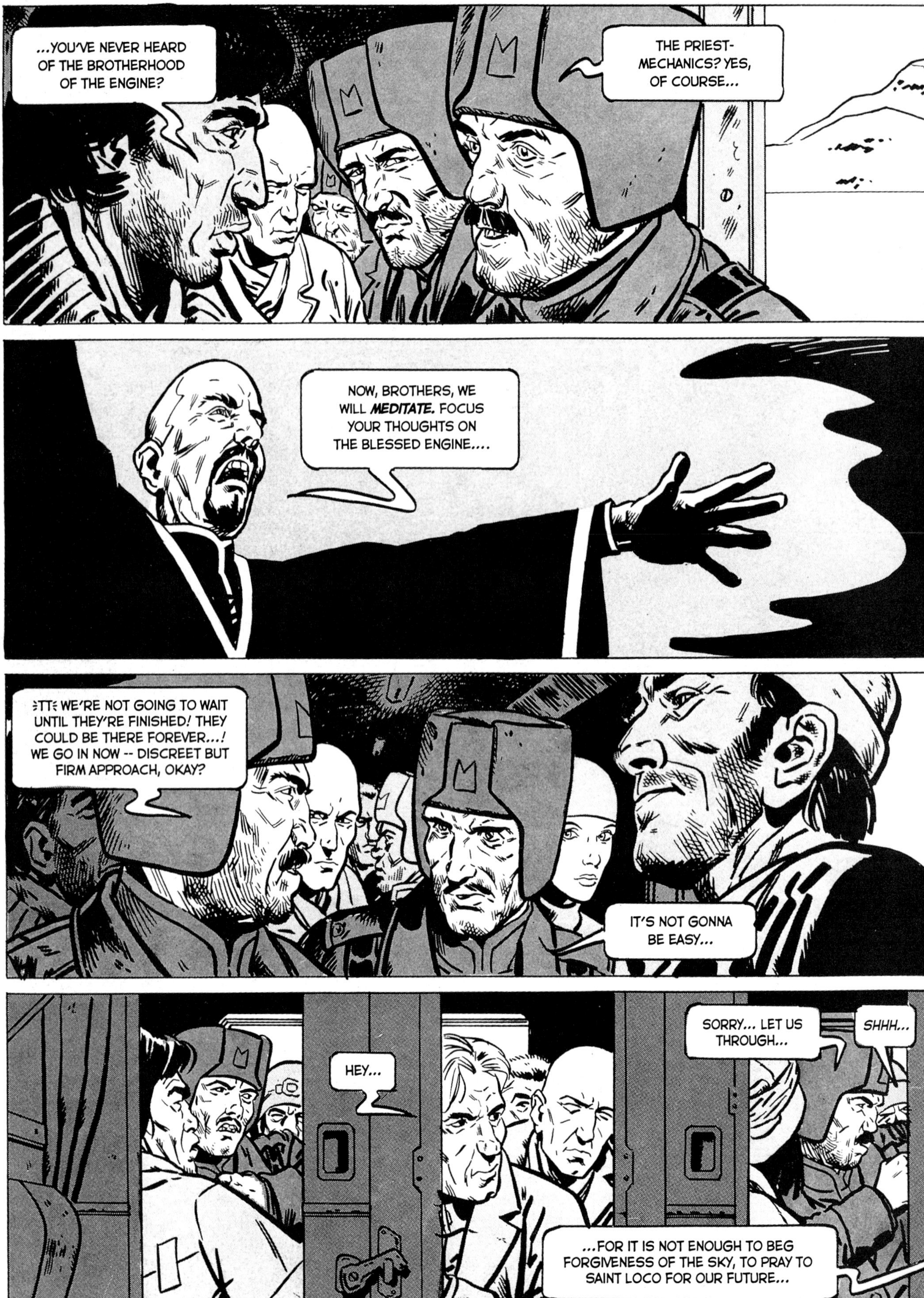
...YOU'VE NEVER HEARD OF THE BROTHERHOOD OF THE ENGINE?
THE PRIEST-MECHANICS? YES, OF COURSE...
NOW, BROTHERS, WE WILL MEDITATE. FOCUS YOUR THOUGHTS ON THE BLESSED ENGINE....
TT WE'RE NOT GOING TO WAIT UNTIL THEY'RE FINISHED! THEY COULD BE THERE FOREVER...! WE GO IN NOW -- DISCREET BUT FIRM APPROACH, OKAY?
IT'S NOT GONNA BE EASY...
HEY...
SORRY... LET US THROUGH...
SHHH...
...FOR IT IS NOT ENOUGH TO BEG FORGIVENESS OF THE SKY, TO PRAY TO SAINT LOCO FOR OUR FUTURE...

WE MUST MOBILIZE ALL OUR MENTAL POWERS... WE WILL TRANSFER THE POWERFUL PSYCHIC ENERGY THAT PERMEATES EVERY ONE OF US -- WE WILL TRANSFER IT FROM OUR BODIES, *INTO THE ENGINE ITSELF!* WE WILL GUIDE HER WITH OUR THOUGHTS, FOCUSING UPON EVERY COG AND BOLT, TO EASE HER STRUGGLE THROUGH THE SNOW...

EXCUSE ME, FATHER, BUT...

≥TSSK≥ WHAT IS IT? THE NEGATIVE VIBRATIONS ARE FLOWING OFF YOU IN WAVES -- I CAN *FEEL* THEM DISTURBING OUR CONCENTRATION...

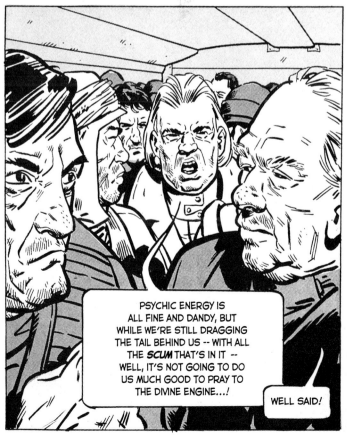

PSYCHIC ENERGY IS ALL FINE AND DANDY, BUT WHILE WE'RE STILL DRAGGING THE TAIL BEHIND US -- WITH ALL THE *SCUM* THAT'S IN IT -- WELL, IT'S NOT GOING TO DO US MUCH GOOD TO PRAY TO THE DIVINE ENGINE...!

WELL SAID!

HEY, *SOLDIER BOYS!* YOU OUGHTTA BE ABLE TO TELL US! WHAT GIVES?! *DUMP THE TAIL ALREADY!*

WHAT ABOUT THE *PEOPLE* BACK THERE?

49

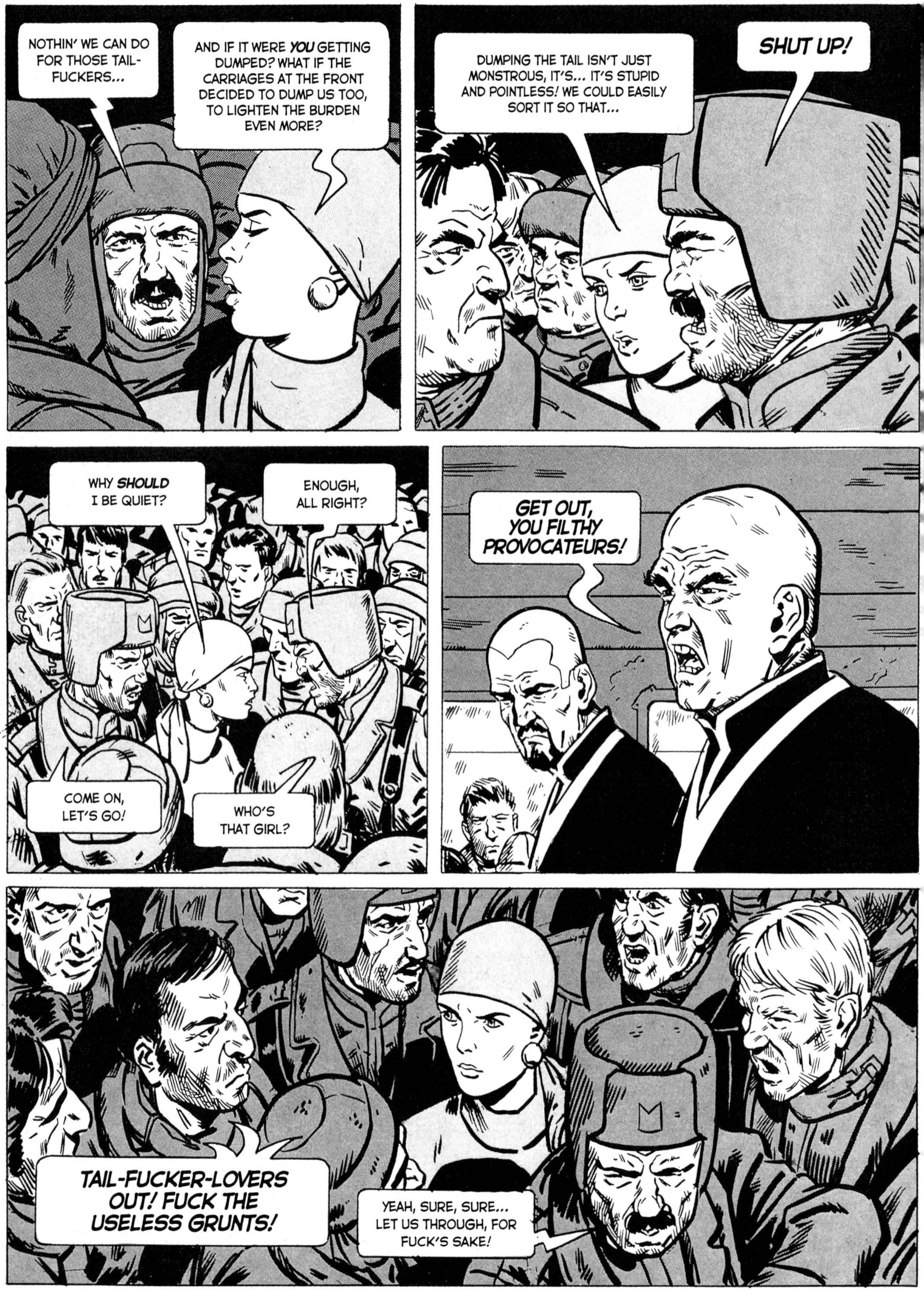
NOTHIN' WE CAN DO FOR THOSE TAIL-FUCKERS...
AND IF IT WERE YOU GETTING DUMPED? WHAT IF THE CARRIAGES AT THE FRONT DECIDED TO DUMP US TOO, TO LIGHTEN THE BURDEN EVEN MORE?
DUMPING THE TAIL ISN'T JUST MONSTROUS, IT'S... IT'S STUPID AND POINTLESS! WE COULD EASILY SORT IT SO THAT...
SHUT UP!
WHY SHOULD I BE QUIET?
ENOUGH, ALL RIGHT?
COME ON, LET'S GO!
WHO'S THAT GIRL?
GET OUT, YOU FILTHY PROVOCATEURS!
TAIL-FUCKER-LOVERS OUT! FUCK THE USELESS GRUNTS!
YEAH, SURE, SURE... LET US THROUGH, FOR FUCK'S SAKE!

NICE WORK! A COUPLE MINUTES LONGER AND WE'D **ALL** HAVE HAD THE SHIT KICKED OUT OF US BECAUSE OF YOU. NEXT TIME, JUST KEEP YOUR SABRE-RATTLING TO YOURSELF...

WHAT ABOUT YOU?

?

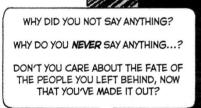

WHY DID YOU NOT SAY ANYTHING?

WHY DO YOU **NEVER** SAY ANYTHING...?

DON'T YOU CARE ABOUT THE FATE OF THE PEOPLE YOU LEFT BEHIND, NOW THAT YOU'VE MADE IT OUT?

...AND YET YOU SAY YOU KNOW WHAT IT'S LIKE OVER THERE... SO WHY DO YOU NEVER TALK ABOUT IT?

THOSE PEOPLE WANT OUT OF THE GHETTO TOO... WHY NOT TRY TO DEFEND THEM? **HELP** THEM?

YOU DON'T KNOW WHAT YOU'RE TALKING ABOUT.

FOR GOD'S SAKE! JUST SHUT UP, BOTH OF YOU, AND KEEP WALKING!

LOOK, YOU CAN TALK ALL YOU WANT WHEN WE GET TO HEADQUARTERS... THE BRASS WILL BE **DELIGHTED** TO LISTEN.

IN THE MEANTIME, JUST KEEP WALKING AND SHUT UP!

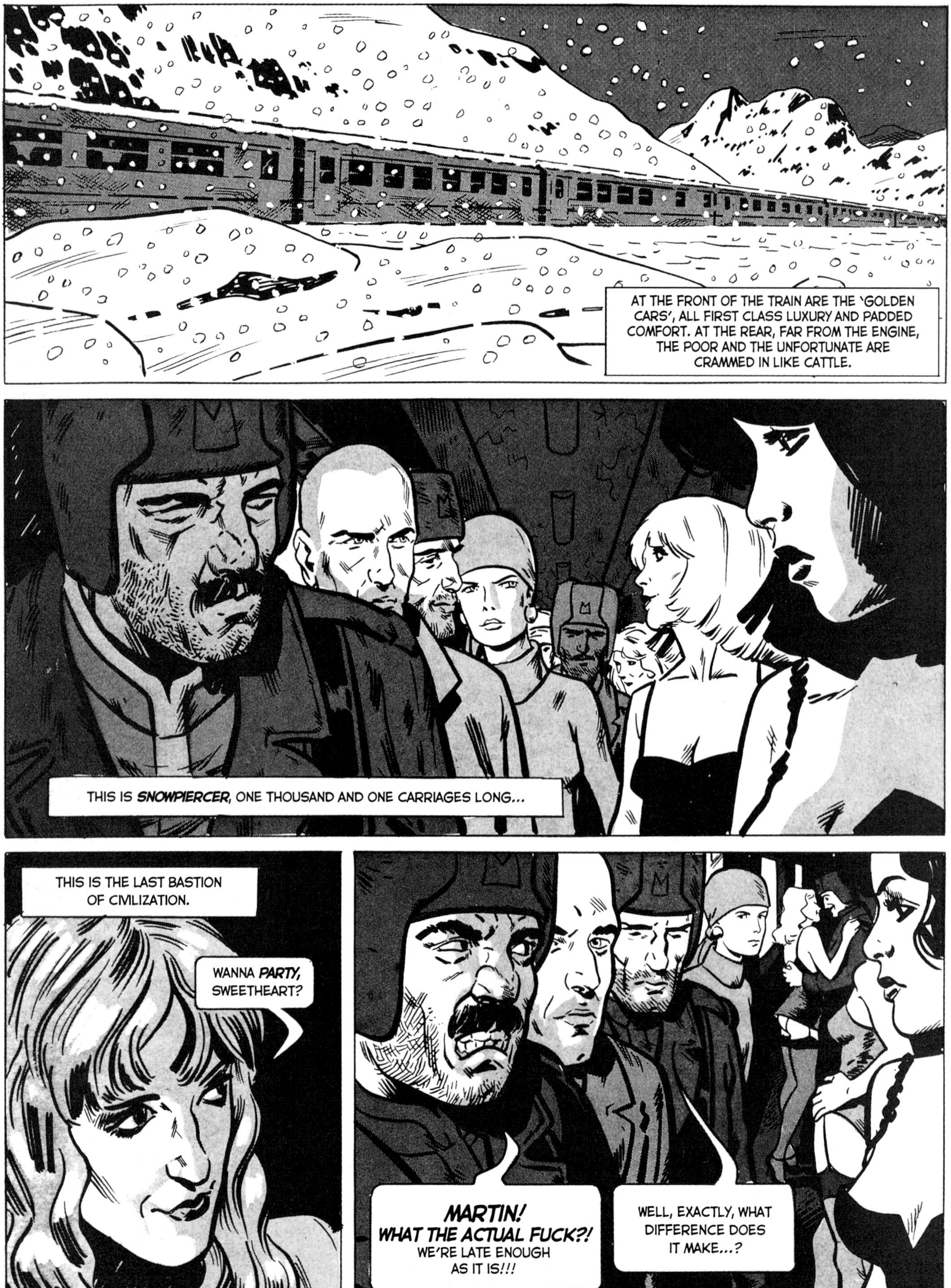
AT THE FRONT OF THE TRAIN ARE THE 'GOLDEN CARS', ALL FIRST CLASS LUXURY AND PADDED COMFORT. AT THE REAR, FAR FROM THE ENGINE, THE POOR AND THE UNFORTUNATE ARE CRAMMED IN LIKE CATTLE.
THIS IS *SNOWPIERCER*, ONE THOUSAND AND ONE CARRIAGES LONG...
THIS IS THE LAST BASTION OF CIVILIZATION.
WANNA *PARTY*, SWEETHEART?
MARTIN! WHAT THE ACTUAL FUCK?! WE'RE LATE ENOUGH AS IT IS!!!
WELL, EXACTLY, WHAT DIFFERENCE DOES IT MAKE...?

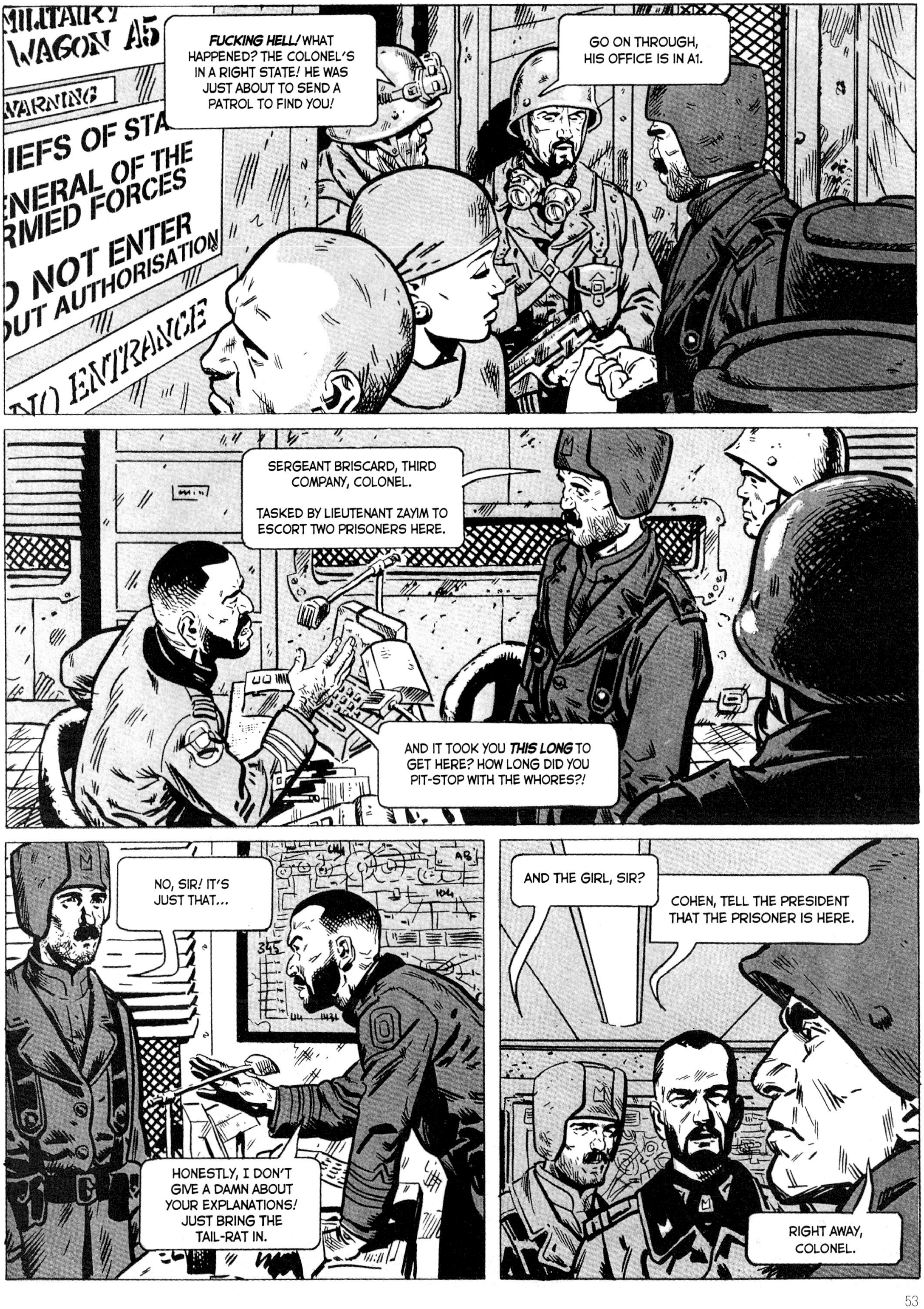

MILITARY WAGON A5
WARNING
...IEFS OF STA...
...ENERAL OF THE ...RMED FORCES
...O NOT ENTER ...OUT AUTHORISATION
NO ENTRANCE
FUCKING HELL! WHAT HAPPENED? THE COLONEL'S IN A RIGHT STATE! HE WAS JUST ABOUT TO SEND A PATROL TO FIND YOU!
GO ON THROUGH, HIS OFFICE IS IN A1.
SERGEANT BRISCARD, THIRD COMPANY, COLONEL.
TASKED BY LIEUTENANT ZAYIM TO ESCORT TWO PRISONERS HERE.
AND IT TOOK YOU THIS LONG TO GET HERE? HOW LONG DID YOU PIT-STOP WITH THE WHORES?!
NO, SIR! IT'S JUST THAT...
HONESTLY, I DON'T GIVE A DAMN ABOUT YOUR EXPLANATIONS! JUST BRING THE TAIL-RAT IN.
AND THE GIRL, SIR?
COHEN, TELL THE PRESIDENT THAT THE PRISONER IS HERE.
RIGHT AWAY, COLONEL.

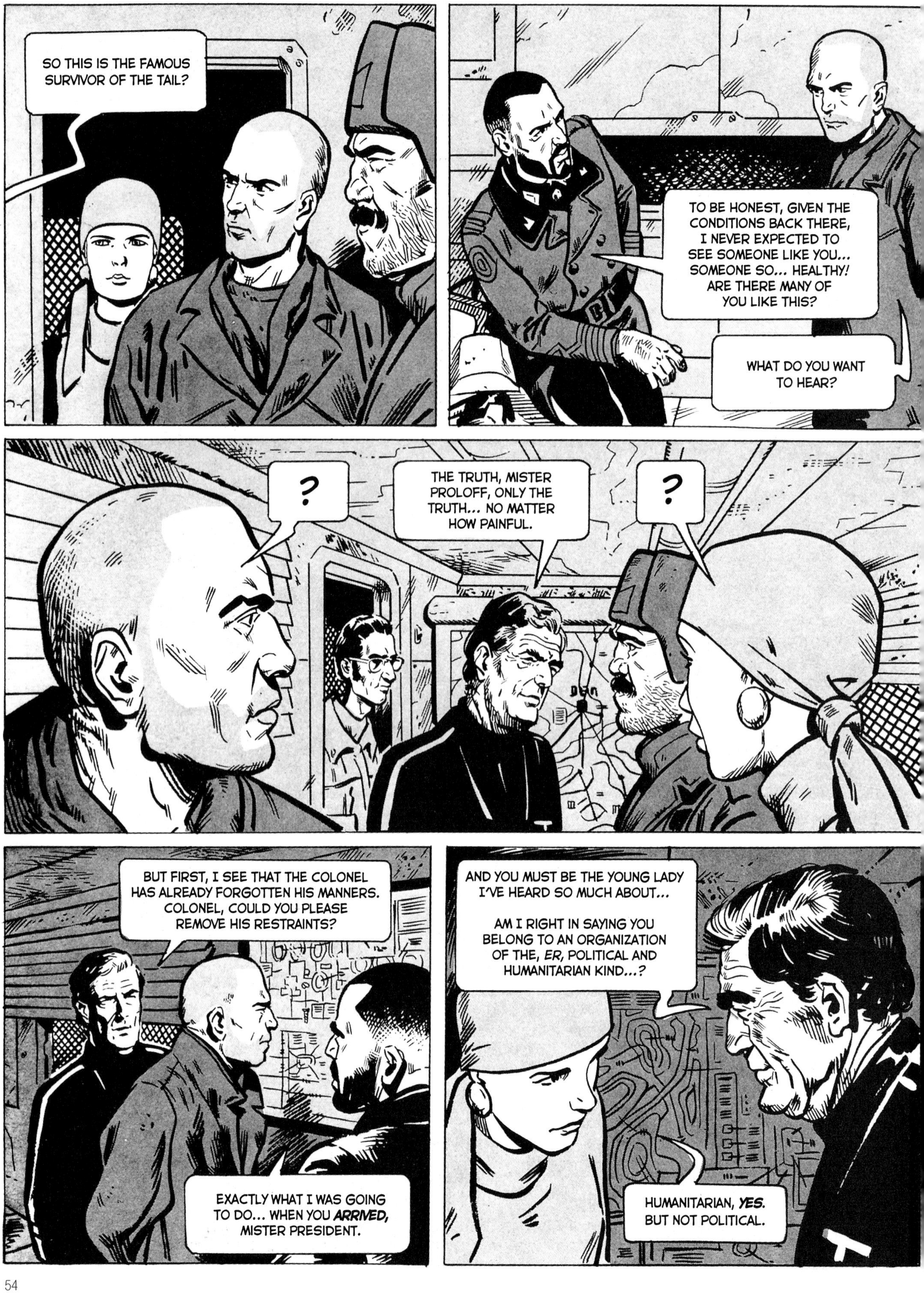
SO THIS IS THE FAMOUS SURVIVOR OF THE TAIL?
TO BE HONEST, GIVEN THE CONDITIONS BACK THERE, I NEVER EXPECTED TO SEE SOMEONE LIKE YOU... SOMEONE SO... HEALTHY! ARE THERE MANY OF YOU LIKE THIS?
WHAT DO YOU WANT TO HEAR?
?
THE TRUTH, MISTER PROLOFF, ONLY THE TRUTH... NO MATTER HOW PAINFUL.
?
BUT FIRST, I SEE THAT THE COLONEL HAS ALREADY FORGOTTEN HIS MANNERS. COLONEL, COULD YOU PLEASE REMOVE HIS RESTRAINTS?
EXACTLY WHAT I WAS GOING TO DO... WHEN YOU ***ARRIVED,*** MISTER PRESIDENT.
AND YOU MUST BE THE YOUNG LADY I'VE HEARD SO MUCH ABOUT...
AM I RIGHT IN SAYING YOU BELONG TO AN ORGANIZATION OF THE, *ER,* POLITICAL AND HUMANITARIAN KIND...?
HUMANITARIAN, ***YES.*** BUT NOT POLITICAL.

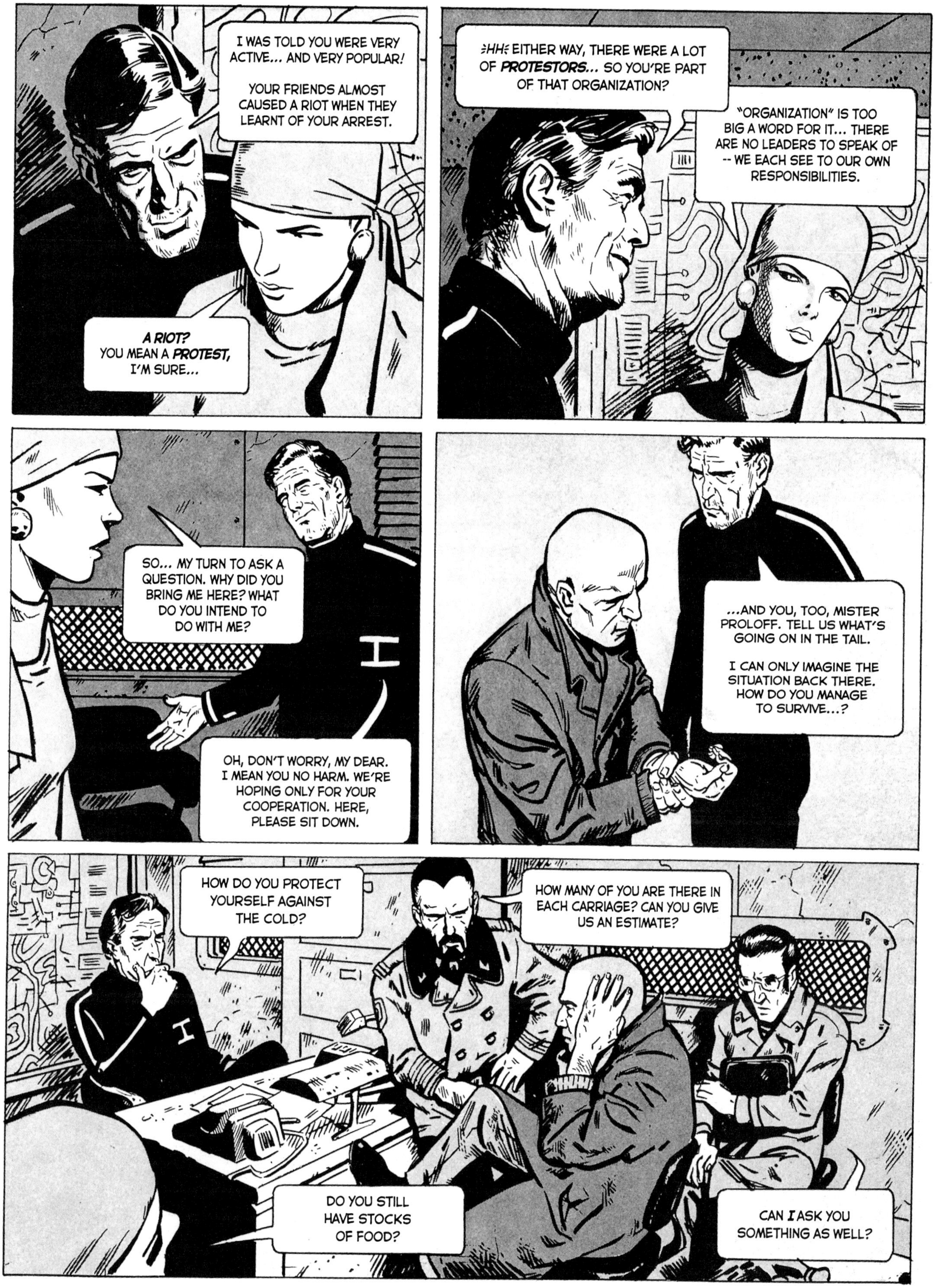
I WAS TOLD YOU WERE VERY ACTIVE... AND VERY POPULAR!
YOUR FRIENDS ALMOST CAUSED A RIOT WHEN THEY LEARNT OF YOUR ARREST.
A RIOT? YOU MEAN A *PROTEST,* I'M SURE...
HH EITHER WAY, THERE WERE A LOT OF *PROTESTORS...* SO YOU'RE PART OF THAT ORGANIZATION?
"ORGANIZATION" IS TOO BIG A WORD FOR IT... THERE ARE NO LEADERS TO SPEAK OF -- WE EACH SEE TO OUR OWN RESPONSIBILITIES.
SO... MY TURN TO ASK A QUESTION. WHY DID YOU BRING ME HERE? WHAT DO YOU INTEND TO DO WITH ME?
OH, DON'T WORRY, MY DEAR. I MEAN YOU NO HARM. WE'RE HOPING ONLY FOR YOUR COOPERATION. HERE, PLEASE SIT DOWN.
...AND YOU, TOO, MISTER PROLOFF. TELL US WHAT'S GOING ON IN THE TAIL.
I CAN ONLY IMAGINE THE SITUATION BACK THERE. HOW DO YOU MANAGE TO SURVIVE...?
HOW DO YOU PROTECT YOURSELF AGAINST THE COLD?
HOW MANY OF YOU ARE THERE IN EACH CARRIAGE? CAN YOU GIVE US AN ESTIMATE?
DO YOU STILL HAVE STOCKS OF FOOD?
CAN *I* ASK YOU SOMETHING AS WELL?

WHAT *I'D* LIKE TO KNOW IS WHY YOU'RE TAKING A SUDDEN INTEREST IN THE LIVING CONDITIONS IN THE REAR CARRIAGES.

WELL, THE MOST OBVIOUS ANSWER IS THE PRESENCE OF MISTER PROLOFF HERE!

IT SEEMS TO ME THAT NOW'S AS GOOD A TIME AS ANY TO OBTAIN SOME UP-TO-DATE, FIRST-HAND INFORMATION...

SURE. BUT WHAT FOR?

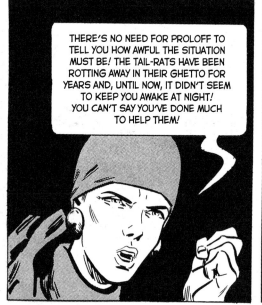

THERE'S NO NEED FOR PROLOFF TO TELL YOU HOW AWFUL THE SITUATION MUST BE! THE TAIL-RATS HAVE BEEN ROTTING AWAY IN THEIR GHETTO FOR YEARS AND, UNTIL NOW, IT DIDN'T SEEM TO KEEP YOU AWAKE AT NIGHT! YOU CAN'T SAY YOU'VE DONE MUCH TO HELP THEM!

NOW HOLD ON--!

STEADY, COLONEL. AND YOU TOO, MISS. YOU'RE NOT HERE TO PUT US ON TRIAL.

ESPECIALLY AS WE'RE NOT DIRECTLY RESPONSIBLE FOR THEIR PLIGHT.

MY ASS YOU'RE NOT! WHO GOT US INTO THIS MESS IN THE FIRST PLACE? WHO STARTED THE WAR THAT ENDED EVERYTHING, IF NOT THE LOUSY MILITARY AND THE FUCKING POLITICIANS...?

PLEASE, MISTER PROLOFF, SPARE US YOUR INSULTING GENERALISATIONS AND SIMPLISTIC ACCUSATIONS. WHAT'S DONE IS DONE. WHAT INTERESTS ME IS THE *PRESENT*. AND THAT CONCERNS YOU TOO. SO AT LEAST LISTEN TO WHAT I HAVE TO SAY!

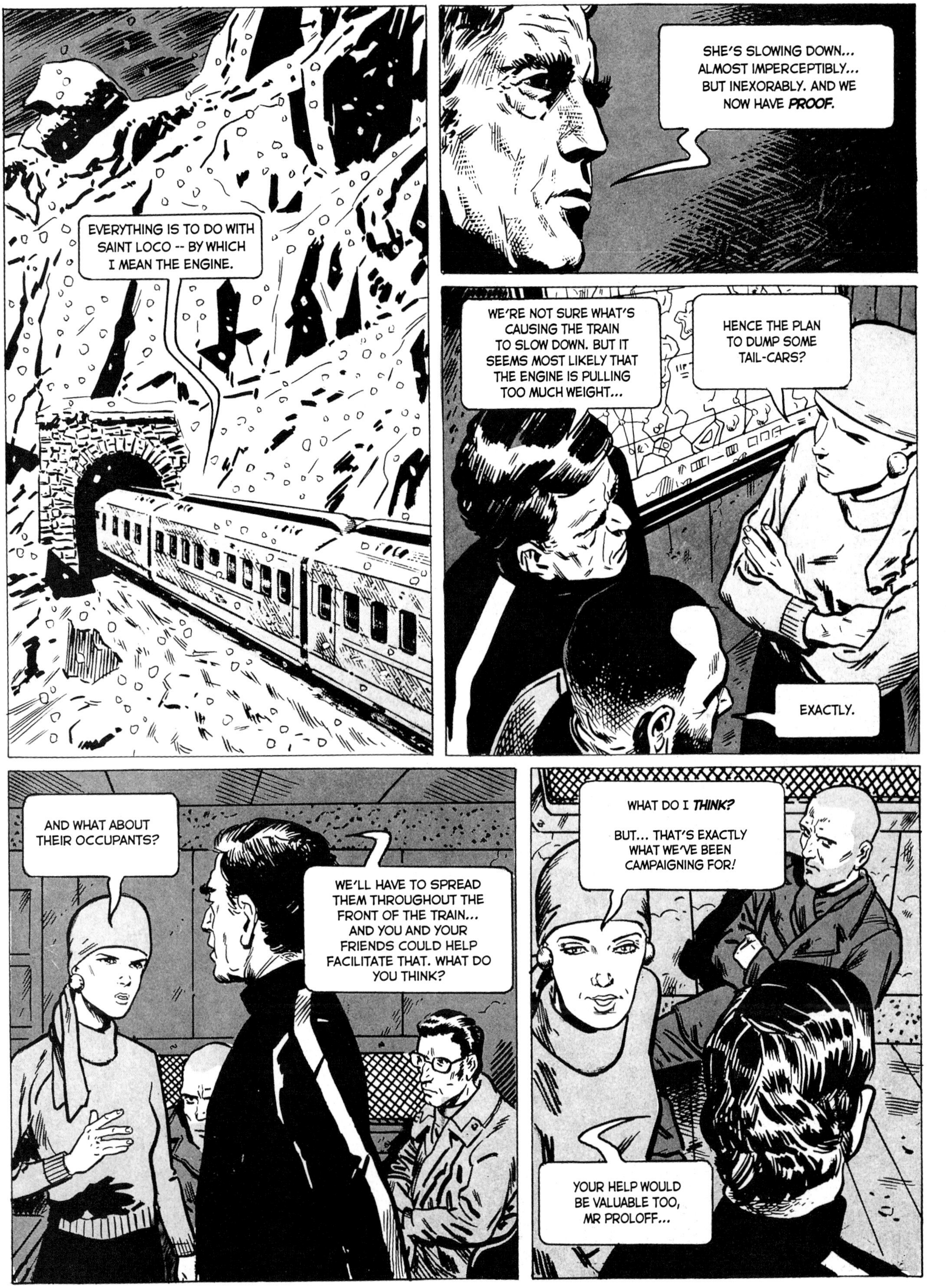
EVERYTHING IS TO DO WITH SAINT LOCO -- BY WHICH I MEAN THE ENGINE.
SHE'S SLOWING DOWN... ALMOST IMPERCEPTIBLY... BUT INEXORABLY. AND WE NOW HAVE PROOF.
WE'RE NOT SURE WHAT'S CAUSING THE TRAIN TO SLOW DOWN. BUT IT SEEMS MOST LIKELY THAT THE ENGINE IS PULLING TOO MUCH WEIGHT...
HENCE THE PLAN TO DUMP SOME TAIL-CARS?
EXACTLY.
AND WHAT ABOUT THEIR OCCUPANTS?
WE'LL HAVE TO SPREAD THEM THROUGHOUT THE FRONT OF THE TRAIN... AND YOU AND YOUR FRIENDS COULD HELP FACILITATE THAT. WHAT DO YOU THINK?
WHAT DO I THINK?
BUT... THAT'S EXACTLY WHAT WE'VE BEEN CAMPAIGNING FOR!
YOUR HELP WOULD BE VALUABLE TOO, MR PROLOFF...

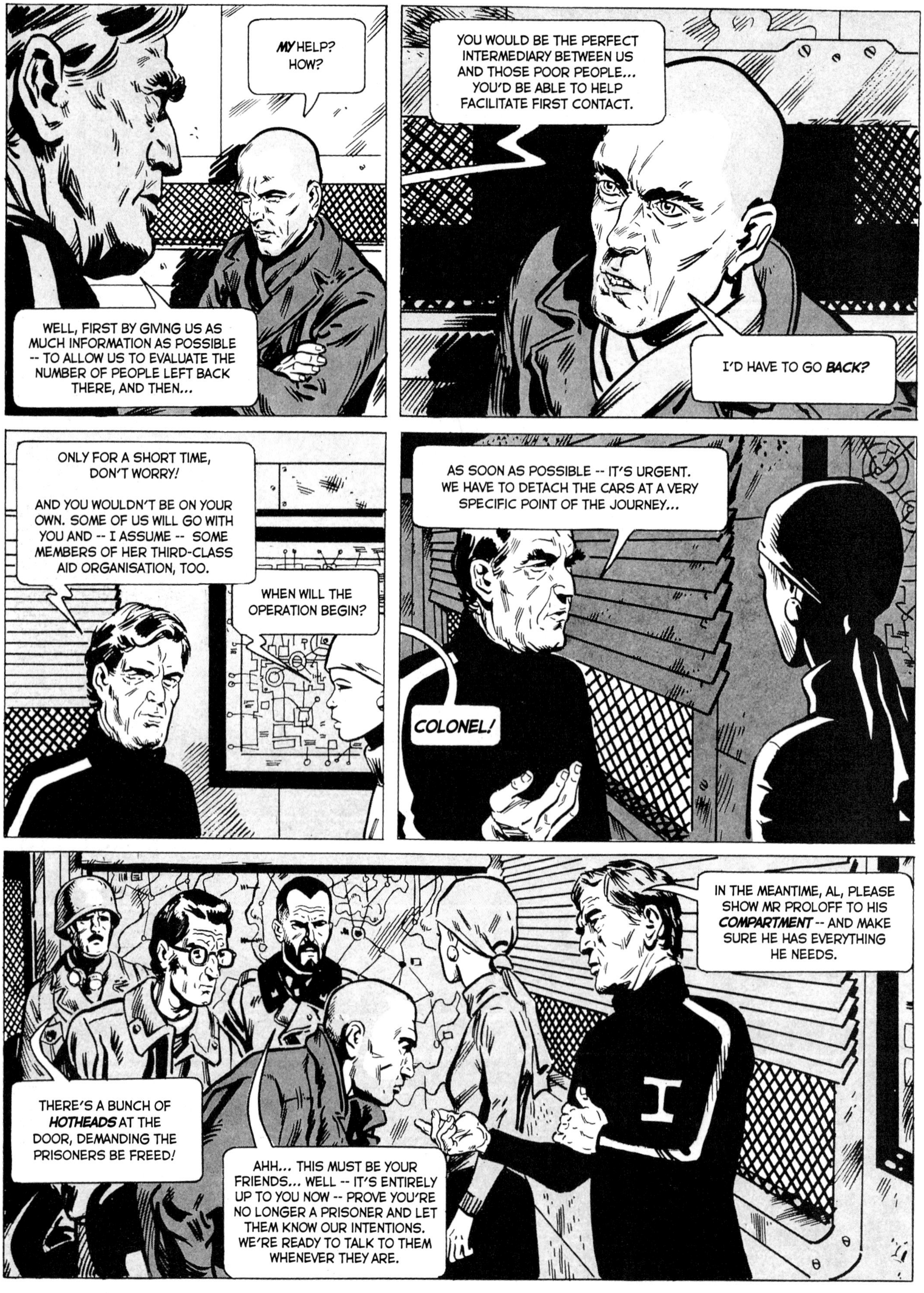

MY HELP? HOW?
WELL, FIRST BY GIVING US AS MUCH INFORMATION AS POSSIBLE -- TO ALLOW US TO EVALUATE THE NUMBER OF PEOPLE LEFT BACK THERE, AND THEN...
YOU WOULD BE THE PERFECT INTERMEDIARY BETWEEN US AND THOSE POOR PEOPLE... YOU'D BE ABLE TO HELP FACILITATE FIRST CONTACT.
I'D HAVE TO GO *BACK?*
ONLY FOR A SHORT TIME, DON'T WORRY! AND YOU WOULDN'T BE ON YOUR OWN. SOME OF US WILL GO WITH YOU AND -- I ASSUME -- SOME MEMBERS OF HER THIRD-CLASS AID ORGANISATION, TOO.
WHEN WILL THE OPERATION BEGIN?
AS SOON AS POSSIBLE -- IT'S URGENT. WE HAVE TO DETACH THE CARS AT A VERY SPECIFIC POINT OF THE JOURNEY...
COLONEL!
THERE'S A BUNCH OF *HOTHEADS* AT THE DOOR, DEMANDING THE PRISONERS BE FREED!
AHH... THIS MUST BE YOUR FRIENDS... WELL -- IT'S ENTIRELY UP TO YOU NOW -- PROVE YOU'RE NO LONGER A PRISONER AND LET THEM KNOW OUR INTENTIONS. WE'RE READY TO TALK TO THEM WHENEVER THEY ARE.
IN THE MEANTIME, AL, PLEASE SHOW MR PROLOFF TO HIS *COMPARTMENT* -- AND MAKE SURE HE HAS EVERYTHING HE NEEDS.

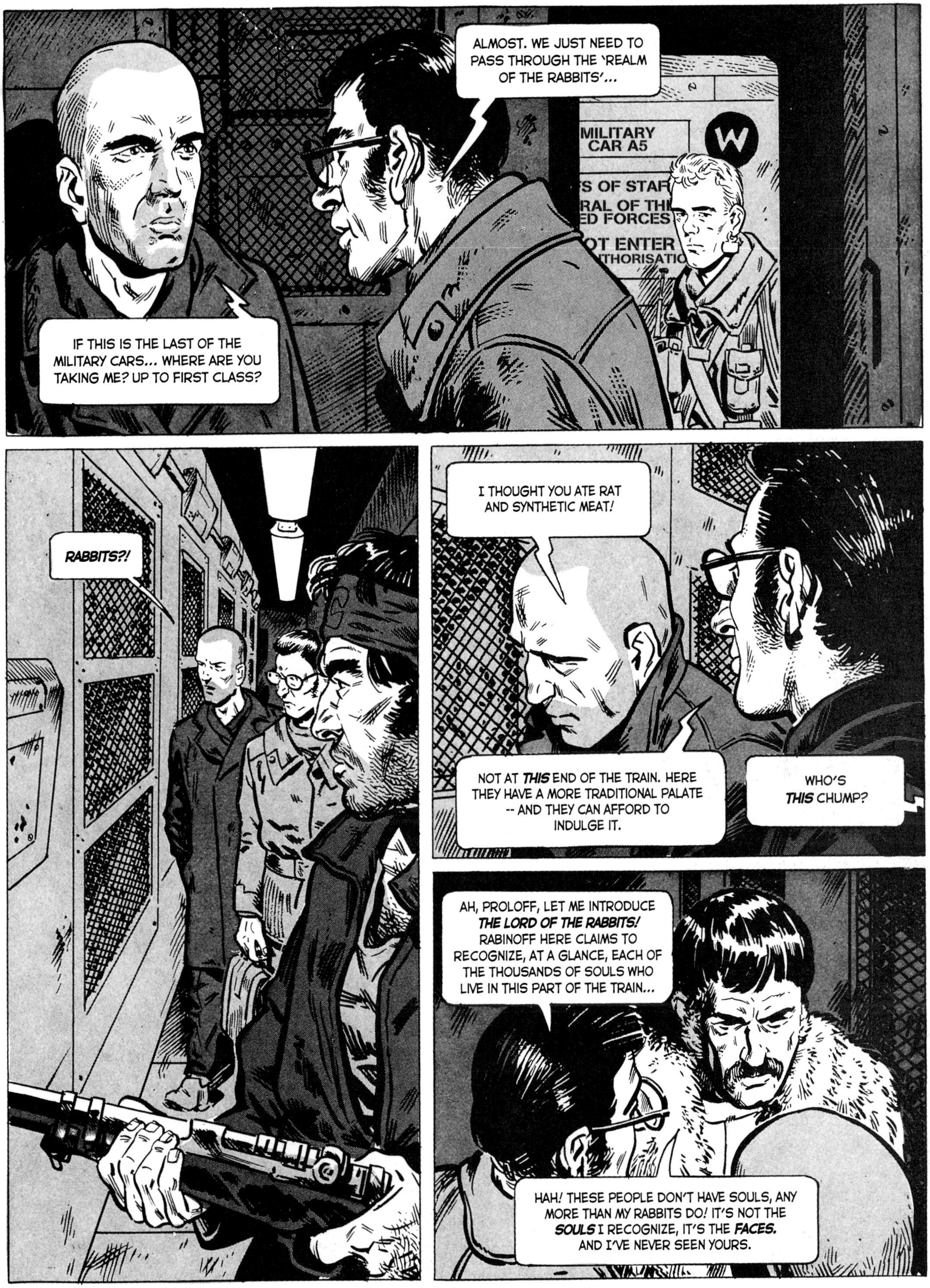

IF THIS IS THE LAST OF THE MILITARY CARS... WHERE ARE YOU TAKING ME? UP TO FIRST CLASS?
ALMOST. WE JUST NEED TO PASS THROUGH THE 'REALM OF THE RABBITS'...
MILITARY CAR A5
W
RABBITS?!
I THOUGHT YOU ATE RAT AND SYNTHETIC MEAT!
NOT AT THIS END OF THE TRAIN. HERE THEY HAVE A MORE TRADITIONAL PALATE -- AND THEY CAN AFFORD TO INDULGE IT.
WHO'S THIS CHUMP?
AH, PROLOFF, LET ME INTRODUCE THE LORD OF THE RABBITS! RABINOFF HERE CLAIMS TO RECOGNIZE, AT A GLANCE, EACH OF THE THOUSANDS OF SOULS WHO LIVE IN THIS PART OF THE TRAIN...
HAH! THESE PEOPLE DON'T HAVE SOULS, ANY MORE THAN MY RABBITS DO! IT'S NOT THE SOULS I RECOGNIZE, IT'S THE FACES. AND I'VE NEVER SEEN YOURS.

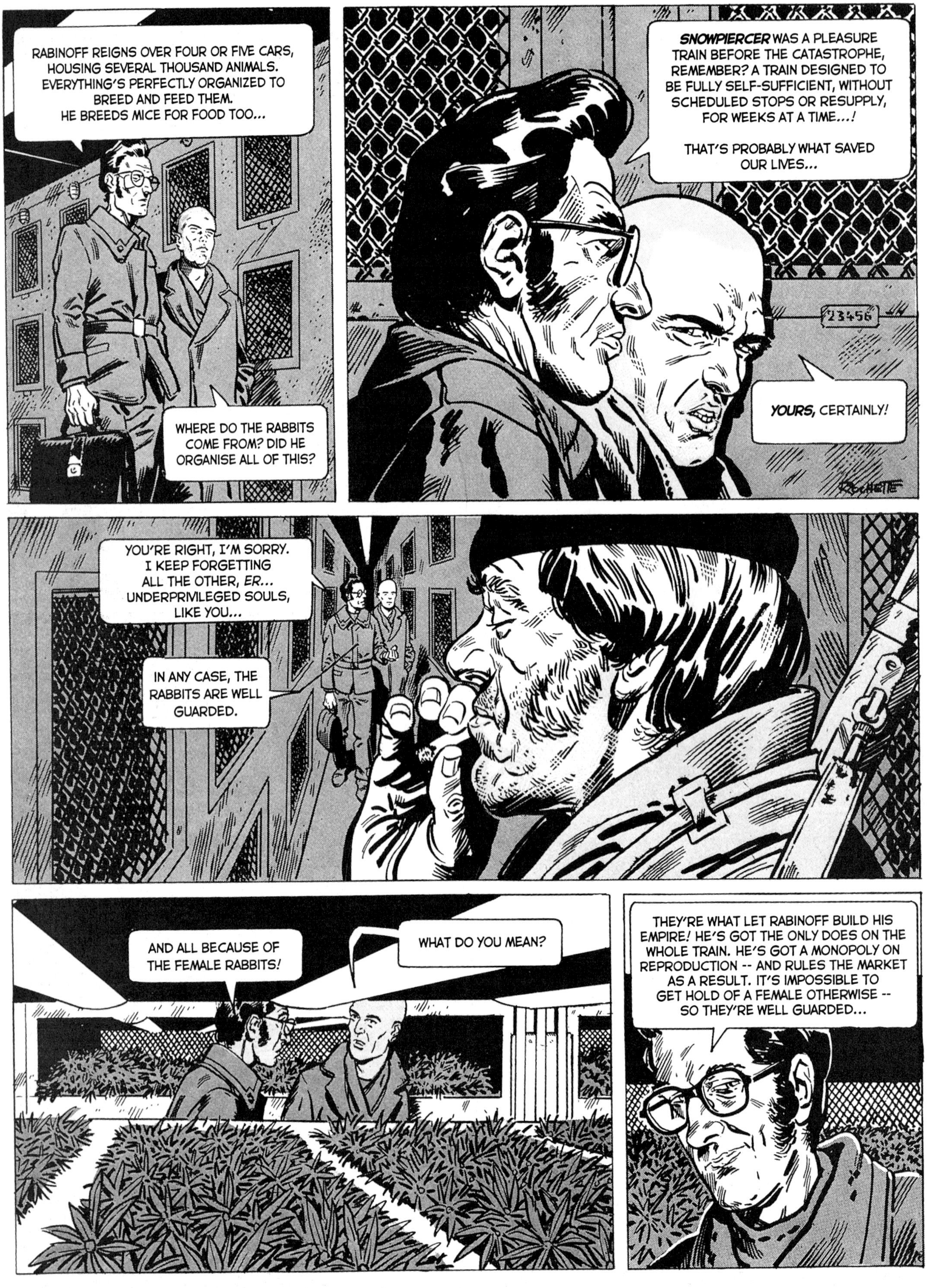
RABINOFF REIGNS OVER FOUR OR FIVE CARS, HOUSING SEVERAL THOUSAND ANIMALS. EVERYTHING'S PERFECTLY ORGANIZED TO BREED AND FEED THEM. HE BREEDS MICE FOR FOOD TOO...
WHERE DO THE RABBITS COME FROM? DID HE ORGANISE ALL OF THIS?
SNOWPIERCER WAS A PLEASURE TRAIN BEFORE THE CATASTROPHE, REMEMBER? A TRAIN DESIGNED TO BE FULLY SELF-SUFFICIENT, WITHOUT SCHEDULED STOPS OR RESUPPLY, FOR WEEKS AT A TIME...! THAT'S PROBABLY WHAT SAVED OUR LIVES...
23456
YOURS, CERTAINLY!
ROCHETTE
YOU'RE RIGHT, I'M SORRY. I KEEP FORGETTING ALL THE OTHER, ER... UNDERPRIVILEGED SOULS, LIKE YOU...
IN ANY CASE, THE RABBITS ARE WELL GUARDED.
AND ALL BECAUSE OF THE FEMALE RABBITS!
WHAT DO YOU MEAN?
THEY'RE WHAT LET RABINOFF BUILD HIS EMPIRE! HE'S GOT THE ONLY DOES ON THE WHOLE TRAIN. HE'S GOT A MONOPOLY ON REPRODUCTION -- AND RULES THE MARKET AS A RESULT. IT'S IMPOSSIBLE TO GET HOLD OF A FEMALE OTHERWISE -- SO THEY'RE WELL GUARDED...

SO THIS IS THE FABLED FIRST CLASS -- THE FAMOUS GOLDEN CARS...

?

OH, SORRY!

CLOSE THE FUCKING DOOR!

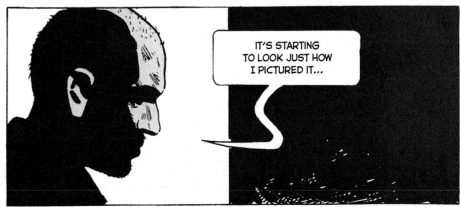

IT'S STARTING TO LOOK JUST HOW I PICTURED IT...

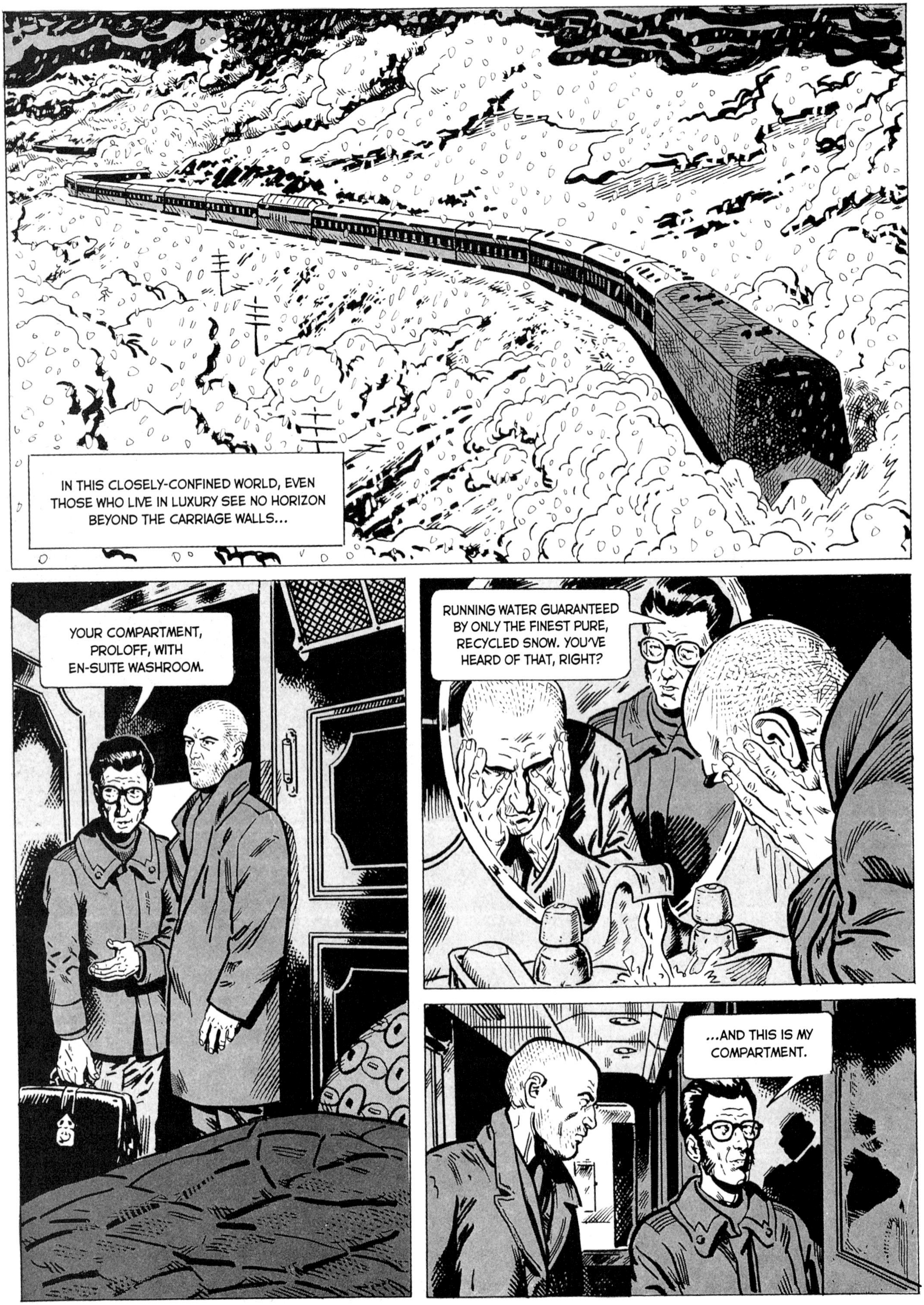
IN THIS CLOSELY-CONFINED WORLD, EVEN THOSE WHO LIVE IN LUXURY SEE NO HORIZON BEYOND THE CARRIAGE WALLS...
YOUR COMPARTMENT, PROLOFF, WITH EN-SUITE WASHROOM.
RUNNING WATER GUARANTEED BY ONLY THE FINEST PURE, RECYCLED SNOW. YOU'VE HEARD OF THAT, RIGHT?
...AND THIS IS MY COMPARTMENT.

ALL THESE **BOOKS**...! THEY'RE ALL YOURS?

SOME CAME FROM THE TRAIN LIBRARY, FROM THE TIME OF THE PLEASURE TRIPS.

MOST OF THEM ARE NOVELS -- NOTHING OF GREAT INTEREST OR LITERARY VALUE, BUT THEY'RE **ALL** PRECIOUS NOW. THE REST WERE MINE TO BEGIN WITH...

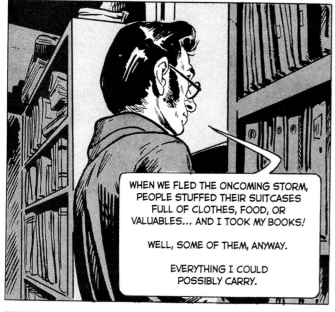

WHEN WE FLED THE ONCOMING STORM, PEOPLE STUFFED THEIR SUITCASES FULL OF CLOTHES, FOOD, OR VALUABLES... AND I TOOK MY BOOKS!

WELL, SOME OF THEM, ANYWAY.

EVERYTHING I COULD POSSIBLY CARRY.

YOU LIKE TO READ?

MMM...

I'VE LIVED AMONG BOOKS MY WHOLE LIFE... I'VE READ ALL OF THESE... AND RE-READ THEM TOO. MANY TIMES.

I'D GIVE... A GREAT DEAL... TO SMELL THE... *INTOXICATING SCENT* OF A NEW BOOK AGAIN.

WHAT ABOUT THIS? DOES IT WORK...?

THE VIEWSCREEN? YES. DO YOU WANT TO WATCH SOMETHING? MOST OF WHAT I HAVE IS NEWS-CLIPS AND DOCUMENTARIES...

I'M **SNOWPIERCER'S** ARCHIVIST AND HISTORIAN, REALLY -- AS MUCH BY ACCIDENT AND CIRCUMSTANCE AS ANYTHING ELSE.

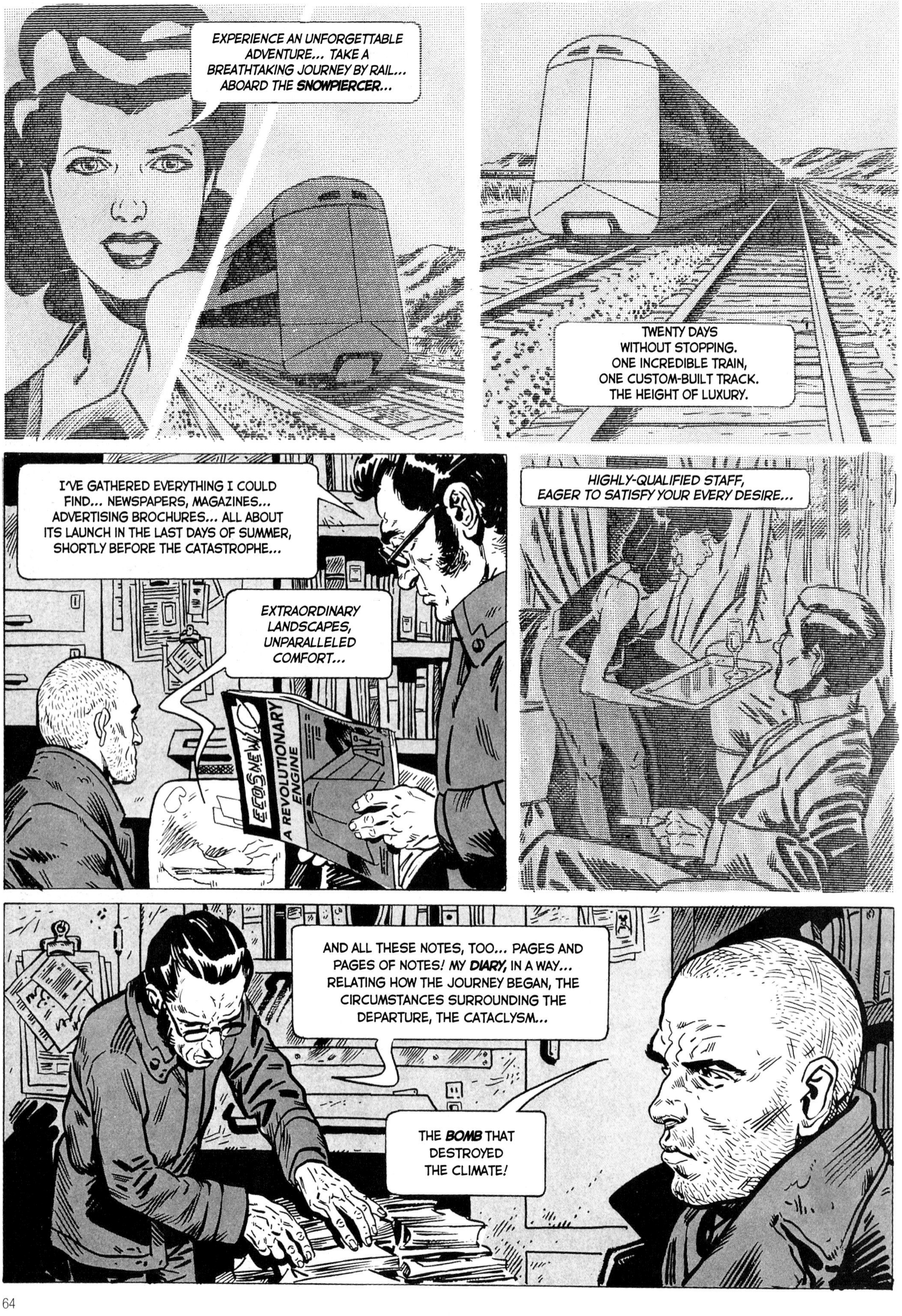
EXPERIENCE AN UNFORGETTABLE ADVENTURE... TAKE A BREATHTAKING JOURNEY BY RAIL... ABOARD THE **SNOWPIERCER**...
TWENTY DAYS WITHOUT STOPPING. ONE INCREDIBLE TRAIN, ONE CUSTOM-BUILT TRACK. THE HEIGHT OF LUXURY.
I'VE GATHERED EVERYTHING I COULD FIND... NEWSPAPERS, MAGAZINES... ADVERTISING BROCHURES... ALL ABOUT ITS LAUNCH IN THE LAST DAYS OF SUMMER, SHORTLY BEFORE THE CATASTROPHE...
EXTRAORDINARY LANDSCAPES, UNPARALLELED COMFORT...
A REVOLUTIONARY ENGINE
HIGHLY-QUALIFIED STAFF, EAGER TO SATISFY YOUR EVERY DESIRE...
AND ALL THESE NOTES, TOO... PAGES AND PAGES OF NOTES! MY ***DIARY***, IN A WAY... RELATING HOW THE JOURNEY BEGAN, THE CIRCUMSTANCES SURROUNDING THE DEPARTURE, THE CATACLYSM...
THE ***BOMB*** THAT DESTROYED THE CLIMATE!

WE'VE NEVER BEEN *SURE* ABOUT THE CATACLYSM'S CAUSE...

BUT KIND OF STRANGE THAT IT HAPPENED JUST WHEN THE *WAR* BROKE OUT, NO?

UNLESS YOU SEE IT AS A MANIFESTATION OF DIVINE JUSTICE...

HEIGHTENED TENSIONS BETWEEN EAST AND WEST AFTER GENERAL'S DECLARATION

BOTH SIDES HAD BEEN SAYING FOR YEARS THAT THEY HAD A WEAPON THAT COULD DEVASTATE THE CLIMATE... BUT THEY'D ALSO BOTH BEEN SAYING THAT IT WORKED *FAR BEYOND* WHAT THEY'D DARED HOPE.

THAT'S NOT *POSSIBLE.* IT WAS AN ACCIDENT...

IT WAS AN ACCIDENT... *RIGHT?*

I STILL REMEMBER WHEN IT STARTED... JUST LIKE THAT. ALL OF A SUDDEN -- BANG IN THE MIDDLE OF THE AFTERNOON... A JULY AFTERNOON!

WHAT I REMEMBER MOST IS THE STRANGE *WIND* THAT STARTED BLOWING. A FREEZING, TERRIFYING BLAST THAT SWEPT EVERYTHING AWAY... LIFE... CIVILIZATION... ALL ERASED... IN JUST A FEW HOURS!

...BUT *SOMEHOW*, THERE WAS A *LUXURY SUPER-TRAIN* WITH AN EXTRAORDINARY ENGINE -- JUST SITTING IN A STATION, READY TO GO. A PROTOTYPE WITH UNHEARD OF ENDURANCE... AND ON-BOARD FACILITIES THAT BORDERED ON THE *PROVIDENTIAL.* EVERYTHING DESIGNED TO RESIST THE RIGORS OF WINTER, AND DRIVE ON INDEFINITELY, FOREVER, THROUGH THE SNOW THAT NO-ONE HAD BELIEVED WOULD EVER FALL...

A MIRACLE INDEED.

YES, A TRAIN *MIRACULOUSLY* READY TO WELCOME THE BIG SHOTS, THE MILITARY AND THE UPPER CLASSES -- ALONG WITH ALL THEIR FAMILIES AND INHERITED WEALTH... LET'S BE *FAIR,* THOUGH: THEY MADE THE EFFORT AT THE LAST-MINUTE FOR THE REST OF US -- HASTILY ADDING ON EXTRA CARRIAGES. THIRD-CLASS CARRIAGES... SUITABLE ONLY FOR LAST-MINUTE SQUATTERS. THE ONES WHO WEREN'T PART OF THE PLAN!

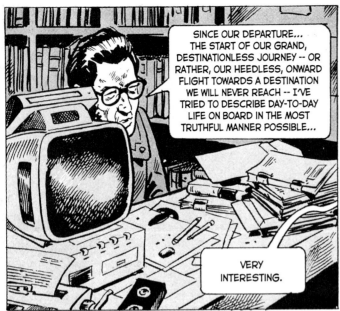

SINCE OUR DEPARTURE... THE START OF OUR GRAND, DESTINATIONLESS JOURNEY -- OR RATHER, OUR HEEDLESS, ONWARD FLIGHT TOWARDS A DESTINATION WE WILL NEVER REACH -- I'VE TRIED TO DESCRIBE DAY-TO-DAY LIFE ON BOARD IN THE MOST TRUTHFUL MANNER POSSIBLE...

VERY INTERESTING.

SO I GUESS I'VE BEEN BROUGHT HERE TO DESCRIBE WHAT'S HAPPENING IN THE TAIL, RIGHT?

YOU DON'T HAVE ANY INFORMATION ON US IN YOUR LITTLE DIARY... AND YOU'RE COUNTING ON ME TO FILL THAT GAP...

INDEED, I...

SORRY, BUT I'M GOING TO DISAPPOINT YOU.

I'VE NO DESIRE TO TELL YOU WHAT'S GOING ON THERE. I JUST WANT TO FORGET...

I... I *UNDERSTAND*, BUT...

NO, YOU *DON'T* UNDERSTAND. YOU CAN'T. INSTEAD, I'D LIKE TO ASK *YOU* A QUESTION...

OF COURSE, GO AHEAD...

ALL THIS: YOUR DIARY, THOSE NOTES... WHAT ARE THEY FOR? *WHO* ARE THEY FOR? WHAT'S THEIR PURPOSE?

YOU'RE NOT VERY *OPTIMISTIC*, ARE YOU?

AND YOU *ARE*?

HMM... WELL... I-- I FEEL LIKE A DRINK. HOW ABOUT YOU?

IT MUST BE NEARLY TIME FOR DINNER. COME ALONG.

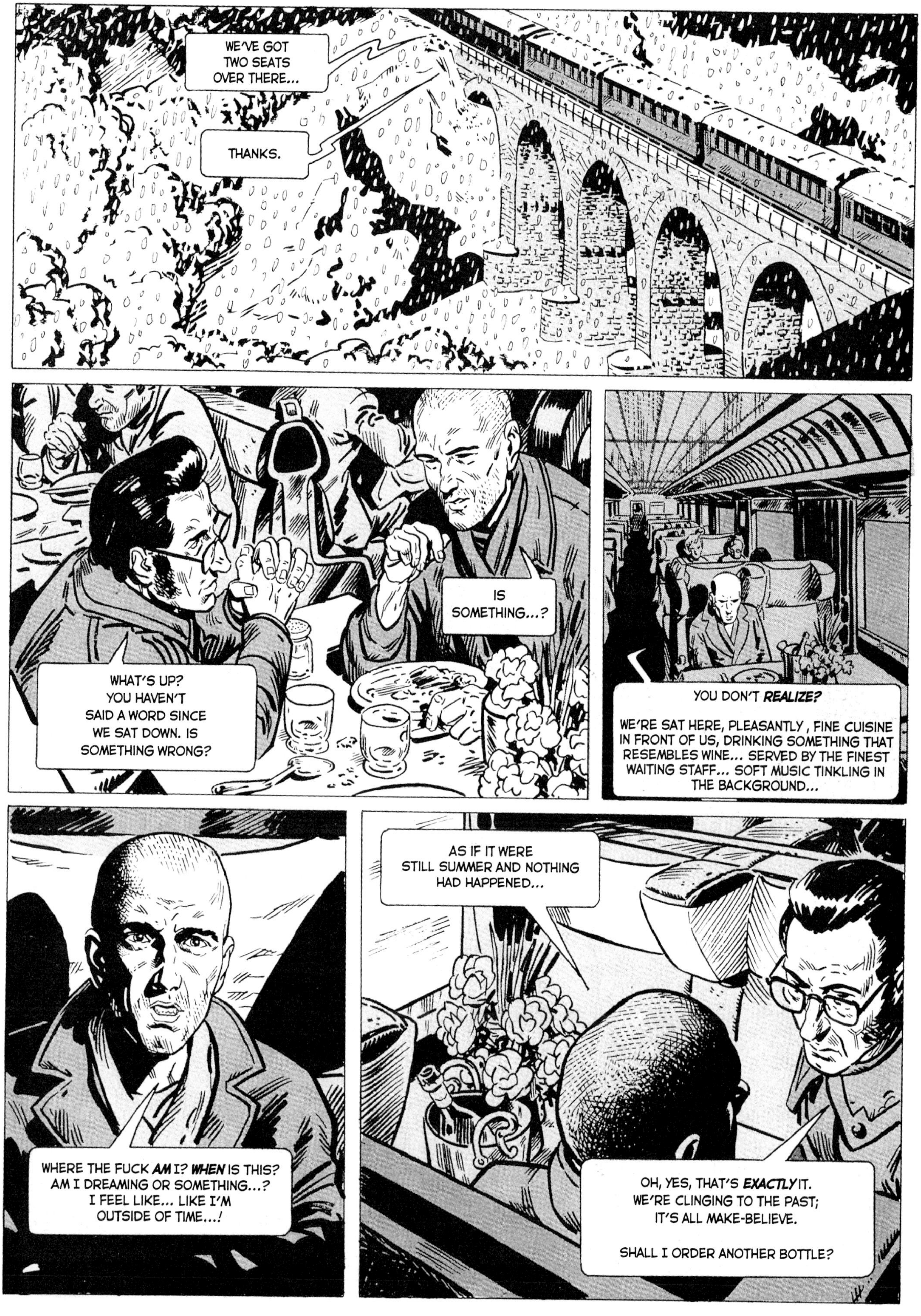
WE'VE GOT TWO SEATS OVER THERE...
THANKS.
WHAT'S UP? YOU HAVEN'T SAID A WORD SINCE WE SAT DOWN. IS SOMETHING WRONG?
IS SOMETHING...?
YOU DON'T ***REALIZE?***
WE'RE SAT HERE, PLEASANTLY, FINE CUISINE IN FRONT OF US, DRINKING SOMETHING THAT RESEMBLES WINE... SERVED BY THE FINEST WAITING STAFF... SOFT MUSIC TINKLING IN THE BACKGROUND...
AS IF IT WERE STILL SUMMER AND NOTHING HAD HAPPENED...
WHERE THE FUCK ***AM*** I? ***WHEN*** IS THIS? AM I DREAMING OR SOMETHING...? I FEEL LIKE... LIKE I'M OUTSIDE OF TIME...!
OH, YES, THAT'S ***EXACTLY*** IT. WE'RE CLINGING TO THE PAST; IT'S ALL MAKE-BELIEVE.
SHALL I ORDER ANOTHER BOTTLE?

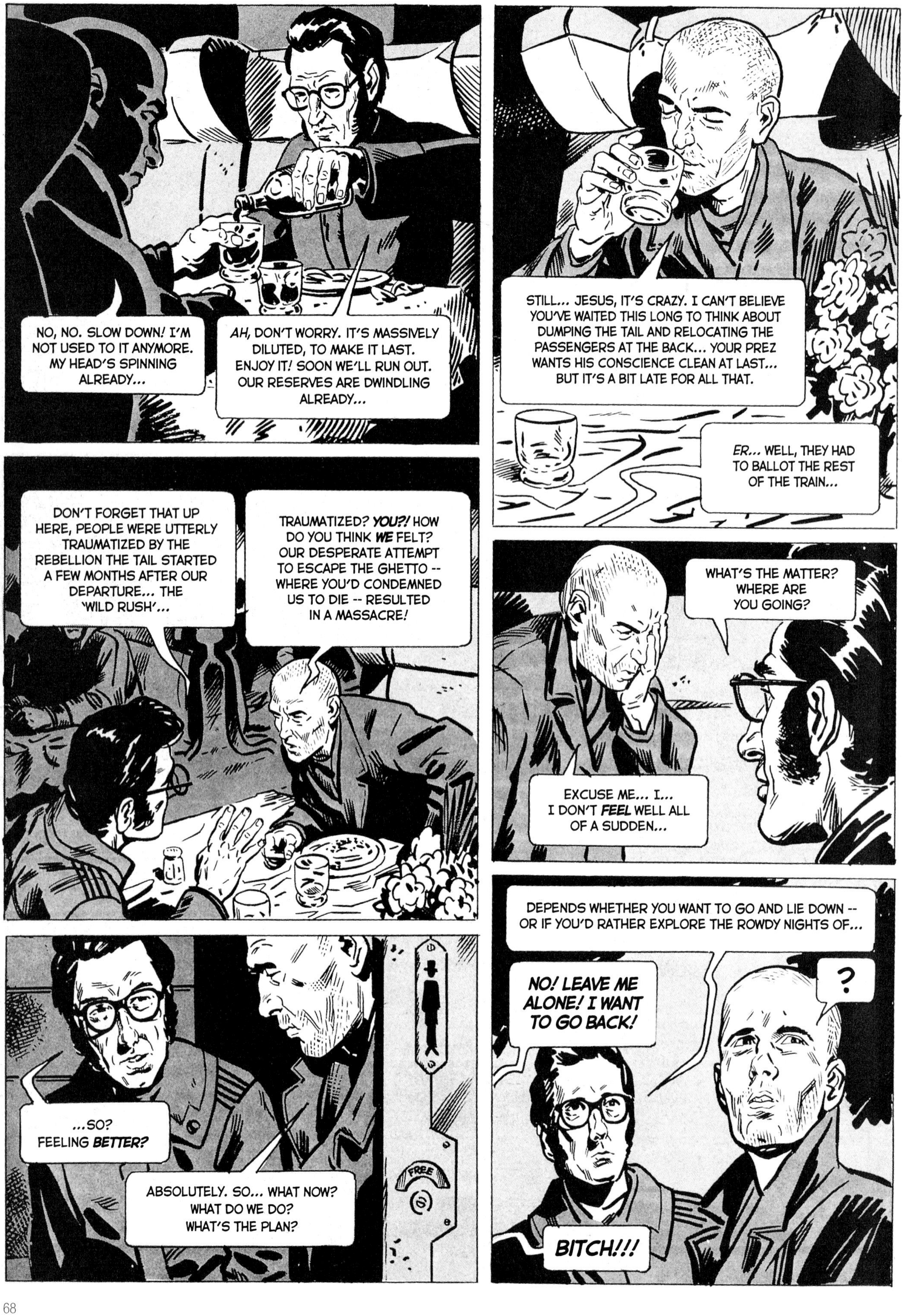
NO, NO. SLOW DOWN! I'M NOT USED TO IT ANYMORE. MY HEAD'S SPINNING ALREADY...
AH, DON'T WORRY. IT'S MASSIVELY DILUTED, TO MAKE IT LAST. ENJOY IT! SOON WE'LL RUN OUT. OUR RESERVES ARE DWINDLING ALREADY...
STILL... JESUS, IT'S CRAZY. I CAN'T BELIEVE YOU'VE WAITED THIS LONG TO THINK ABOUT DUMPING THE TAIL AND RELOCATING THE PASSENGERS AT THE BACK... YOUR PREZ WANTS HIS CONSCIENCE CLEAN AT LAST... BUT IT'S A BIT LATE FOR ALL THAT.
ER... WELL, THEY HAD TO BALLOT THE REST OF THE TRAIN...
DON'T FORGET THAT UP HERE, PEOPLE WERE UTTERLY TRAUMATIZED BY THE REBELLION THE TAIL STARTED A FEW MONTHS AFTER OUR DEPARTURE... THE 'WILD RUSH'...
TRAUMATIZED? YOU?! HOW DO YOU THINK WE FELT? OUR DESPERATE ATTEMPT TO ESCAPE THE GHETTO -- WHERE YOU'D CONDEMNED US TO DIE -- RESULTED IN A MASSACRE!
WHAT'S THE MATTER? WHERE ARE YOU GOING?
EXCUSE ME... I... I DON'T FEEL WELL ALL OF A SUDDEN...
...SO? FEELING BETTER?
ABSOLUTELY. SO... WHAT NOW? WHAT DO WE DO? WHAT'S THE PLAN?
FREE
DEPENDS WHETHER YOU WANT TO GO AND LIE DOWN -- OR IF YOU'D RATHER EXPLORE THE ROWDY NIGHTS OF...
NO! LEAVE ME ALONE! I WANT TO GO BACK!
?
BITCH!!!

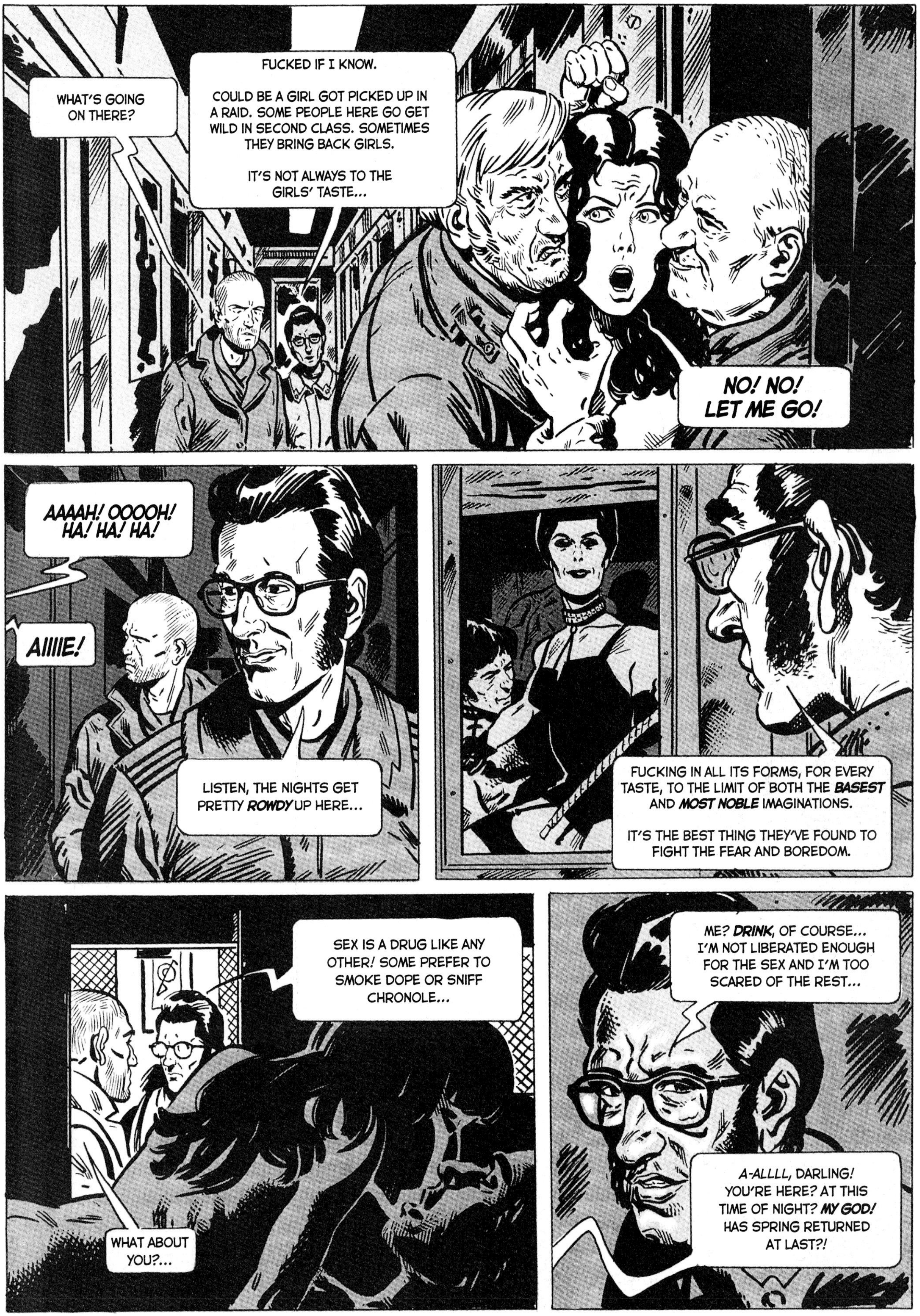
WHAT'S GOING ON THERE?
FUCKED IF I KNOW.
COULD BE A GIRL GOT PICKED UP IN A RAID. SOME PEOPLE HERE GO GET WILD IN SECOND CLASS. SOMETIMES THEY BRING BACK GIRLS.
IT'S NOT ALWAYS TO THE GIRLS' TASTE...
NO! NO! LET ME GO!
AAAAH! OOOOH! HA! HA! HA!
AIIIIE!
LISTEN, THE NIGHTS GET PRETTY ROWDY UP HERE...
FUCKING IN ALL ITS FORMS, FOR EVERY TASTE, TO THE LIMIT OF BOTH THE BASEST AND MOST NOBLE IMAGINATIONS.
IT'S THE BEST THING THEY'VE FOUND TO FIGHT THE FEAR AND BOREDOM.
SEX IS A DRUG LIKE ANY OTHER! SOME PREFER TO SMOKE DOPE OR SNIFF CHRONOLE...
WHAT ABOUT YOU?...
ME? DRINK, OF COURSE... I'M NOT LIBERATED ENOUGH FOR THE SEX AND I'M TOO SCARED OF THE REST...
A-ALLLL, DARLING! YOU'RE HERE? AT THIS TIME OF NIGHT? MY GOD! HAS SPRING RETURNED AT LAST?!

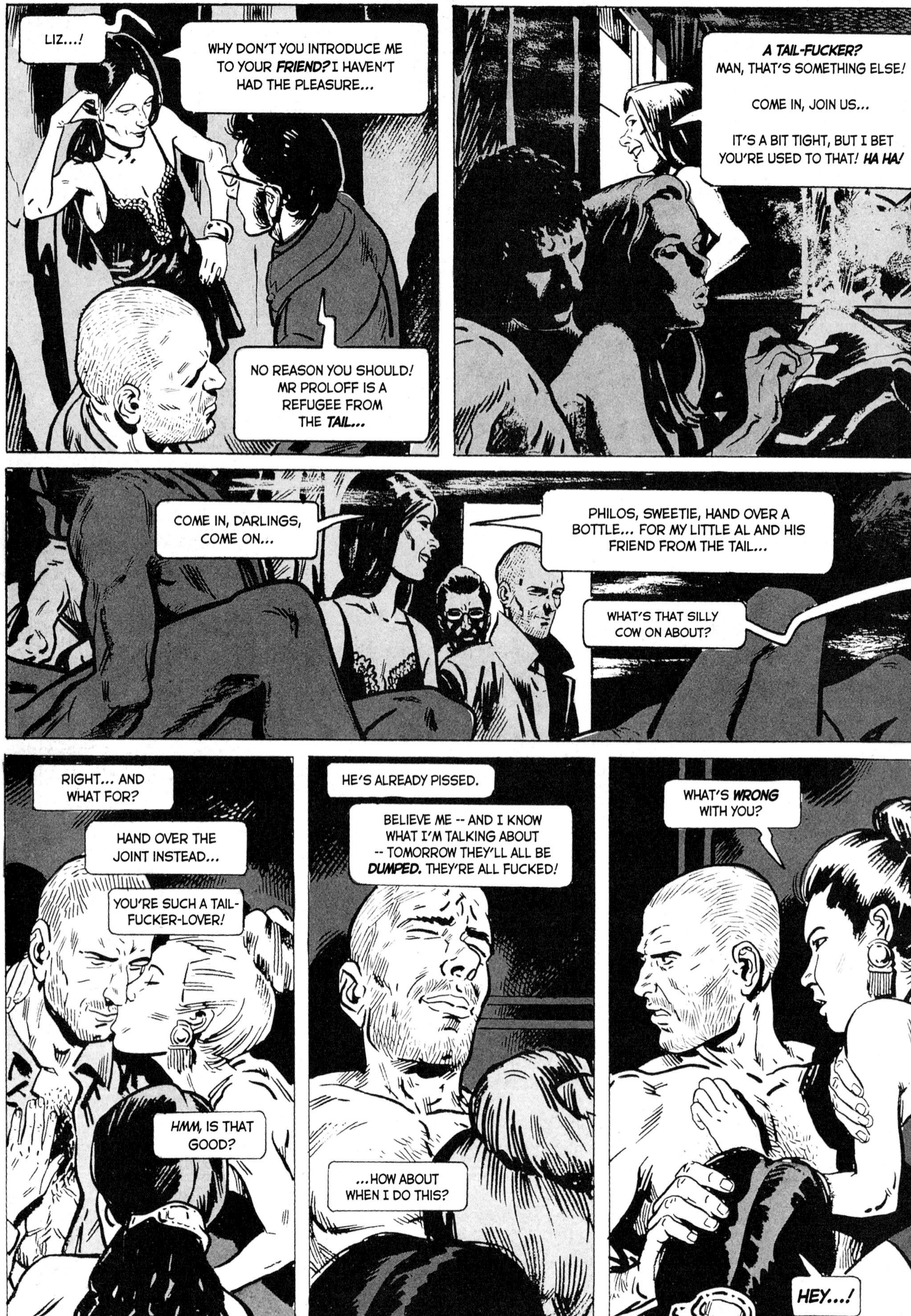
LIZ...!
WHY DON'T YOU INTRODUCE ME TO YOUR FRIEND? I HAVEN'T HAD THE PLEASURE...
NO REASON YOU SHOULD! MR PROLOFF IS A REFUGEE FROM THE TAIL...
A TAIL-FUCKER? MAN, THAT'S SOMETHING ELSE!
COME IN, JOIN US...
IT'S A BIT TIGHT, BUT I BET YOU'RE USED TO THAT! HA HA!
COME IN, DARLINGS, COME ON...
PHILOS, SWEETIE, HAND OVER A BOTTLE... FOR MY LITTLE AL AND HIS FRIEND FROM THE TAIL...
WHAT'S THAT SILLY COW ON ABOUT?
RIGHT... AND WHAT FOR?
HAND OVER THE JOINT INSTEAD...
YOU'RE SUCH A TAIL-FUCKER-LOVER!
HMM, IS THAT GOOD?
HE'S ALREADY PISSED.
BELIEVE ME -- AND I KNOW WHAT I'M TALKING ABOUT -- TOMORROW THEY'LL ALL BE DUMPED. THEY'RE ALL FUCKED!
...HOW ABOUT WHEN I DO THIS?
WHAT'S WRONG WITH YOU?
HEY...!

WHAT ARE YOU *TALKING* ABOUT?

WHAT? ME? ⋝HIC!⋜ NOTHING AT ALL!

FUCK IT, I *HEARD* YOU: "THEY'LL ALL BE DUMPED, THEY'RE ALL FUCKED". *WHAT ARE YOU TALKING ABOUT?*

OH, *FUCK IT,* THEN -- IT'S NOTHING TO DO WITH ME...! IT'S TRUE. THE PRESIDENT AND THE COLONEL ARE BULLSHITTING YOU... THEY NEVER INTENDED TO RELOCATE THE PEOPLE IN THE TAIL.

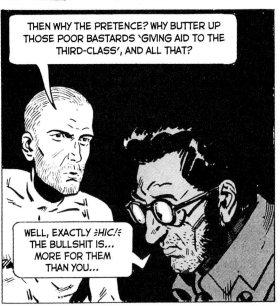

THEN WHY THE PRETENCE? WHY BUTTER UP THOSE POOR BASTARDS 'GIVING AID TO THE THIRD-CLASS', AND ALL THAT?

WELL, EXACTLY ⋝HIC!⋜ THE BULLSHIT IS... MORE FOR THEM THAN YOU...

THEY'RE HOPING TO GET RID OF THE MOST IMPORTANT OF THEM, THE WORST PAINS-IN-THE-ASS, BY LURING THEM BACK TO THE TAIL -- AND DUMPING THEM ALONG WITH THE REST!

BUT *WHY?*

HEY! YOU GONNA CARRY ON MUCH LONGER WITH THIS BORING PREACHY SHIT?! SOME OF US ARE TRYING TO *FUCK* HERE!

...OH IT'S NOT COMPLICATED...

THE PRESIDENT IS CONVINCED -- RIGHTLY OR WRONGLY -- THAT THOSE GIVING AID TO THE THIRD CLASS ARE A POLITICAL THREAT... A THREAT TO THE PRIVILEGED CLASS, LIKE US -- AND THAT, SOONER RATHER THAN LATER, THEY'LL TRY TO GET RID OF US AND TAKE POWER FOR THEMSELVES.

?

OF COURSE, I WASN'T MEANT TO TELL YOU *ANY* OF THIS...

WHAT ARE YOU GOING TO DO NOW?

PROLOFF!

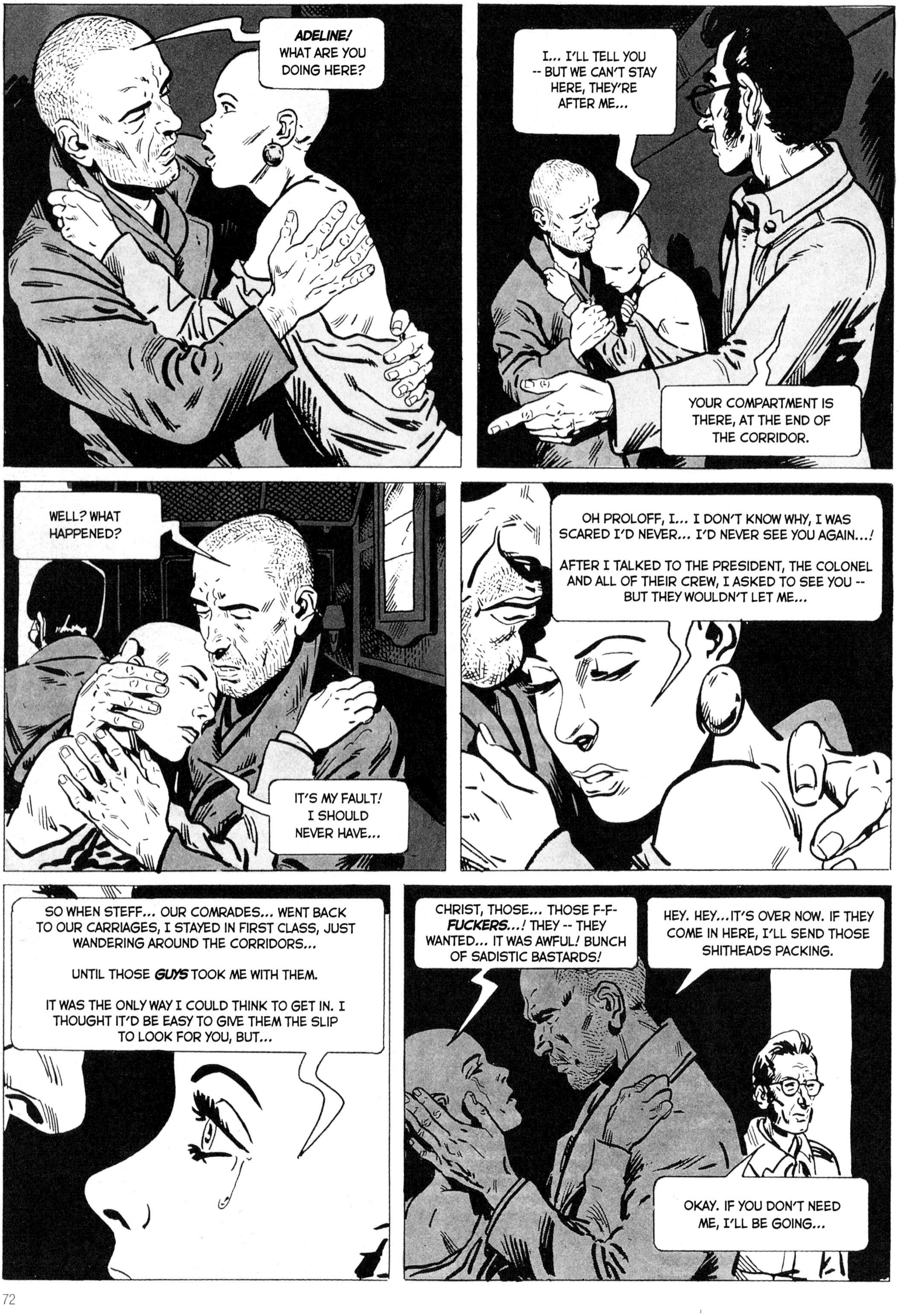
ADELINE! WHAT ARE YOU DOING HERE?
I... I'LL TELL YOU -- BUT WE CAN'T STAY HERE, THEY'RE AFTER ME...
YOUR COMPARTMENT IS THERE, AT THE END OF THE CORRIDOR.
WELL? WHAT HAPPENED?
IT'S MY FAULT! I SHOULD NEVER HAVE...
OH PROLOFF, I... I DON'T KNOW WHY, I WAS SCARED I'D NEVER... I'D NEVER SEE YOU AGAIN...!
AFTER I TALKED TO THE PRESIDENT, THE COLONEL AND ALL OF THEIR CREW, I ASKED TO SEE YOU -- BUT THEY WOULDN'T LET ME...
SO WHEN STEFF... OUR COMRADES... WENT BACK TO OUR CARRIAGES, I STAYED IN FIRST CLASS, JUST WANDERING AROUND THE CORRIDORS...
UNTIL THOSE GUYS TOOK ME WITH THEM.
IT WAS THE ONLY WAY I COULD THINK TO GET IN. I THOUGHT IT'D BE EASY TO GIVE THEM THE SLIP TO LOOK FOR YOU, BUT...
CHRIST, THOSE... THOSE F-F-FUCKERS...! THEY -- THEY WANTED... IT WAS AWFUL! BUNCH OF SADISTIC BASTARDS!
HEY. HEY...IT'S OVER NOW. IF THEY COME IN HERE, I'LL SEND THOSE SHITHEADS PACKING.
OKAY. IF YOU DON'T NEED ME, I'LL BE GOING...

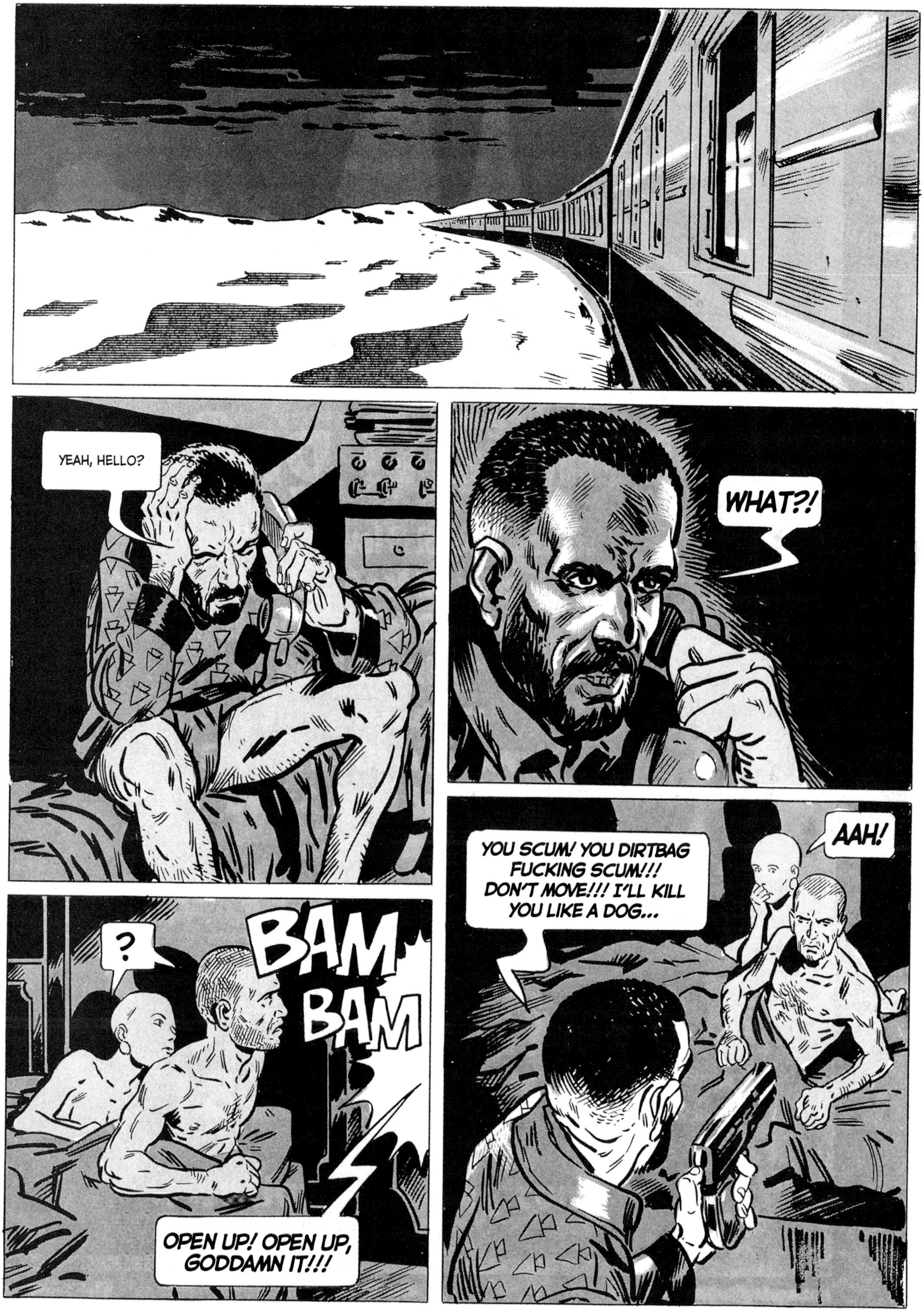
YEAH, HELLO?
WHAT?!
?
BAM
BAM
OPEN UP! OPEN UP, GODDAMN IT!!!
YOU SCUM! YOU DIRTBAG FUCKING SCUM!!! DON'T MOVE!!! I'LL KILL YOU LIKE A DOG...
AAH!

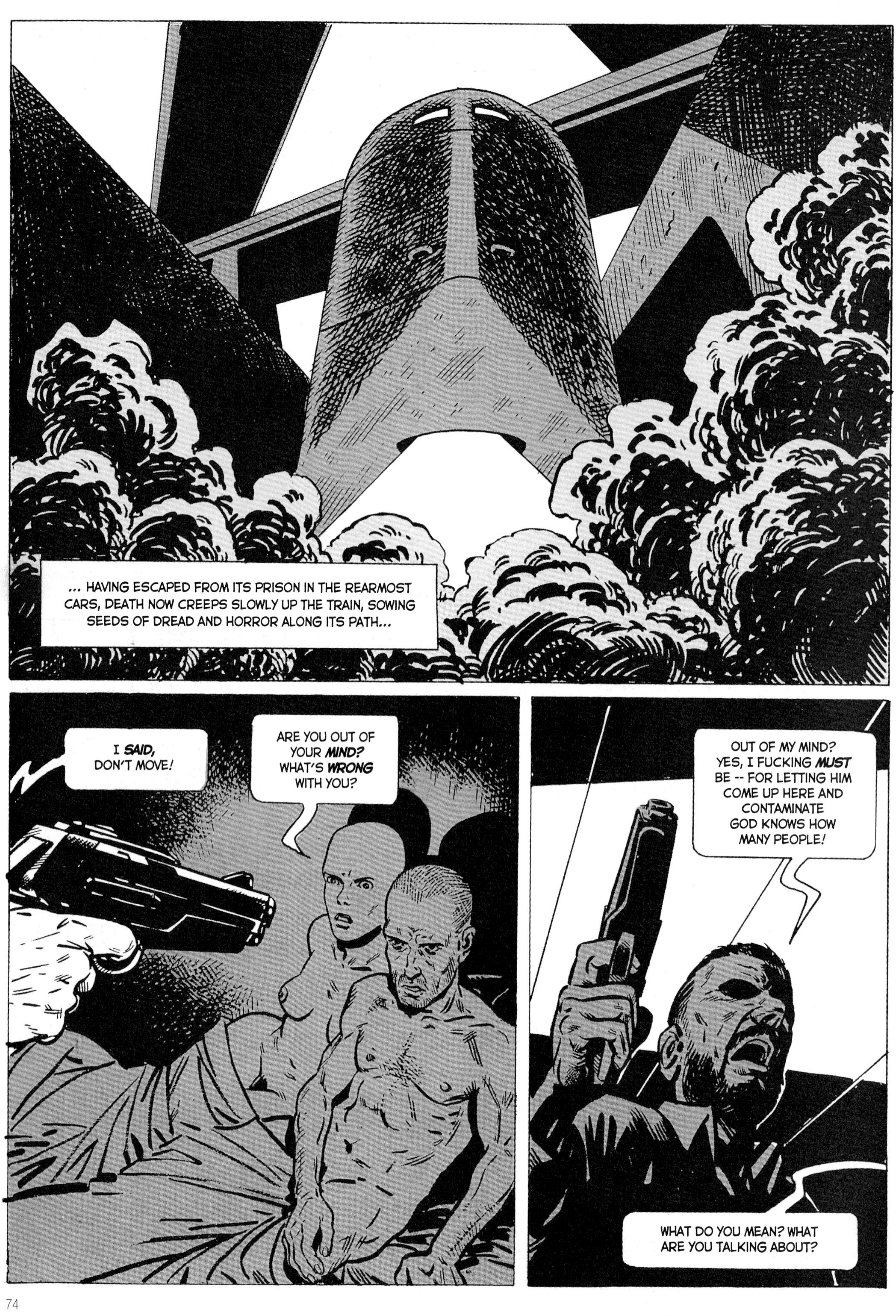
... HAVING ESCAPED FROM ITS PRISON IN THE REARMOST CARS, DEATH NOW CREEPS SLOWLY UP THE TRAIN, SOWING SEEDS OF DREAD AND HORROR ALONG ITS PATH...
I *SAID,* DON'T MOVE!
ARE YOU OUT OF YOUR *MIND?* WHAT'S *WRONG* WITH YOU?
OUT OF MY MIND? YES, I FUCKING *MUST* BE -- FOR LETTING HIM COME UP HERE AND CONTAMINATE GOD KNOWS HOW MANY PEOPLE!
WHAT DO YOU MEAN? WHAT ARE YOU TALKING ABOUT?

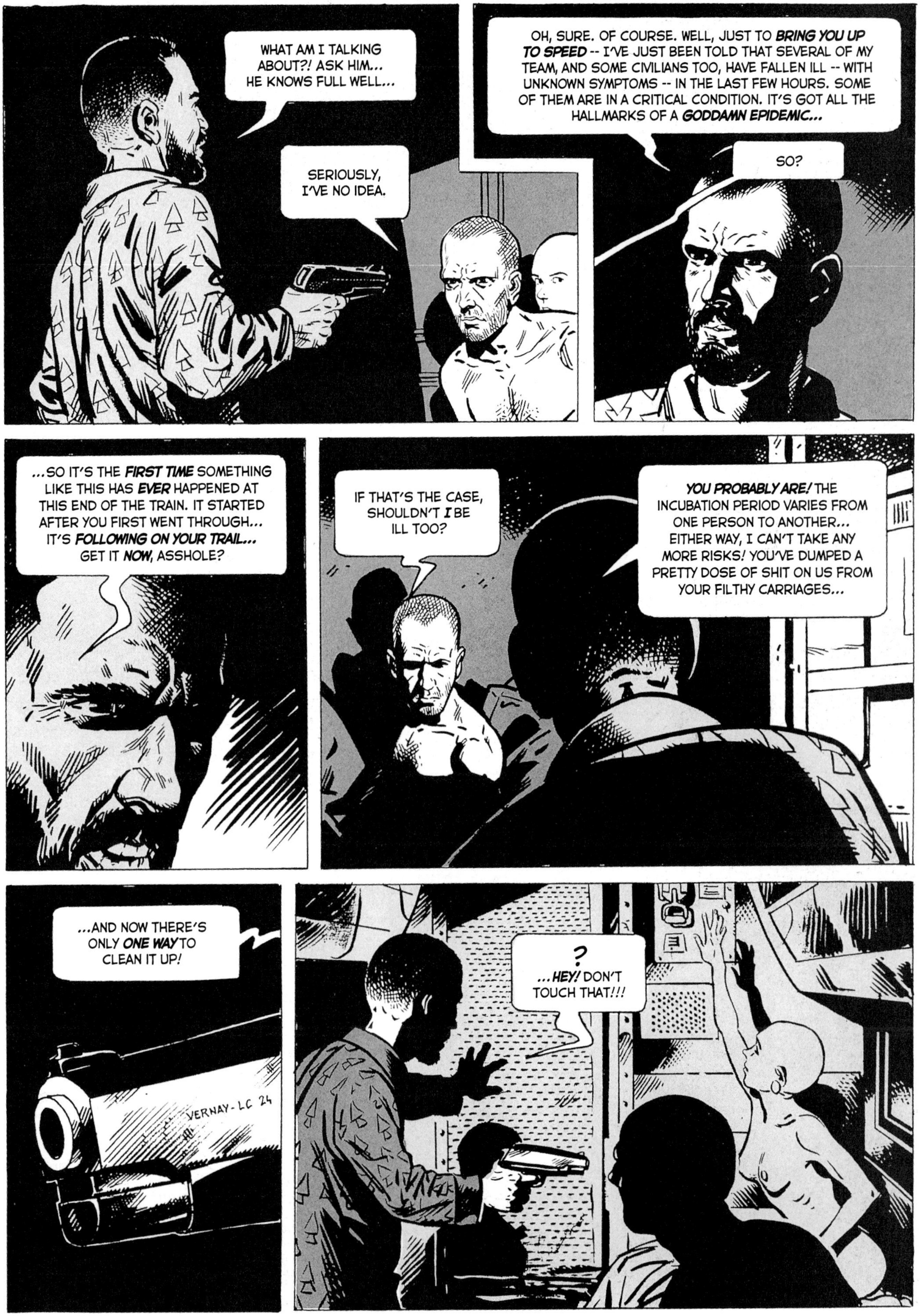
WHAT AM I TALKING ABOUT?! ASK HIM... HE KNOWS FULL WELL...
SERIOUSLY, I'VE NO IDEA.
OH, SURE. OF COURSE. WELL, JUST TO **BRING YOU UP TO SPEED** -- I'VE JUST BEEN TOLD THAT SEVERAL OF MY TEAM, AND SOME CIVILIANS TOO, HAVE FALLEN ILL -- WITH UNKNOWN SYMPTOMS -- IN THE LAST FEW HOURS. SOME OF THEM ARE IN A CRITICAL CONDITION. IT'S GOT ALL THE HALLMARKS OF A **GODDAMN EPIDEMIC...**
SO?
...SO IT'S THE **FIRST TIME** SOMETHING LIKE THIS HAS **EVER** HAPPENED AT THIS END OF THE TRAIN. IT STARTED AFTER YOU FIRST WENT THROUGH... IT'S **FOLLOWING ON YOUR TRAIL...** GET IT **NOW**, ASSHOLE?
IF THAT'S THE CASE, SHOULDN'T **I** BE ILL TOO?
YOU PROBABLY ARE! THE INCUBATION PERIOD VARIES FROM ONE PERSON TO ANOTHER... EITHER WAY, I CAN'T TAKE ANY MORE RISKS! YOU'VE DUMPED A PRETTY DOSE OF SHIT ON US FROM YOUR FILTHY CARRIAGES...
...AND NOW THERE'S ONLY **ONE WAY** TO CLEAN IT UP!
VERNAY - LC 24
?
...HEY! DON'T TOUCH THAT!!!

BLAM

BOK

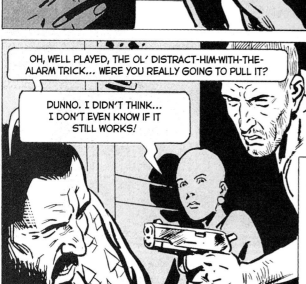

OH, WELL PLAYED, THE OL' DISTRACT-HIM-WITH-THE-ALARM TRICK... WERE YOU REALLY GOING TO PULL IT?

DUNNO. I DIDN'T THINK... I DON'T EVEN KNOW IF IT STILL WORKS!

GREAT JOB, ALL THE SAME.

C'MON, LET'S SPLIT!

PROLOFF...

WHAT?

IS IT TRUE WHAT HE SAID...? ABOUT THE *DISEASE*...

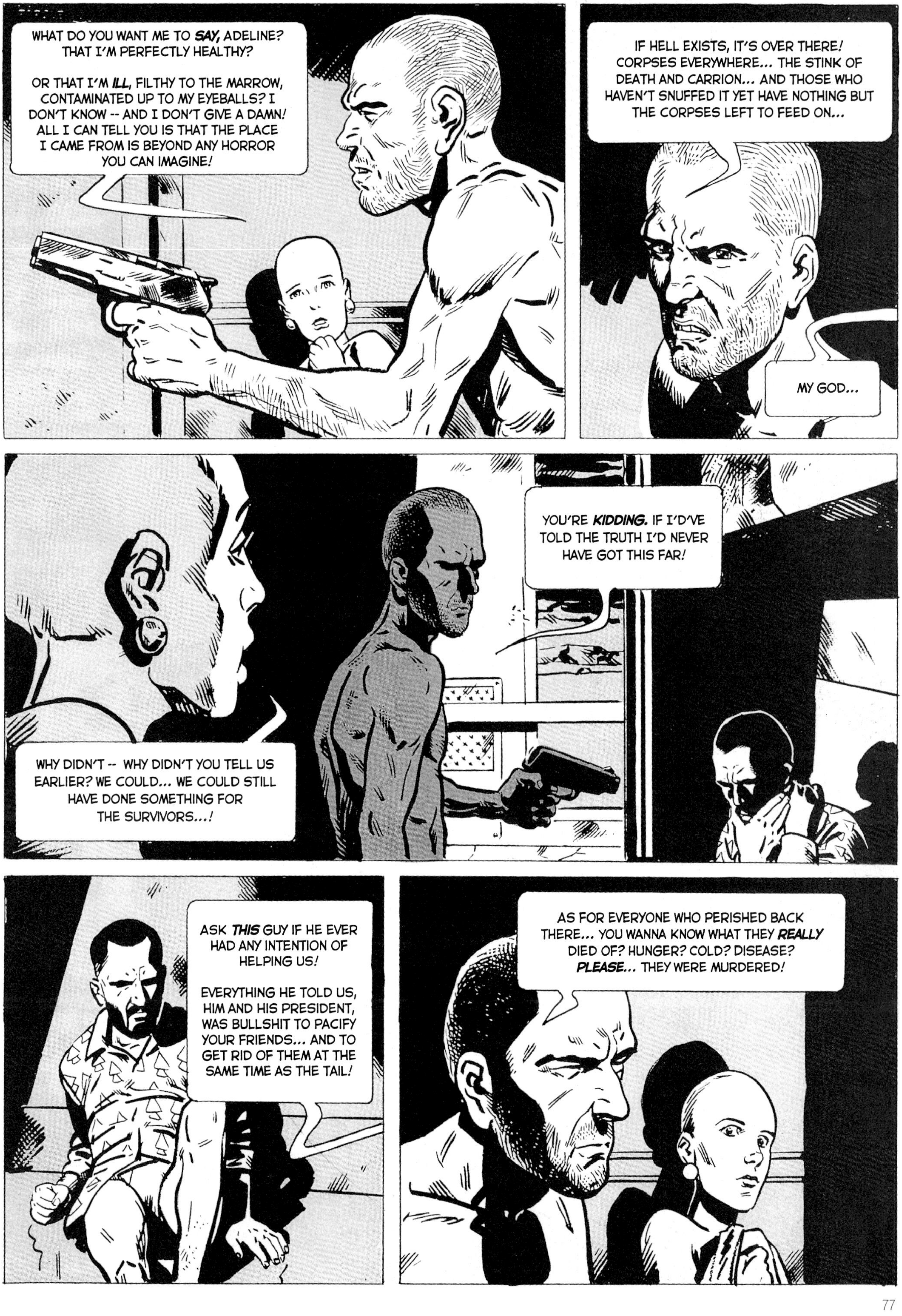
WHAT DO YOU WANT ME TO SAY, ADELINE? THAT I'M PERFECTLY HEALTHY?
OR THAT I'M ILL, FILTHY TO THE MARROW, CONTAMINATED UP TO MY EYEBALLS? I DON'T KNOW -- AND I DON'T GIVE A DAMN! ALL I CAN TELL YOU IS THAT THE PLACE I CAME FROM IS BEYOND ANY HORROR YOU CAN IMAGINE!
IF HELL EXISTS, IT'S OVER THERE! CORPSES EVERYWHERE... THE STINK OF DEATH AND CARRION... AND THOSE WHO HAVEN'T SNUFFED IT YET HAVE NOTHING BUT THE CORPSES LEFT TO FEED ON...
MY GOD...
WHY DIDN'T -- WHY DIDN'T YOU TELL US EARLIER? WE COULD... WE COULD STILL HAVE DONE SOMETHING FOR THE SURVIVORS...!
YOU'RE KIDDING. IF I'D'VE TOLD THE TRUTH I'D NEVER HAVE GOT THIS FAR!
ASK THIS GUY IF HE EVER HAD ANY INTENTION OF HELPING US!
EVERYTHING HE TOLD US, HIM AND HIS PRESIDENT, WAS BULLSHIT TO PACIFY YOUR FRIENDS... AND TO GET RID OF THEM AT THE SAME TIME AS THE TAIL!
AS FOR EVERYONE WHO PERISHED BACK THERE... YOU WANNA KNOW WHAT THEY REALLY DIED OF? HUNGER? COLD? DISEASE? PLEASE... THEY WERE MURDERED!

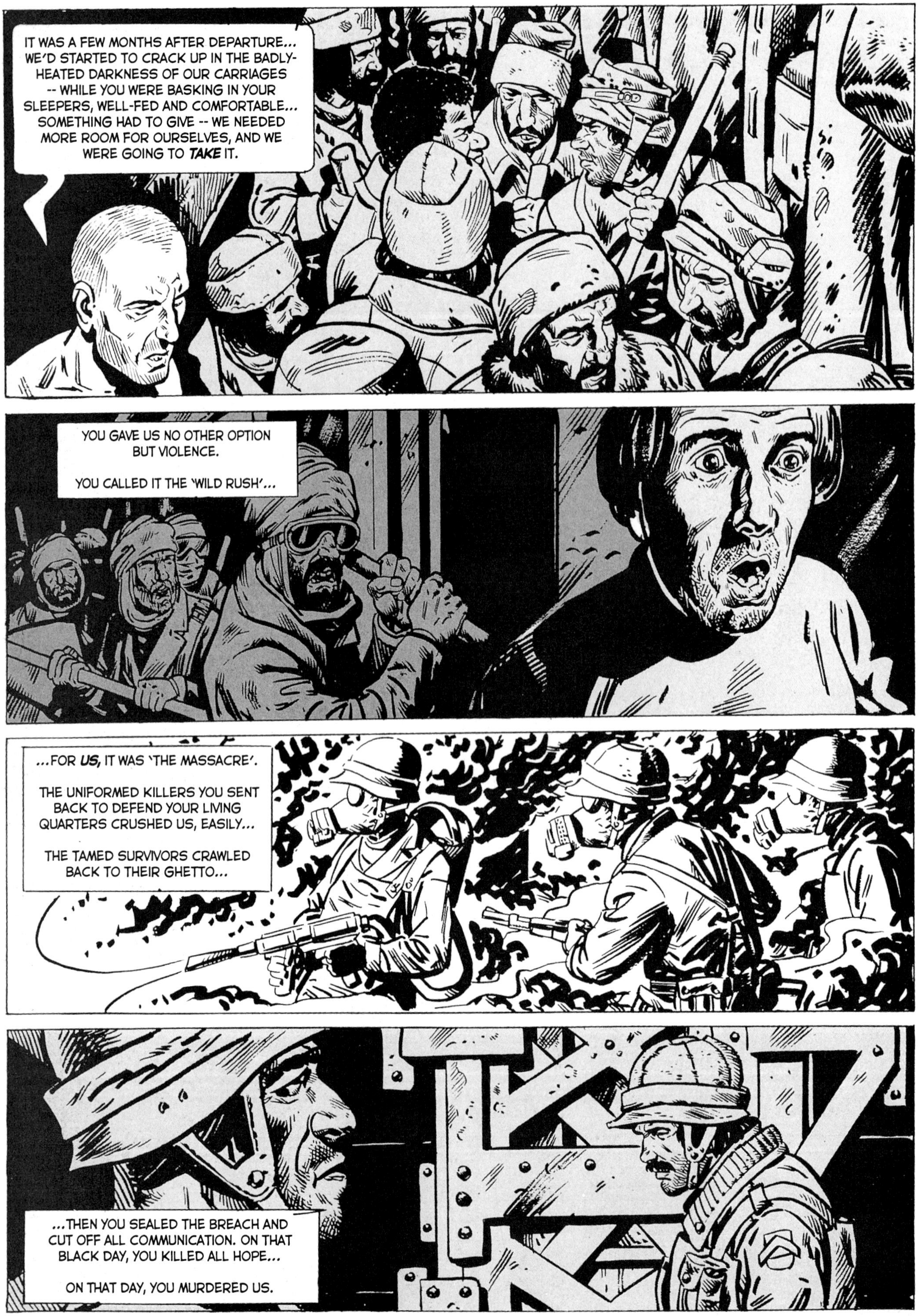
IT WAS A FEW MONTHS AFTER DEPARTURE... WE'D STARTED TO CRACK UP IN THE BADLY-HEATED DARKNESS OF OUR CARRIAGES -- WHILE YOU WERE BASKING IN YOUR SLEEPERS, WELL-FED AND COMFORTABLE... SOMETHING HAD TO GIVE -- WE NEEDED MORE ROOM FOR OURSELVES, AND WE WERE GOING TO *TAKE* IT.
YOU GAVE US NO OTHER OPTION BUT VIOLENCE.
YOU CALLED IT THE 'WILD RUSH'...
...FOR *US*, IT WAS 'THE MASSACRE'.
THE UNIFORMED KILLERS YOU SENT BACK TO DEFEND YOUR LIVING QUARTERS CRUSHED US, EASILY...
THE TAMED SURVIVORS CRAWLED BACK TO THEIR GHETTO...
...THEN YOU SEALED THE BREACH AND CUT OFF ALL COMMUNICATION. ON THAT BLACK DAY, YOU KILLED ALL HOPE...
ON THAT DAY, YOU MURDERED US.

THERE'S NOTHING HERE FOR ME ANYMORE. ADELINE... DON'T FEEL YOU HAVE TO COME WITH ME...

AND *YOU* -- JUST BE GLAD I HAVEN'T BLOWN YOUR BRAINS OUT TO COVER OUR ESCAPE!

PROLOFF... I'M NOT THINKING OF ME. I'M THINKING ABOUT STEFF AND THE OTHERS. I'VE GOT TO *WARN* THEM BEFORE IT'S TOO LATE... THEY HAVE TO KNOW THAT THEY WERE TRICKED AND THAT THEY'RE IN DANGER.

WHERE ARE THEY?

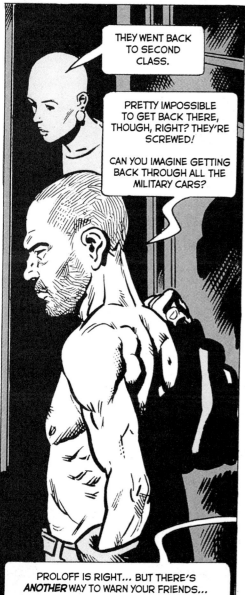

THEY WENT BACK TO SECOND CLASS.

PRETTY IMPOSSIBLE TO GET BACK THERE, THOUGH, RIGHT? THEY'RE SCREWED!

CAN YOU IMAGINE GETTING BACK THROUGH ALL THE MILITARY CARS?

YOU'VE BEEN HERE THE WHOLE TIME?!

THERE'S A *RADIO BOOTH* IN ONE OF THE CARS JUST A LITTLE FURTHER UP... A COMMS BOOTH WITH A MICROPHONE. YOU'LL BE HEARD THROUGHOUT THE WHOLE TRAIN, EVEN BACK IN SECOND CLASS...

THANKS FOR THE TIP... AND SEE YA!

AL! WHAT THE FUCK ARE YOU DOING? STOP THEM, GODDAMN IT!!!

PROLOFF IS RIGHT... BUT THERE'S *ANOTHER* WAY TO WARN YOUR FRIENDS...

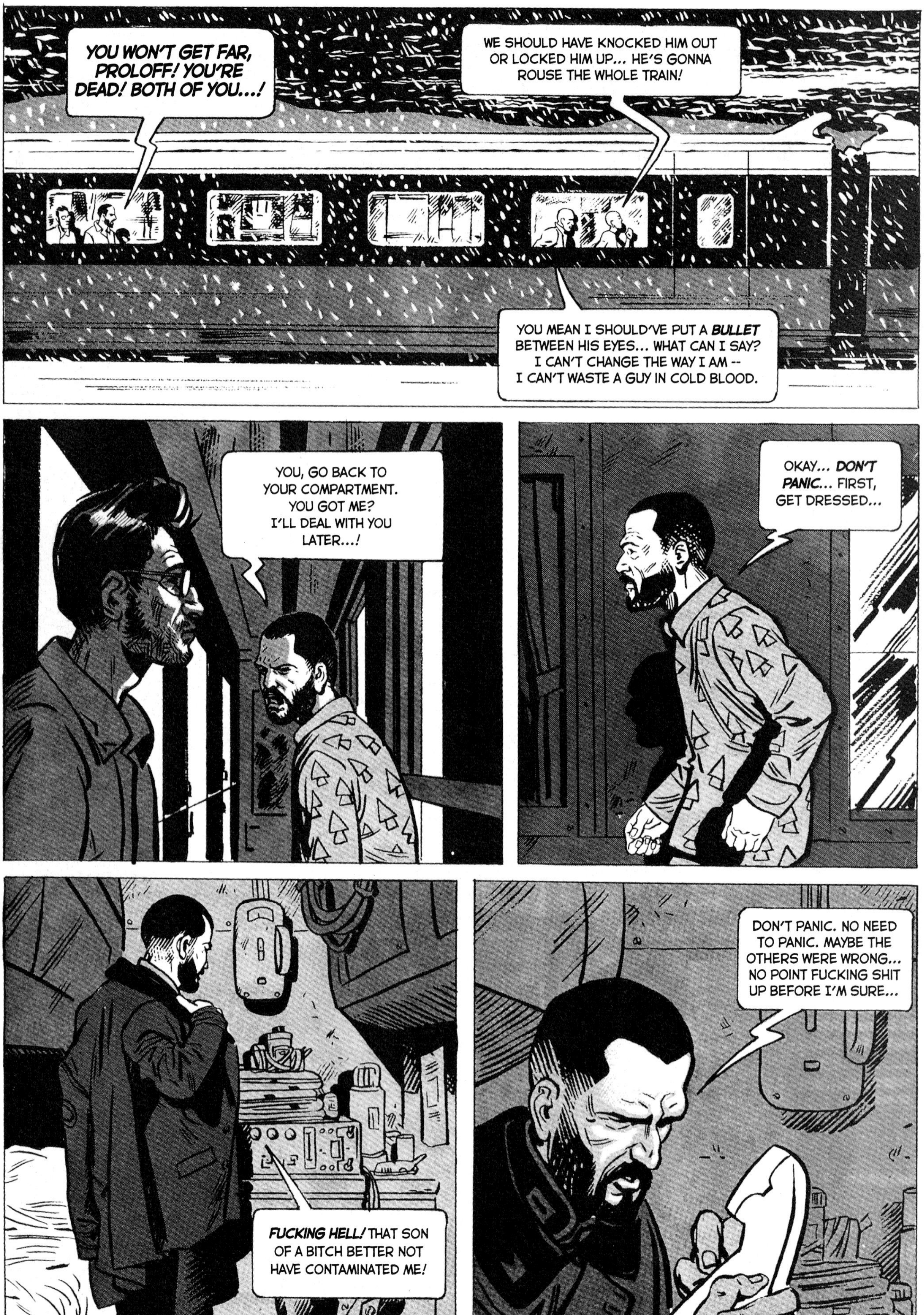
YOU WON'T GET FAR, PROLOFF! YOU'RE DEAD! BOTH OF YOU...!
WE SHOULD HAVE KNOCKED HIM OUT OR LOCKED HIM UP... HE'S GONNA ROUSE THE WHOLE TRAIN!
YOU MEAN I SHOULD'VE PUT A BULLET BETWEEN HIS EYES... WHAT CAN I SAY? I CAN'T CHANGE THE WAY I AM -- I CAN'T WASTE A GUY IN COLD BLOOD.
YOU, GO BACK TO YOUR COMPARTMENT. YOU GOT ME? I'LL DEAL WITH YOU LATER...!
OKAY... DON'T PANIC... FIRST, GET DRESSED...
FUCKING HELL! THAT SON OF A BITCH BETTER NOT HAVE CONTAMINATED ME!
DON'T PANIC. NO NEED TO PANIC. MAYBE THE OTHERS WERE WRONG... NO POINT FUCKING SHIT UP BEFORE I'M SURE...

...NO, COLONEL, IT'S NOT GETTING BETTER -- ANYTHING BUT! WE'VE GOT A FISTFUL OF NEW CASES -- AND ONE OF THE SICK GUYS DIED THIS MORNING... HANG ON, I'LL PASS YOU OVER TO THE DOC.

...I'M HERE. YES, IT SEEMS TO BE A PARTICULARLY VIRULENT TYPE OF PNEUMOPATHY. AN INFECTIOUS BASTARD THAT STRIKES FAST AND HARD! THE FIRST *SYMPTOMS?* FEVER...

IT STARTS WITH A VIOLENT HEADACHE... PROBLEMS BREATHING... DRY COUGH, CHEST OR STOMACH PAINS.

SOME PEOPLE DISPLAY EXTREME AGITATION...

THE PROBLEM IS, WE'RE NOT EQUIPPED TO DEAL WITH A REAL EPIDEMIC -- LOCO PRESERVE US. PREVENTATIVE MEASURES? IT MAY BE TOO LATE FOR THAT.

BY THE WAY, WHAT HAVE YOU DONE WITH THE PRISONER -- AND THE GIRL WHO WAS WITH HIM? DON'T FORGET, COLONEL, THAT IT WAS UNDER *YOUR* RESPONSIBILITY AND AGAINST *MY* ADVICE THAT THEY WERE TAKEN OUT OF OBSERVATION...

CLICK!

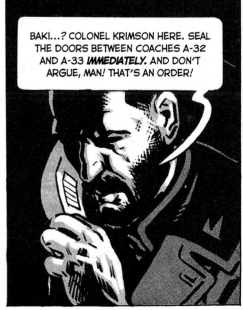

BAKI...? COLONEL KRIMSON HERE. SEAL THE DOORS BETWEEN COACHES A-32 AND A-33 *IMMEDIATELY.* AND DON'T ARGUE, MAN! THAT'S AN ORDER!

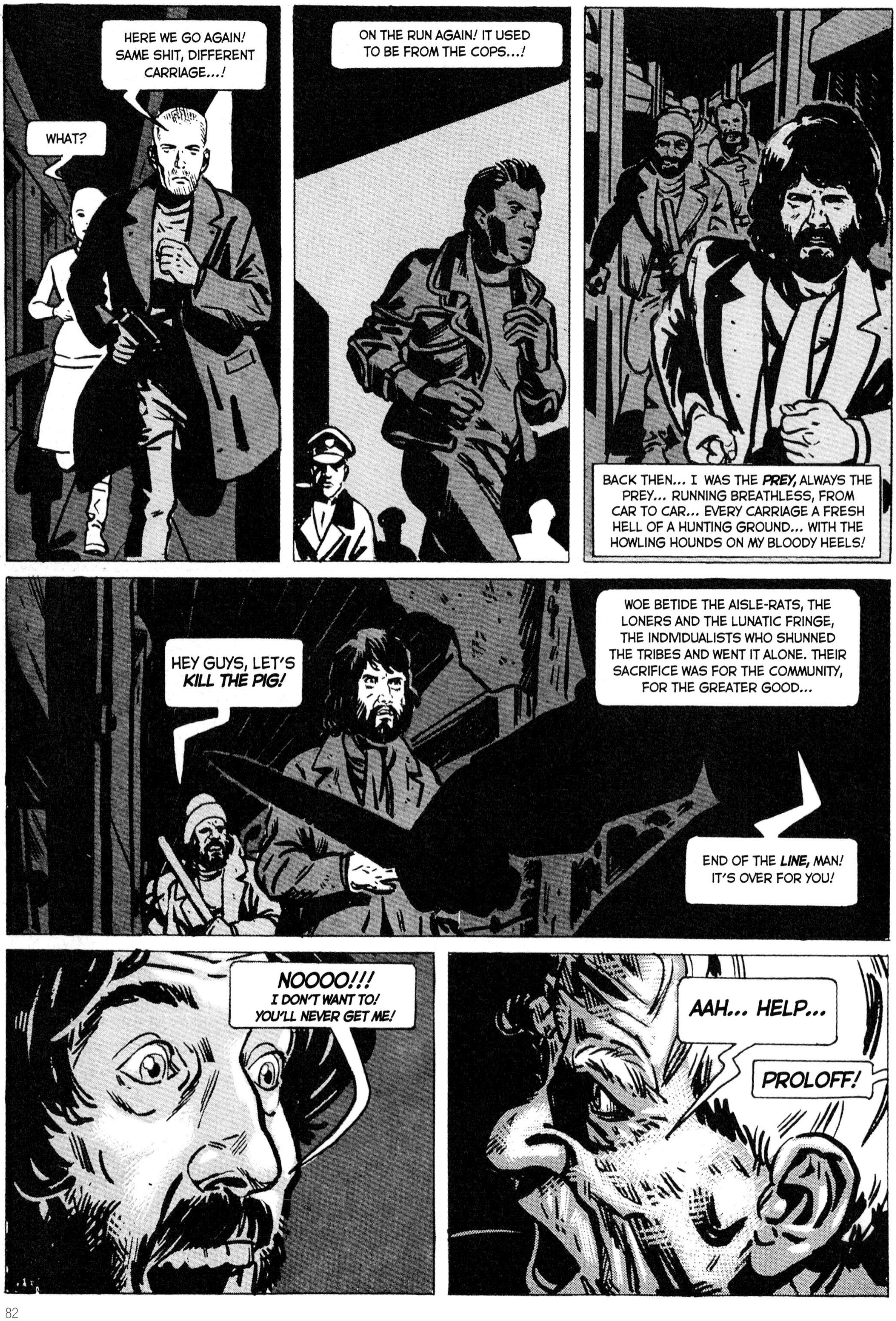
HERE WE GO AGAIN! SAME SHIT, DIFFERENT CARRIAGE...!
WHAT?
ON THE RUN AGAIN! IT USED TO BE FROM THE COPS...!
BACK THEN... I WAS THE PREY, ALWAYS THE PREY... RUNNING BREATHLESS, FROM CAR TO CAR... EVERY CARRIAGE A FRESH HELL OF A HUNTING GROUND... WITH THE HOWLING HOUNDS ON MY BLOODY HEELS!
HEY GUYS, LET'S KILL THE PIG!
WOE BETIDE THE AISLE-RATS, THE LONERS AND THE LUNATIC FRINGE, THE INDIVIDUALISTS WHO SHUNNED THE TRIBES AND WENT IT ALONE. THEIR SACRIFICE WAS FOR THE COMMUNITY, FOR THE GREATER GOOD...
END OF THE LINE, MAN! IT'S OVER FOR YOU!
NOOOO!!! I DON'T WANT TO! YOU'LL NEVER GET ME!
AAH... HELP...
PROLOFF!

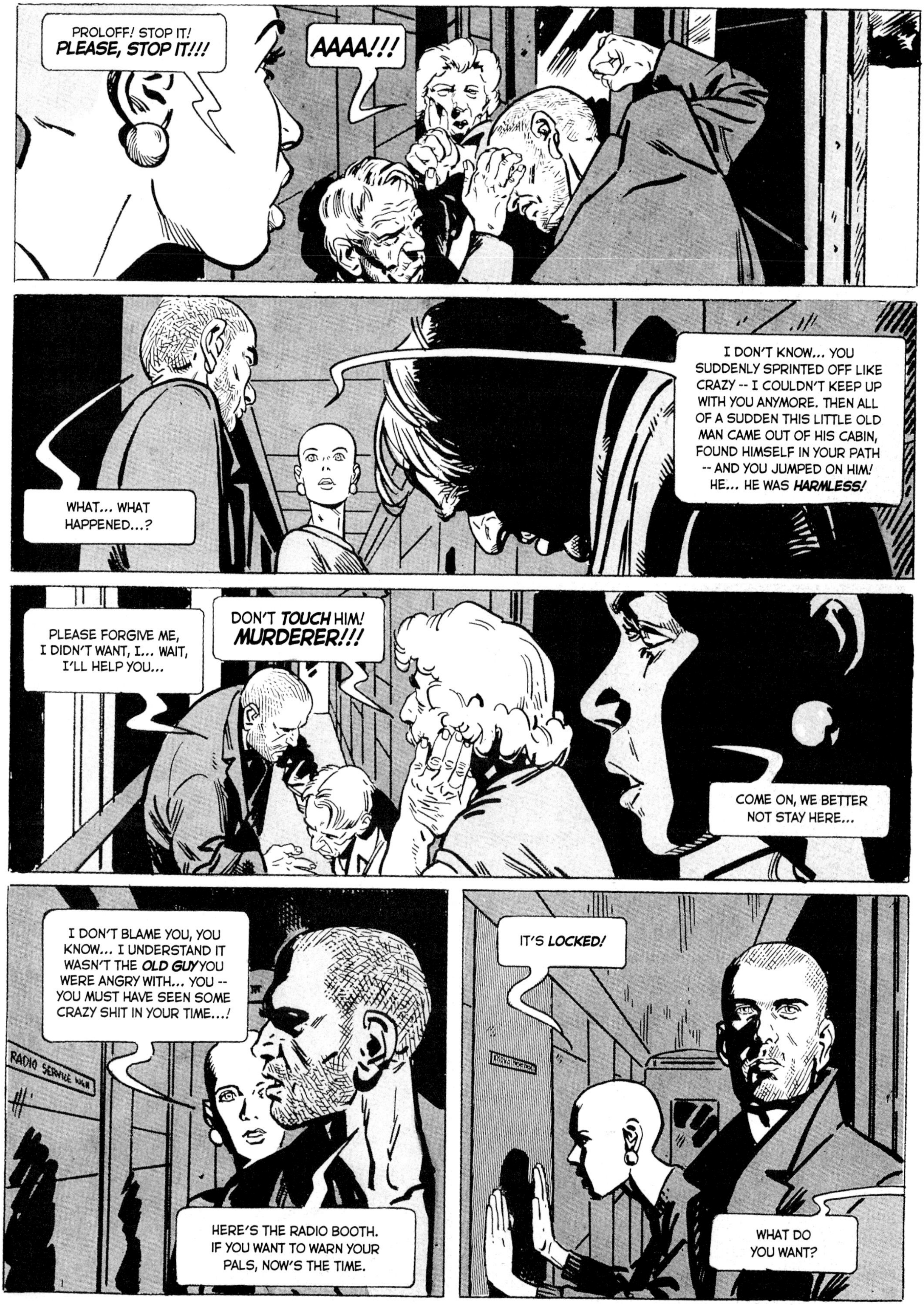
PROLOFF! STOP IT! PLEASE, STOP IT!!!
AAAA!!!
WHAT... WHAT HAPPENED...?
I DON'T KNOW... YOU SUDDENLY SPRINTED OFF LIKE CRAZY -- I COULDN'T KEEP UP WITH YOU ANYMORE. THEN ALL OF A SUDDEN THIS LITTLE OLD MAN CAME OUT OF HIS CABIN, FOUND HIMSELF IN YOUR PATH -- AND YOU JUMPED ON HIM! HE... HE WAS HARMLESS!
PLEASE FORGIVE ME, I DIDN'T WANT, I... WAIT, I'LL HELP YOU...
DON'T TOUCH HIM! MURDERER!!!
COME ON, WE BETTER NOT STAY HERE...
I DON'T BLAME YOU, YOU KNOW... I UNDERSTAND IT WASN'T THE OLD GUY YOU WERE ANGRY WITH... YOU -- YOU MUST HAVE SEEN SOME CRAZY SHIT IN YOUR TIME...!
RADIO SERVICE
HERE'S THE RADIO BOOTH. IF YOU WANT TO WARN YOUR PALS, NOW'S THE TIME.
IT'S LOCKED!
WHAT DO YOU WANT?

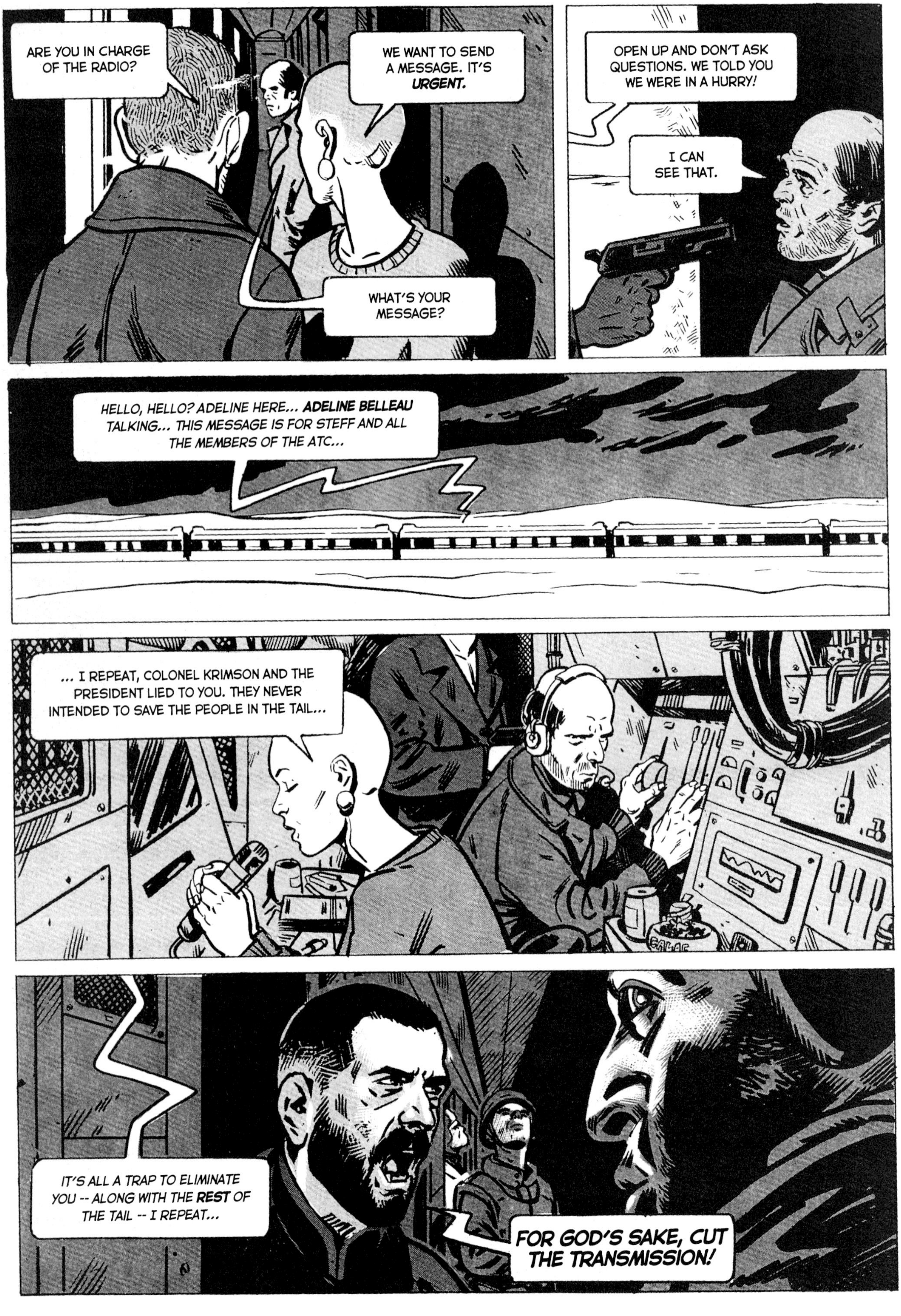
ARE YOU IN CHARGE OF THE RADIO?
WE WANT TO SEND A MESSAGE. IT'S URGENT.
WHAT'S YOUR MESSAGE?
OPEN UP AND DON'T ASK QUESTIONS. WE TOLD YOU WE WERE IN A HURRY!
I CAN SEE THAT.
HELLO, HELLO? ADELINE HERE... ADELINE BELLEAU TALKING... THIS MESSAGE IS FOR STEFF AND ALL THE MEMBERS OF THE ATC...
... I REPEAT, COLONEL KRIMSON AND THE PRESIDENT LIED TO YOU. THEY NEVER INTENDED TO SAVE THE PEOPLE IN THE TAIL...
IT'S ALL A TRAP TO ELIMINATE YOU -- ALONG WITH THE REST OF THE TAIL -- I REPEAT...
FOR GOD'S SAKE, CUT THE TRANSMISSION!

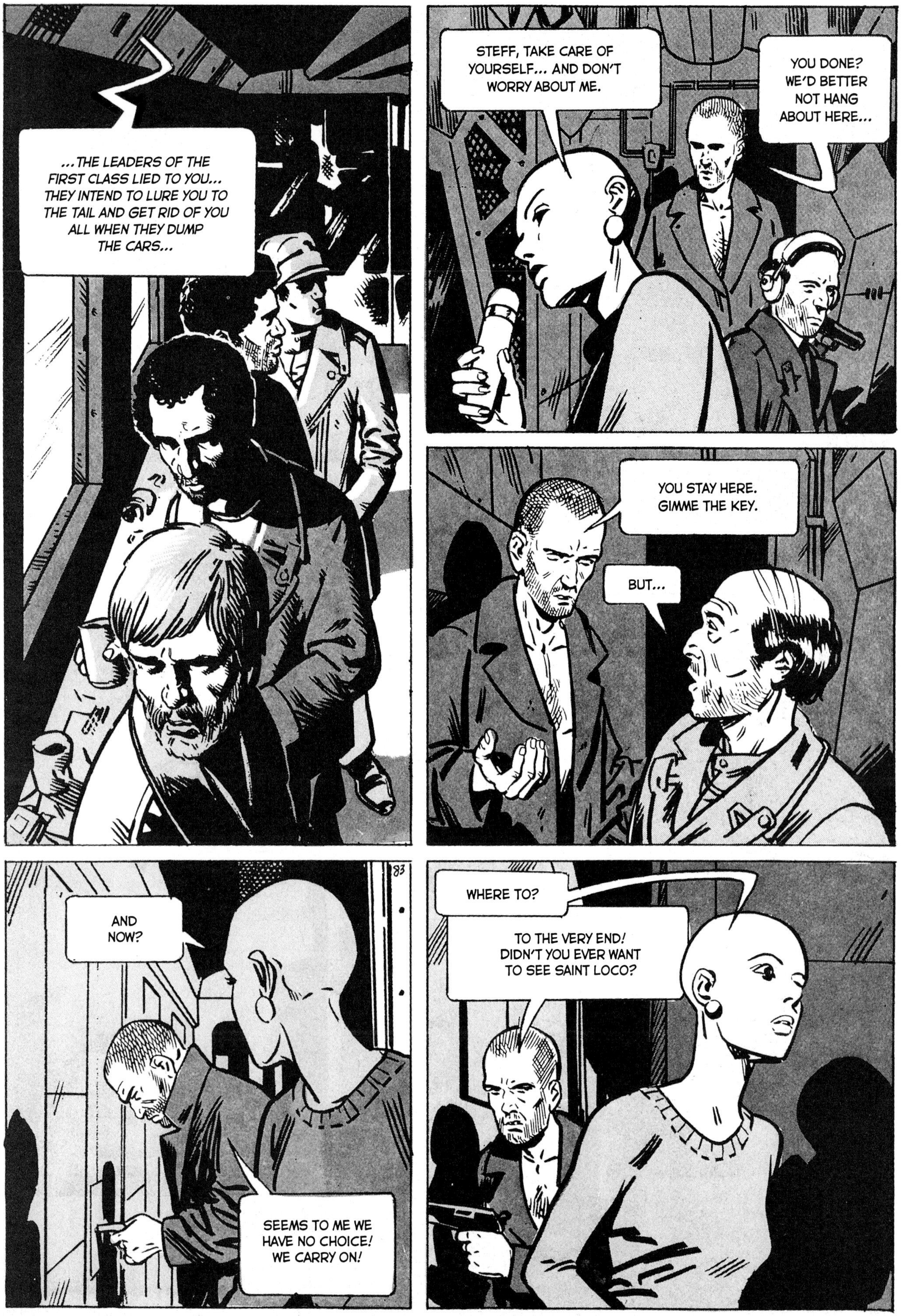
...THE LEADERS OF THE FIRST CLASS LIED TO YOU... THEY INTEND TO LURE YOU TO THE TAIL AND GET RID OF YOU ALL WHEN THEY DUMP THE CARS...
STEFF, TAKE CARE OF YOURSELF... AND DON'T WORRY ABOUT ME.
YOU DONE? WE'D BETTER NOT HANG ABOUT HERE...
YOU STAY HERE. GIMME THE KEY.
BUT...
AND NOW?
SEEMS TO ME WE HAVE NO CHOICE! WE CARRY ON!
WHERE TO?
TO THE VERY END! DIDN'T YOU EVER WANT TO SEE SAINT LOCO?

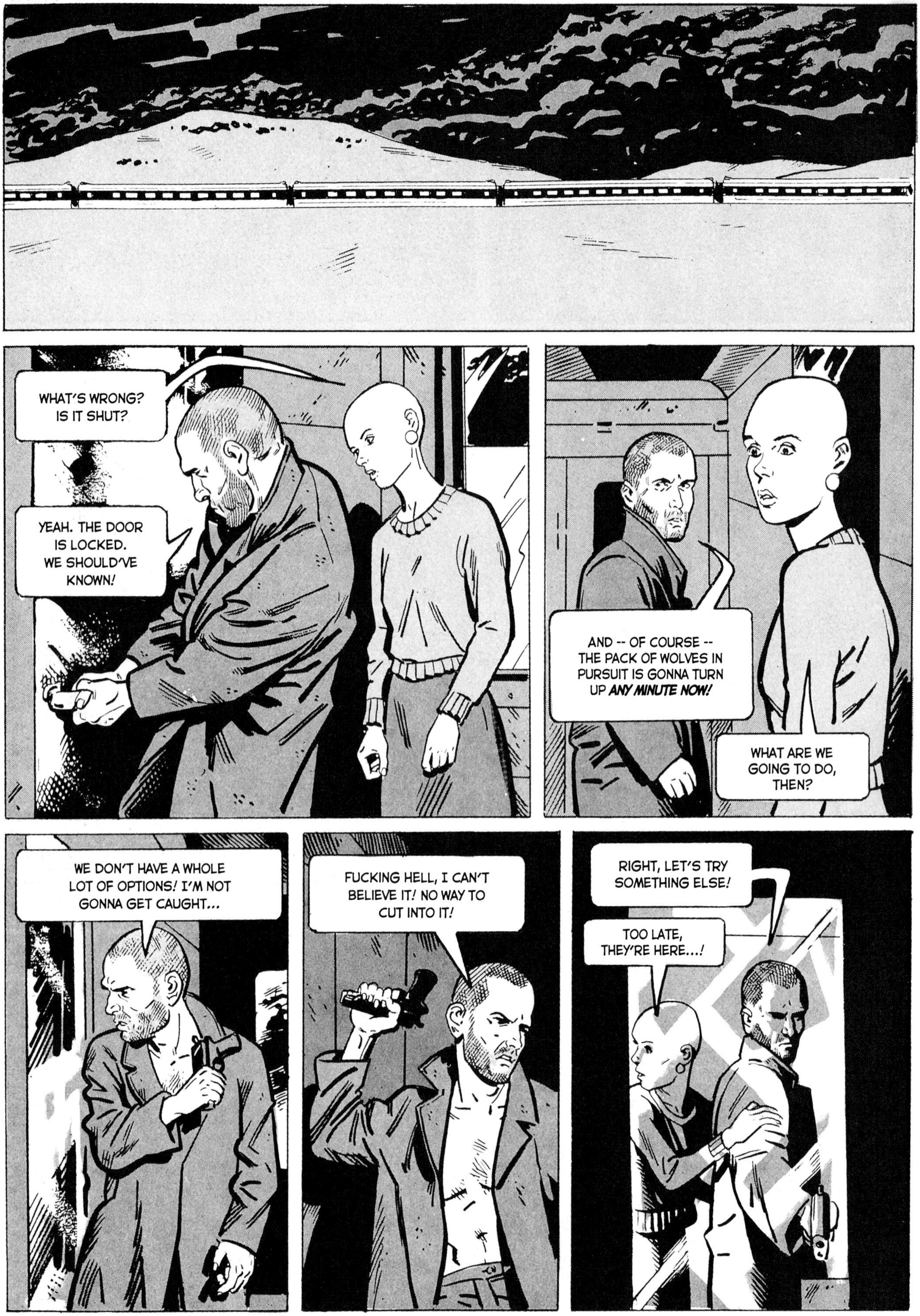
WHAT'S WRONG? IS IT SHUT?
YEAH. THE DOOR IS LOCKED. WE SHOULD'VE KNOWN!
AND -- OF COURSE -- THE PACK OF WOLVES IN PURSUIT IS GONNA TURN UP ANY MINUTE NOW!
WHAT ARE WE GOING TO DO, THEN?
WE DON'T HAVE A WHOLE LOT OF OPTIONS! I'M NOT GONNA GET CAUGHT...
FUCKING HELL, I CAN'T BELIEVE IT! NO WAY TO CUT INTO IT!
RIGHT, LET'S TRY SOMETHING ELSE!
TOO LATE, THEY'RE HERE...!

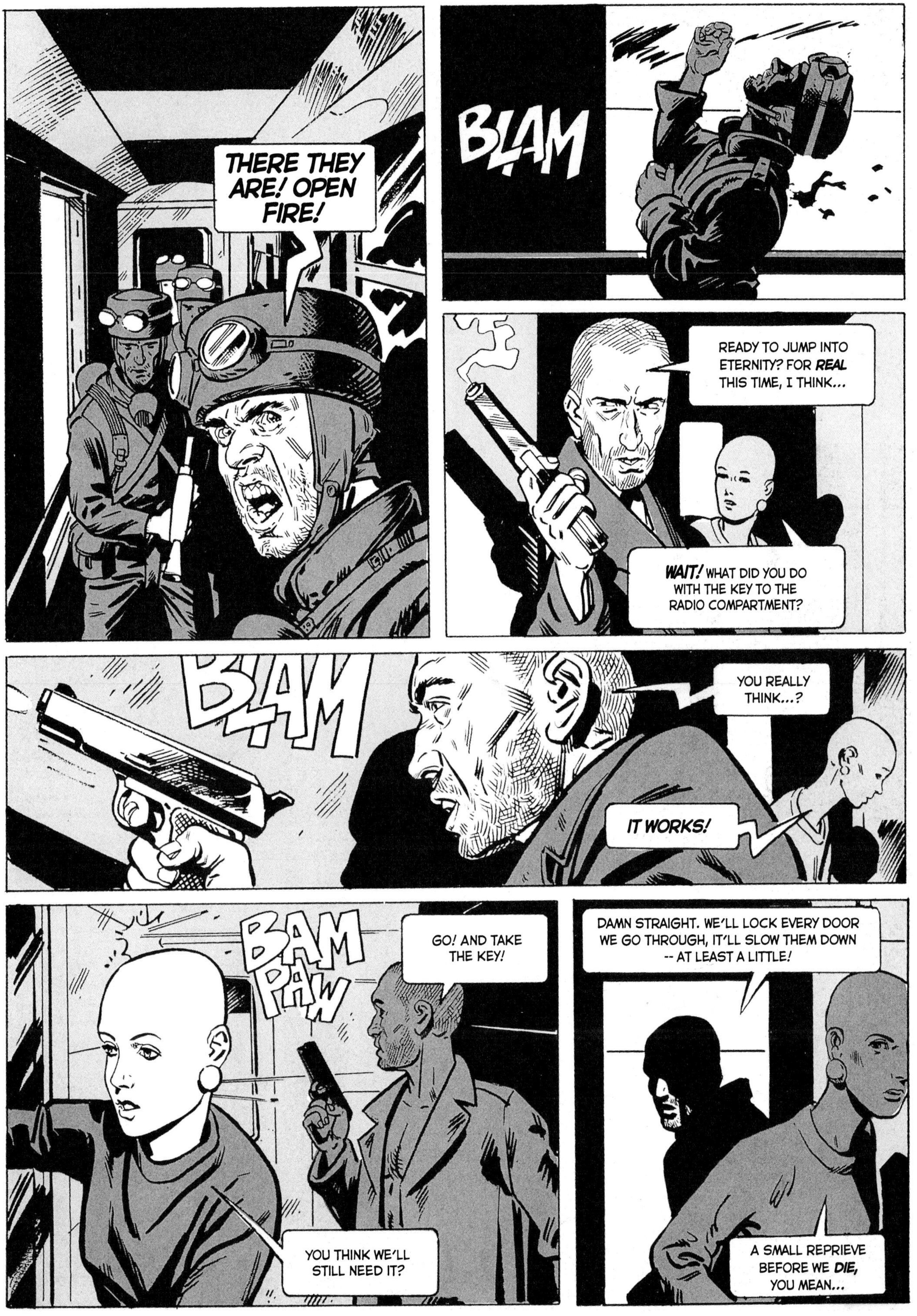
THERE THEY ARE! OPEN FIRE!
BLAM
READY TO JUMP INTO ETERNITY? FOR REAL THIS TIME, I THINK...
WAIT! WHAT DID YOU DO WITH THE KEY TO THE RADIO COMPARTMENT?
BLAM
BLAM
YOU REALLY THINK...?
IT WORKS!
BAM
PAW
GO! AND TAKE THE KEY!
YOU THINK WE'LL STILL NEED IT?
DAMN STRAIGHT. WE'LL LOCK EVERY DOOR WE GO THROUGH, IT'LL SLOW THEM DOWN -- AT LEAST A LITTLE!
A SMALL REPRIEVE BEFORE WE DIE, YOU MEAN...

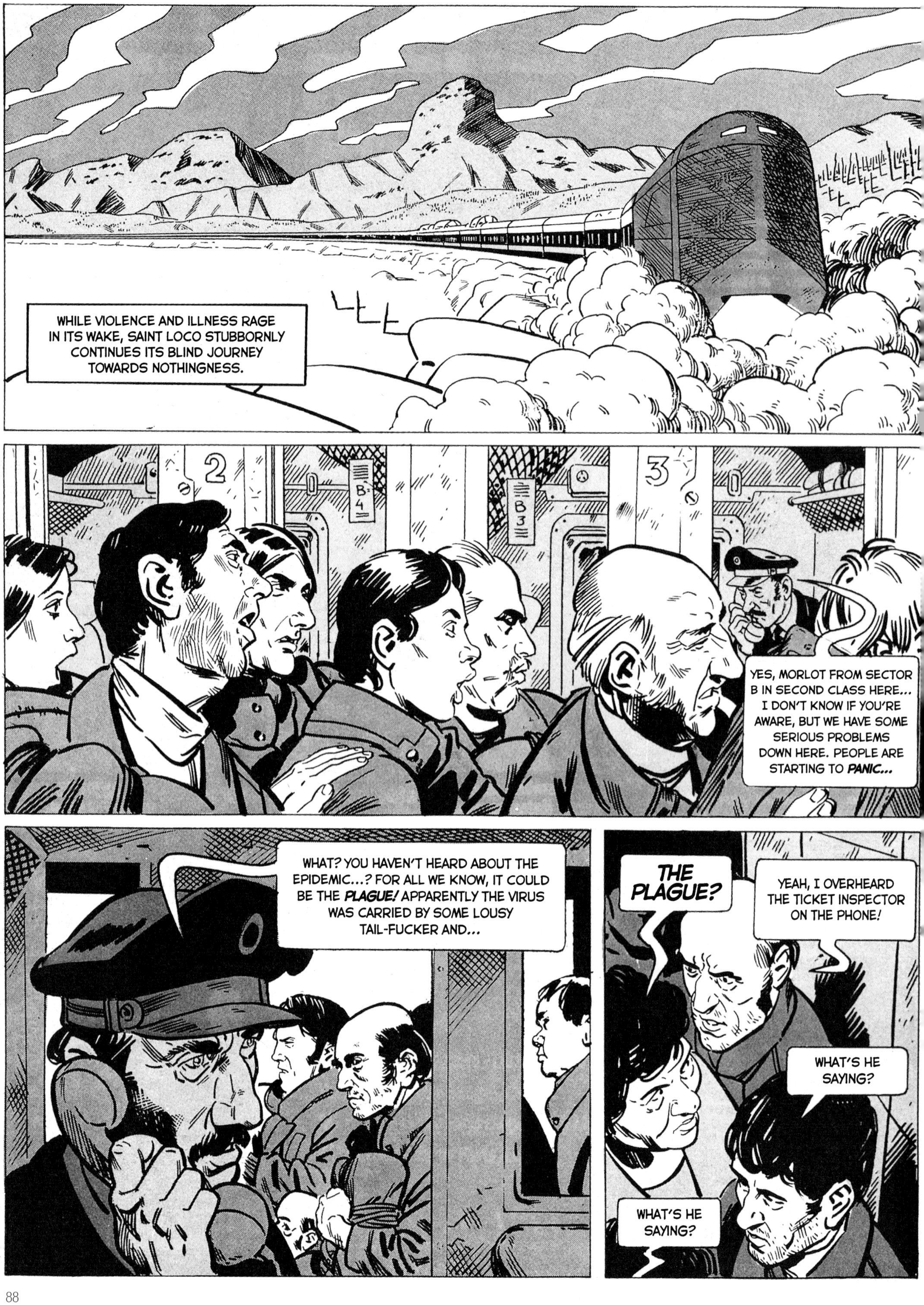
WHILE VIOLENCE AND ILLNESS RAGE IN ITS WAKE, SAINT LOCO STUBBORNLY CONTINUES ITS BLIND JOURNEY TOWARDS NOTHINGNESS.
YES, MORLOT FROM SECTOR B IN SECOND CLASS HERE... I DON'T KNOW IF YOU'RE AWARE, BUT WE HAVE SOME SERIOUS PROBLEMS DOWN HERE. PEOPLE ARE STARTING TO *PANIC...*
WHAT? YOU HAVEN'T HEARD ABOUT THE EPIDEMIC...? FOR ALL WE KNOW, IT COULD BE THE *PLAGUE!* APPARENTLY THE VIRUS WAS CARRIED BY SOME LOUSY TAIL-FUCKER AND...
THE PLAGUE?
YEAH, I OVERHEARD THE TICKET INSPECTOR ON THE PHONE!
WHAT'S HE SAYING?
WHAT'S HE SAYING?

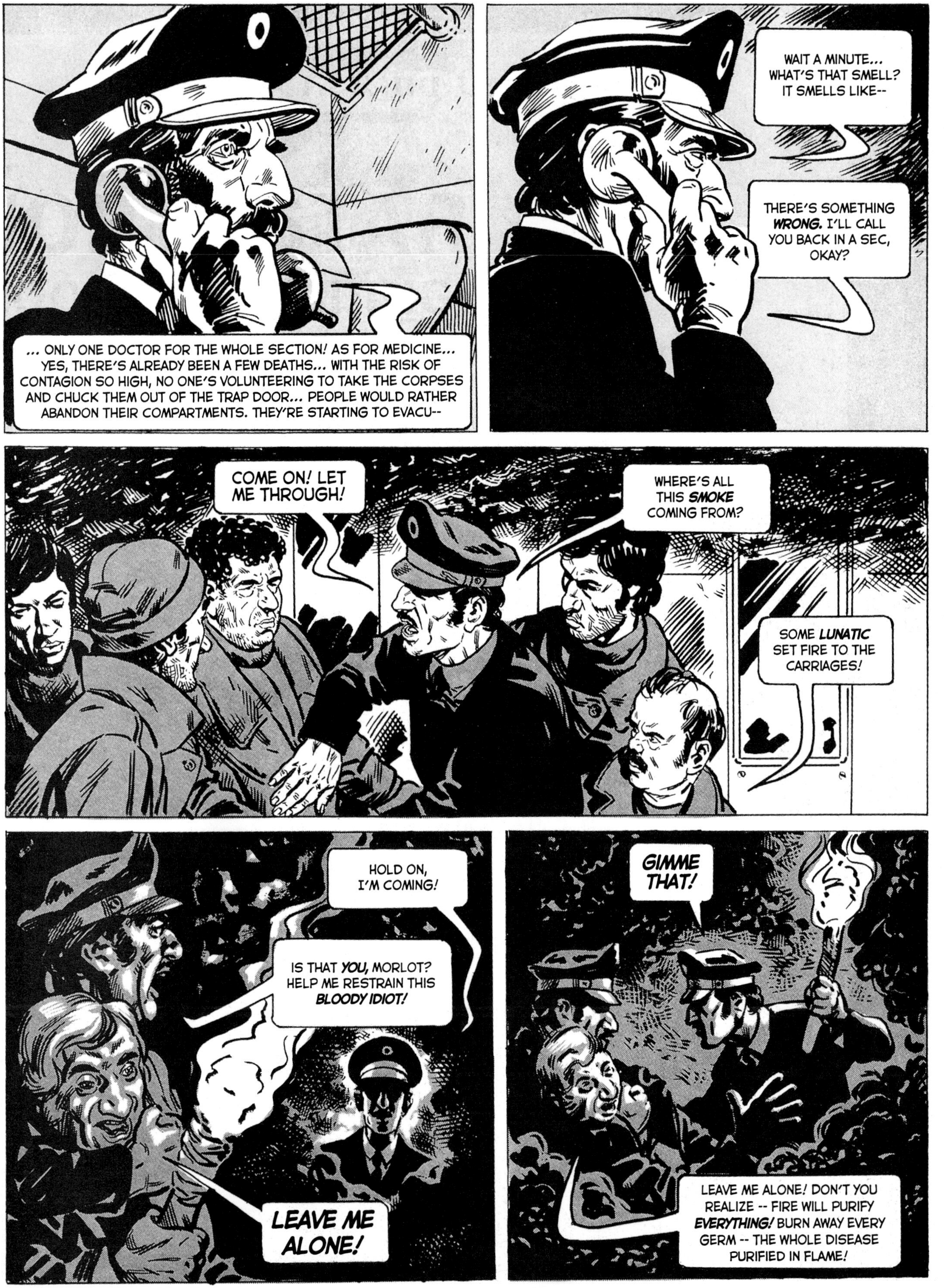

... ONLY ONE DOCTOR FOR THE WHOLE SECTION! AS FOR MEDICINE... YES, THERE'S ALREADY BEEN A FEW DEATHS... WITH THE RISK OF CONTAGION SO HIGH, NO ONE'S VOLUNTEERING TO TAKE THE CORPSES AND CHUCK THEM OUT OF THE TRAP DOOR... PEOPLE WOULD RATHER ABANDON THEIR COMPARTMENTS. THEY'RE STARTING TO EVACU--
WAIT A MINUTE... WHAT'S THAT SMELL? IT SMELLS LIKE--
THERE'S SOMETHING ***WRONG.*** I'LL CALL YOU BACK IN A SEC, OKAY?
COME ON! LET ME THROUGH!
WHERE'S ALL THIS ***SMOKE*** COMING FROM?
SOME ***LUNATIC*** SET FIRE TO THE CARRIAGES!
HOLD ON, I'M COMING!
IS THAT ***YOU,*** MORLOT? HELP ME RESTRAIN THIS ***BLOODY IDIOT!***
LEAVE ME ALONE!
GIMME THAT!
LEAVE ME ALONE! DON'T YOU REALIZE -- FIRE WILL PURIFY ***EVERYTHING!*** BURN AWAY EVERY GERM -- THE WHOLE DISEASE PURIFIED IN FLAME!

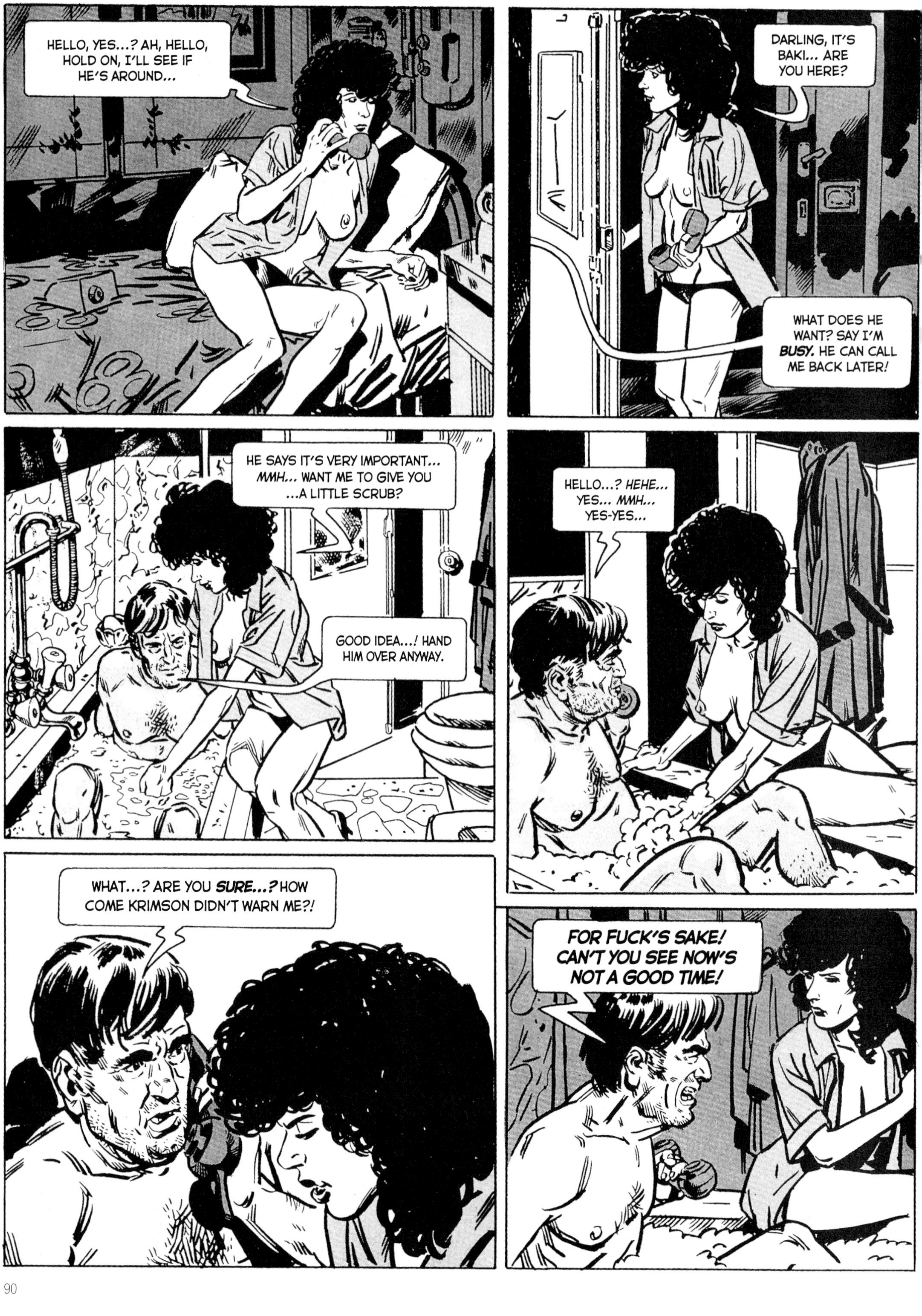
HELLO, YES...? AH, HELLO, HOLD ON, I'LL SEE IF HE'S AROUND...
DARLING, IT'S BAKI... ARE YOU HERE?
WHAT DOES HE WANT? SAY I'M BUSY. HE CAN CALL ME BACK LATER!
HE SAYS IT'S VERY IMPORTANT... MMH... WANT ME TO GIVE YOU ...A LITTLE SCRUB?
GOOD IDEA...! HAND HIM OVER ANYWAY.
HELLO...? HEHE... YES... MMH... YES-YES...
WHAT...? ARE YOU SURE...? HOW COME KRIMSON DIDN'T WARN ME?!
FOR FUCK'S SAKE! CAN'T YOU SEE NOW'S NOT A GOOD TIME!

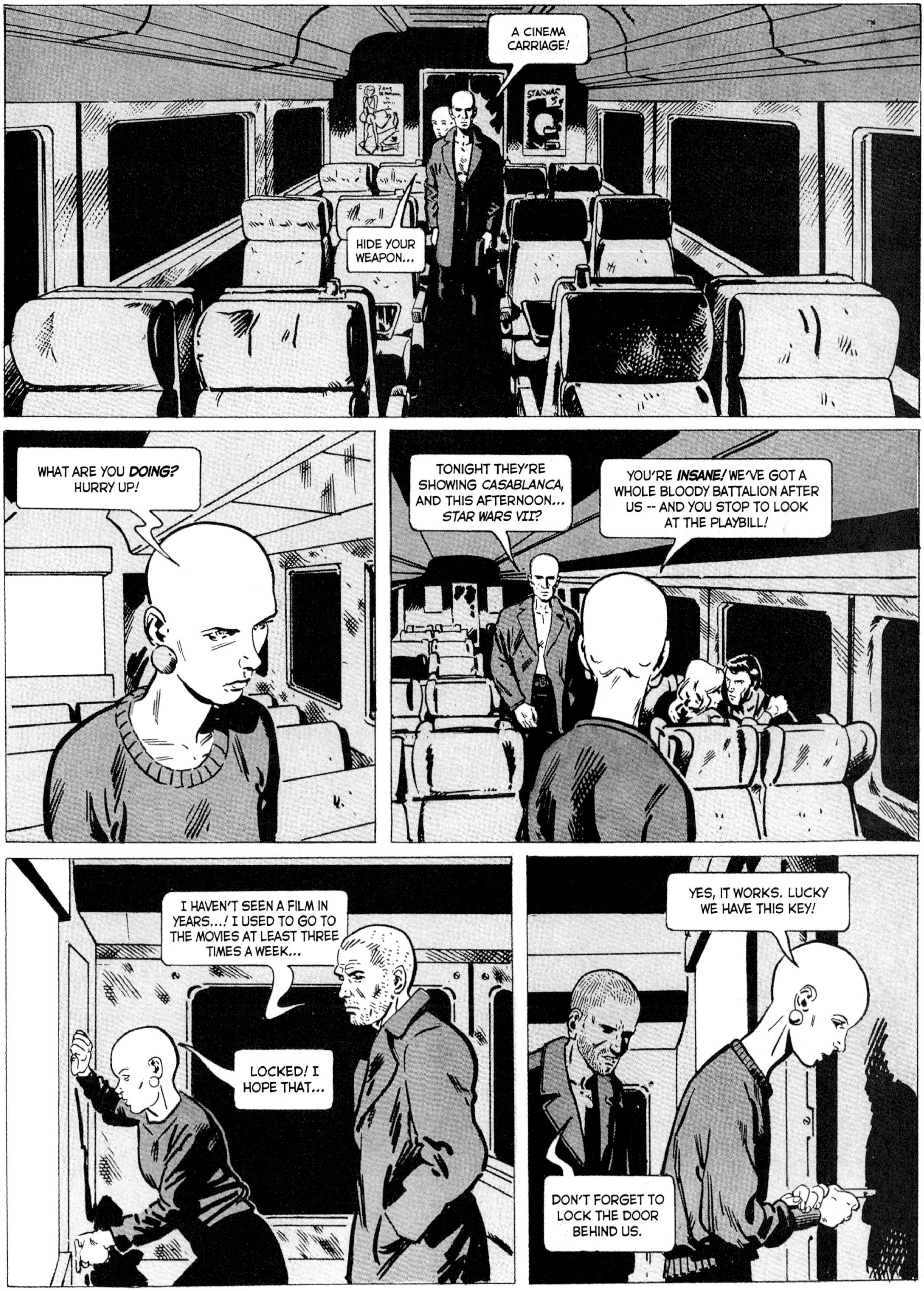
A CINEMA CARRIAGE!
HIDE YOUR WEAPON...
WHAT ARE YOU *DOING?* HURRY UP!
TONIGHT THEY'RE SHOWING *CASABLANCA*, AND THIS AFTERNOON... *STAR WARS VII?*
YOU'RE ***INSANE!*** WE'VE GOT A WHOLE BLOODY BATTALION AFTER US -- AND YOU STOP TO LOOK AT THE PLAYBILL!
I HAVEN'T SEEN A FILM IN YEARS...! I USED TO GO TO THE MOVIES AT LEAST THREE TIMES A WEEK...
LOCKED! I HOPE THAT...
YES, IT WORKS. LUCKY WE HAVE THIS KEY!
DON'T FORGET TO LOCK THE DOOR BEHIND US.

HELLO? PRESIDENT DEWILL HERE. I'D LIKE TO SPEAK TO COLONEL KRIMSON.

THE COLONEL IS ON THE OTHER LINE AT PRESENT, SIR. DO YOU WANT HIM TO CALL YOU BACK?

WHAT ARE YOU TALKING ABOUT? WHERE IS LIEUTENANT ZAYIM? I WANT TO TALK TO *HIM!*

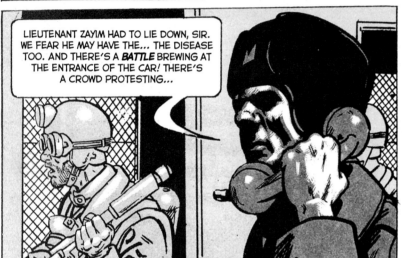

LIEUTENANT ZAYIM HAD TO LIE DOWN, SIR. WE FEAR HE MAY HAVE THE... THE DISEASE TOO. AND THERE'S A *BATTLE* BREWING AT THE ENTRANCE OF THE CAR! THERE'S A CROWD PROTESTING...

...THEY WANT TO DETACH THE TAIL. NOT SURE WE'LL BE ABLE TO CONTAIN THEM MUCH LONGER! I'D RATHER AVOID...

PAW

DIRTBAGS!

MURDERERS!

FOR SAINT LOCO, LET'S GO!!!

STOP IT!

DOWN WITH THE TAIL-FUCKER-LOVERS!

DON'T SHOOT!

WE'LL DUMP YOU ALL WITH THE TAIL-BUMS!

MOVE BACK!

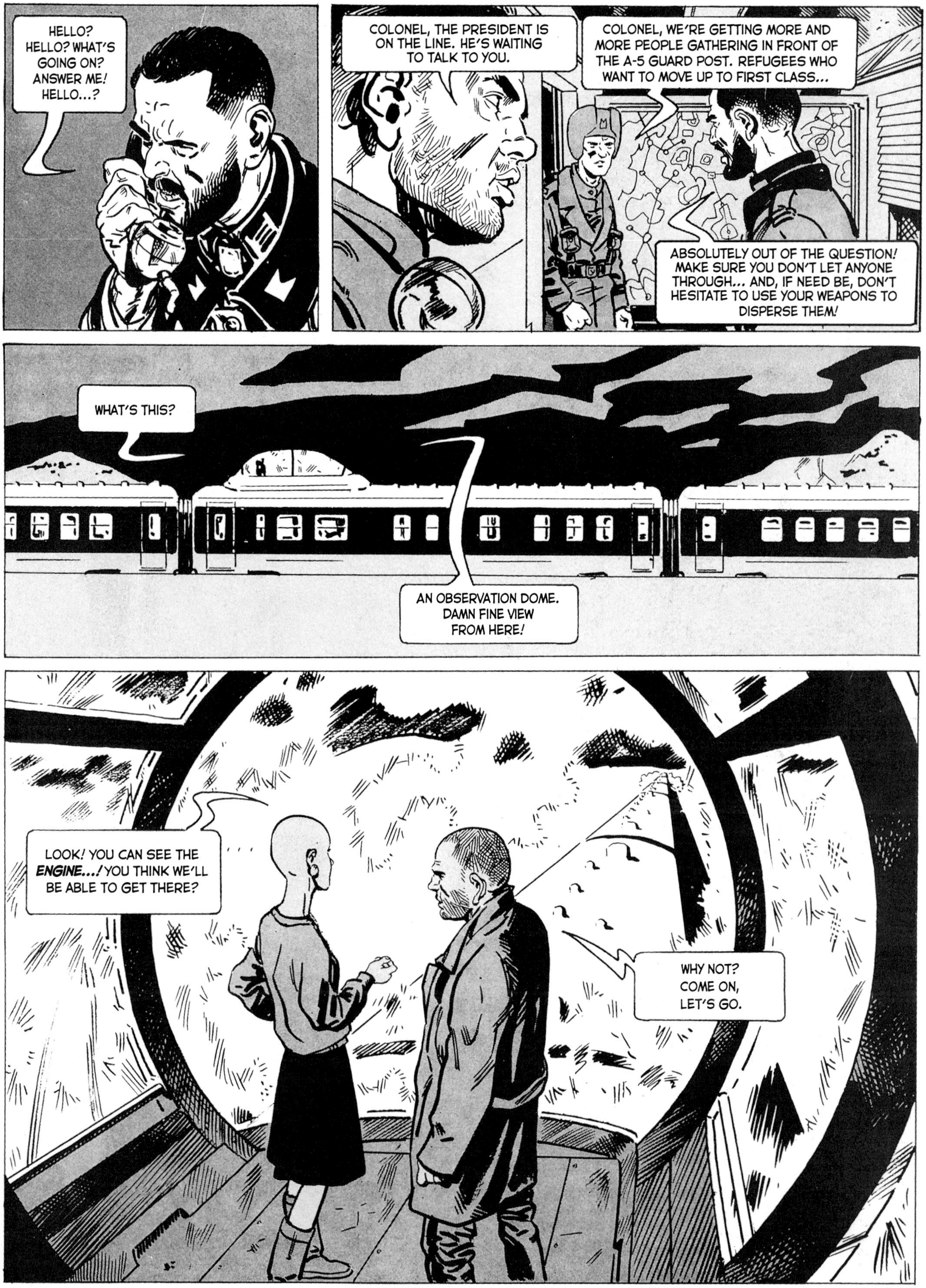
HELLO? HELLO? WHAT'S GOING ON? ANSWER ME! HELLO...?
COLONEL, THE PRESIDENT IS ON THE LINE. HE'S WAITING TO TALK TO YOU.
COLONEL, WE'RE GETTING MORE AND MORE PEOPLE GATHERING IN FRONT OF THE A-5 GUARD POST. REFUGEES WHO WANT TO MOVE UP TO FIRST CLASS...
ABSOLUTELY OUT OF THE QUESTION! MAKE SURE YOU DON'T LET ANYONE THROUGH... AND, IF NEED BE, DON'T HESITATE TO USE YOUR WEAPONS TO DISPERSE THEM!
WHAT'S THIS?
AN OBSERVATION DOME. DAMN FINE VIEW FROM HERE!
LOOK! YOU CAN SEE THE ENGINE...! YOU THINK WE'LL BE ABLE TO GET THERE?
WHY NOT? COME ON, LET'S GO.

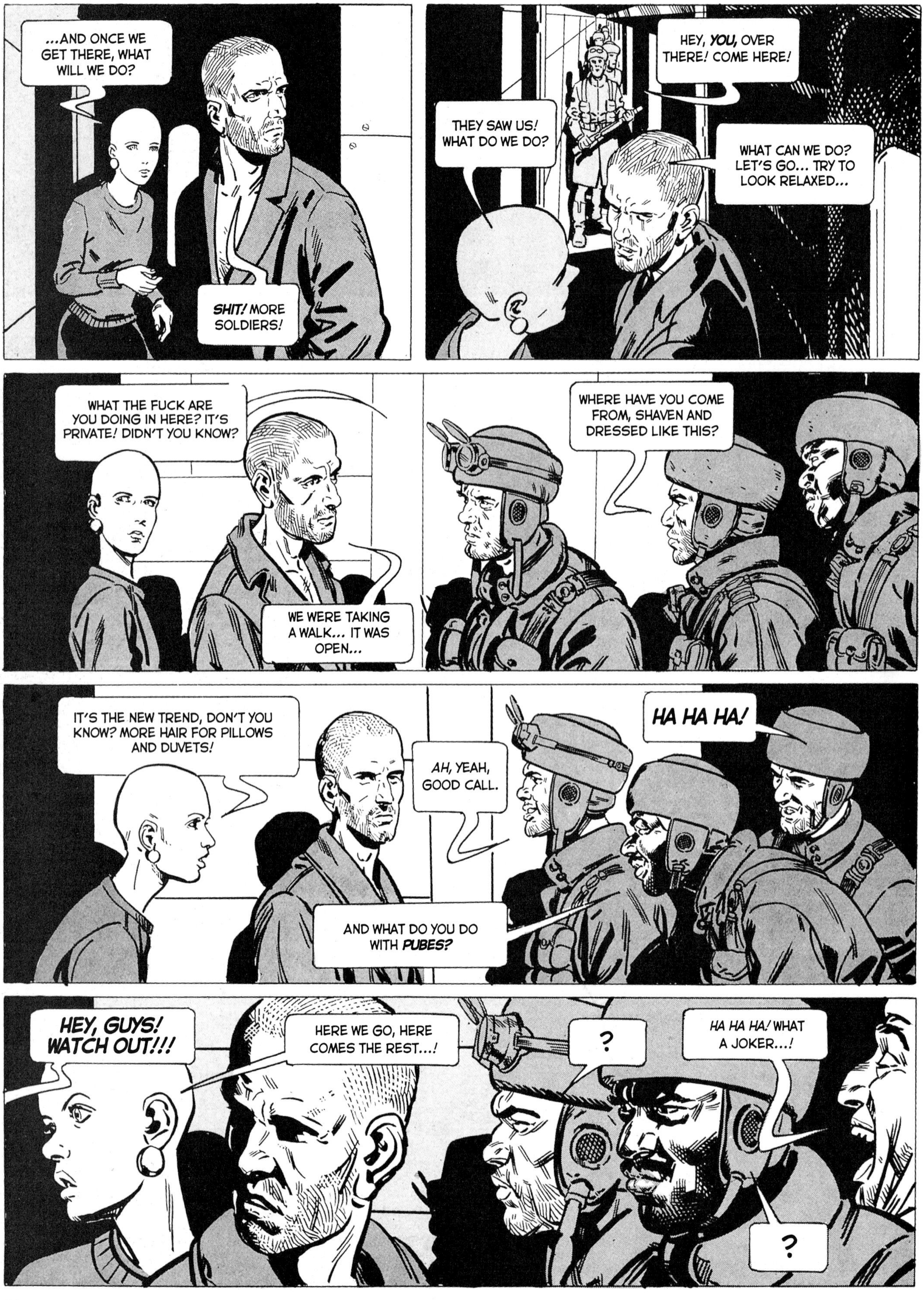
...AND ONCE WE GET THERE, WHAT WILL WE DO?
SHIT! MORE SOLDIERS!
HEY, YOU, OVER THERE! COME HERE!
THEY SAW US! WHAT DO WE DO?
WHAT CAN WE DO? LET'S GO... TRY TO LOOK RELAXED...
WHAT THE FUCK ARE YOU DOING IN HERE? IT'S PRIVATE! DIDN'T YOU KNOW?
WE WERE TAKING A WALK... IT WAS OPEN...
WHERE HAVE YOU COME FROM, SHAVEN AND DRESSED LIKE THIS?
IT'S THE NEW TREND, DON'T YOU KNOW? MORE HAIR FOR PILLOWS AND DUVETS!
AH, YEAH, GOOD CALL.
HA HA HA!
AND WHAT DO YOU DO WITH PUBES?
HEY, GUYS! WATCH OUT!!!
HERE WE GO, HERE COMES THE REST...!
?
HA HA HA! WHAT A JOKER...!
?

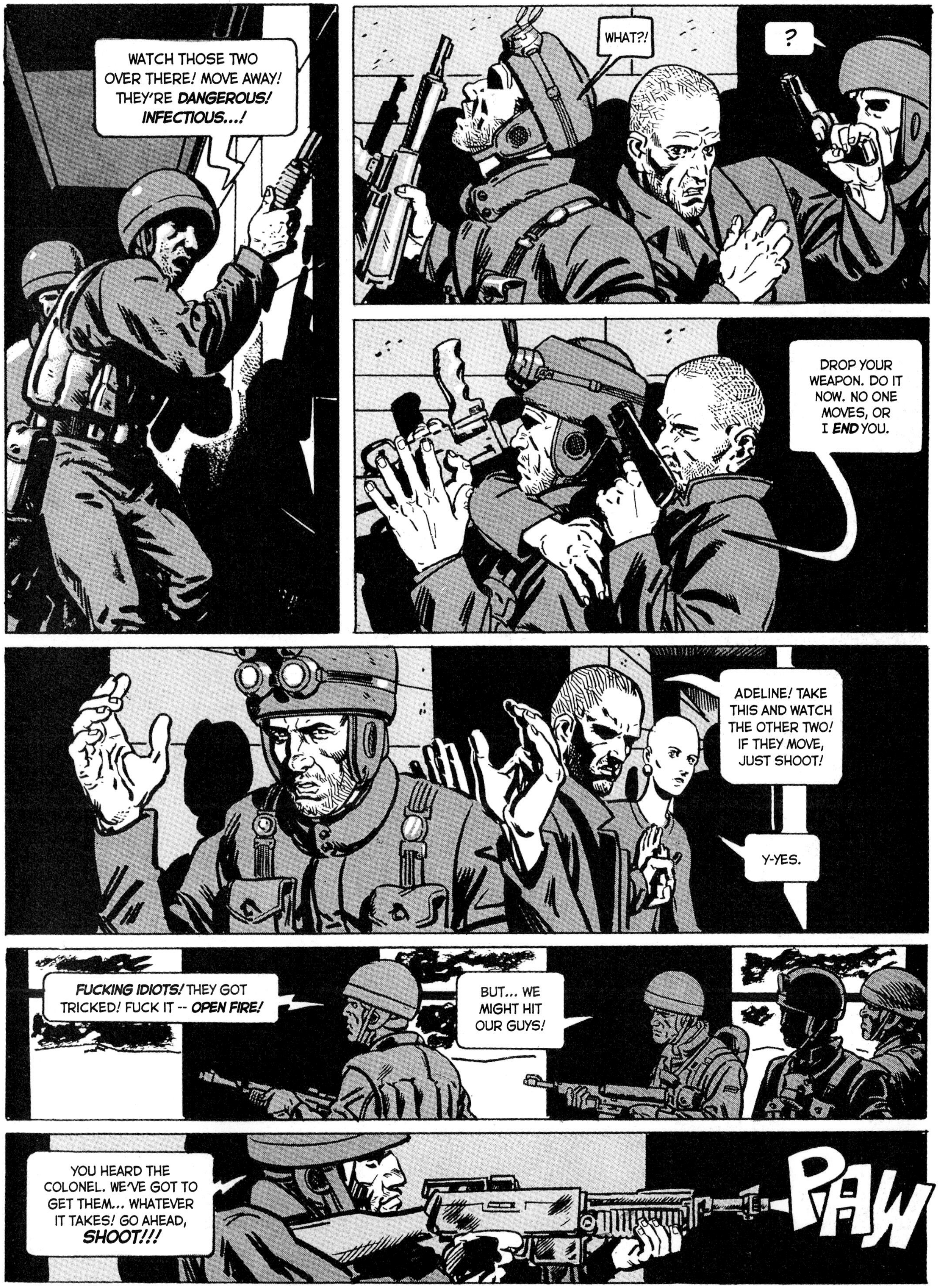

WATCH THOSE TWO OVER THERE! MOVE AWAY! THEY'RE DANGEROUS! INFECTIOUS...!
WHAT?!
?
DROP YOUR WEAPON. DO IT NOW. NO ONE MOVES, OR I END YOU.
ADELINE! TAKE THIS AND WATCH THE OTHER TWO! IF THEY MOVE, JUST SHOOT!
Y-YES.
FUCKING IDIOTS! THEY GOT TRICKED! FUCK IT -- OPEN FIRE!
BUT... WE MIGHT HIT OUR GUYS!
YOU HEARD THE COLONEL. WE'VE GOT TO GET THEM... WHATEVER IT TAKES! GO AHEAD, SHOOT!!!
PAW

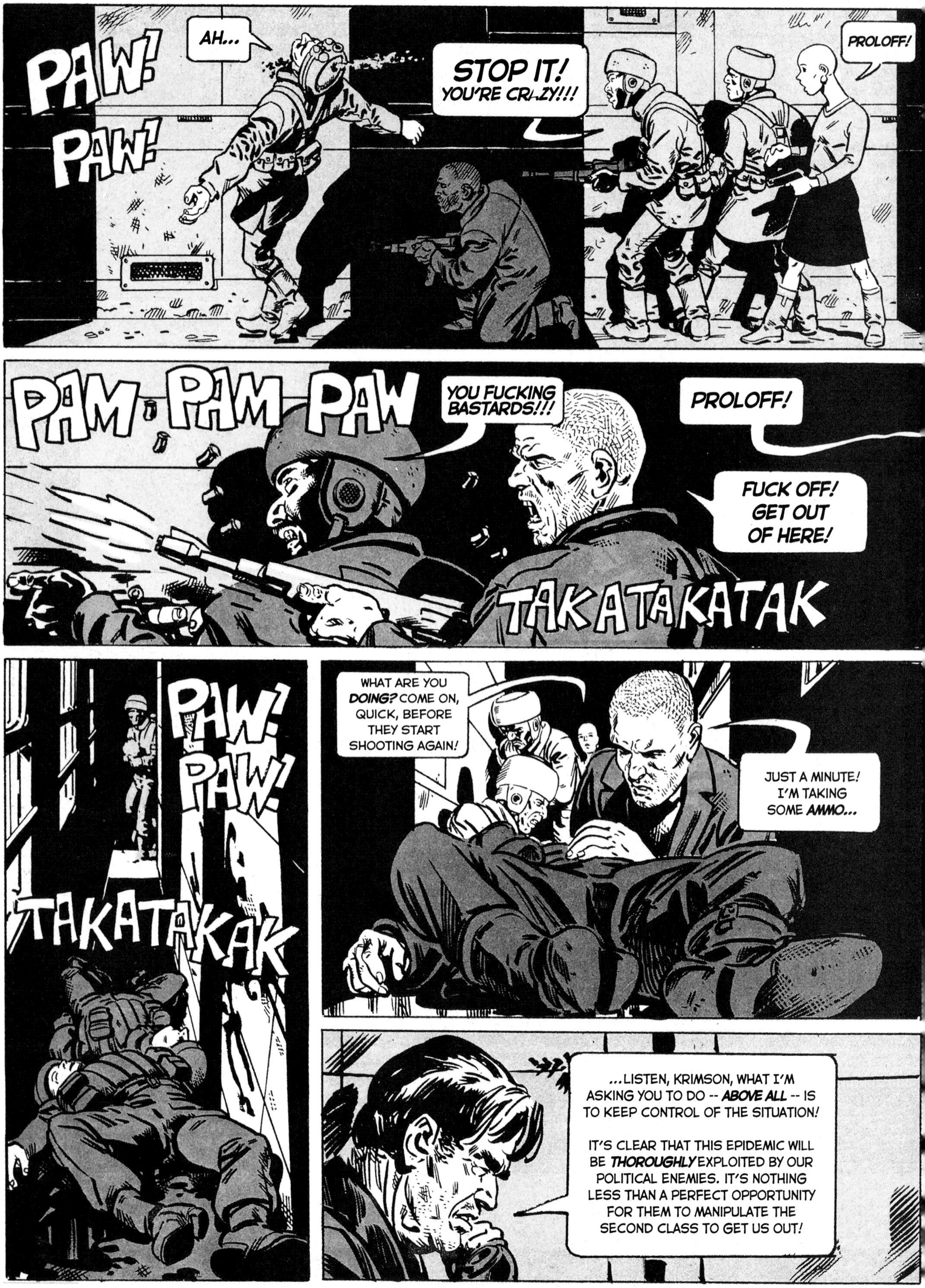

PAW!
PAW!
AH...
STOP IT! YOU'RE CRAZY!!!
PROLOFF!
PAM PAM PAW
YOU FUCKING BASTARDS!!!
PROLOFF!
FUCK OFF! GET OUT OF HERE!
TAKATAKATAK
PAW! PAW!
TAKATAKAK
WHAT ARE YOU DOING? COME ON, QUICK, BEFORE THEY START SHOOTING AGAIN!
JUST A MINUTE! I'M TAKING SOME AMMO...
...LISTEN, KRIMSON, WHAT I'M ASKING YOU TO DO -- ABOVE ALL -- IS TO KEEP CONTROL OF THE SITUATION!
IT'S CLEAR THAT THIS EPIDEMIC WILL BE THOROUGHLY EXPLOITED BY OUR POLITICAL ENEMIES. IT'S NOTHING LESS THAN A PERFECT OPPORTUNITY FOR THEM TO MANIPULATE THE SECOND CLASS TO GET US OUT!

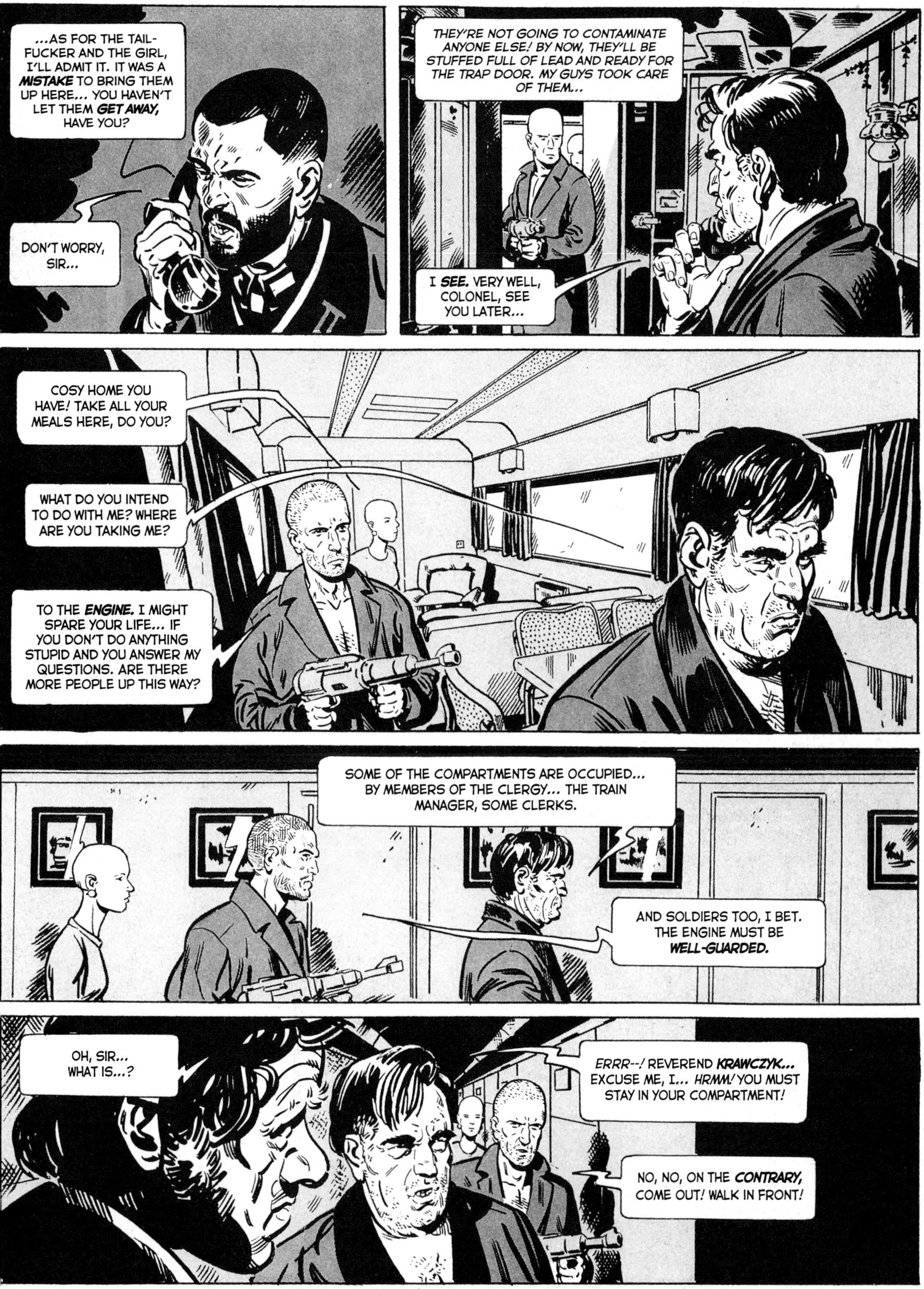

...AS FOR THE TAIL-FUCKER AND THE GIRL, I'LL ADMIT IT. IT WAS A **MISTAKE** TO BRING THEM UP HERE... YOU HAVEN'T LET THEM **GET AWAY,** HAVE YOU?
DON'T WORRY, SIR...
THEY'RE NOT GOING TO CONTAMINATE ANYONE ELSE! BY NOW, THEY'LL BE STUFFED FULL OF LEAD AND READY FOR THE TRAP DOOR. MY GUYS TOOK CARE OF THEM...
I **SEE.** VERY WELL, COLONEL, SEE YOU LATER...
COSY HOME YOU HAVE! TAKE ALL YOUR MEALS HERE, DO YOU?
WHAT DO YOU INTEND TO DO WITH ME? WHERE ARE YOU TAKING ME?
TO THE **ENGINE.** I MIGHT SPARE YOUR LIFE... IF YOU DON'T DO ANYTHING STUPID AND YOU ANSWER MY QUESTIONS. ARE THERE MORE PEOPLE UP THIS WAY?
SOME OF THE COMPARTMENTS ARE OCCUPIED... BY MEMBERS OF THE CLERGY... THE TRAIN MANAGER, SOME CLERKS.
AND SOLDIERS TOO, I BET. THE ENGINE MUST BE **WELL-GUARDED.**
OH, SIR... WHAT IS...?
ERRR--! REVEREND **KRAWCZYK...** EXCUSE ME, I... *HRMM!* YOU MUST STAY IN YOUR COMPARTMENT!
NO, NO, ON THE ***CONTRARY,*** COME OUT! WALK IN FRONT!

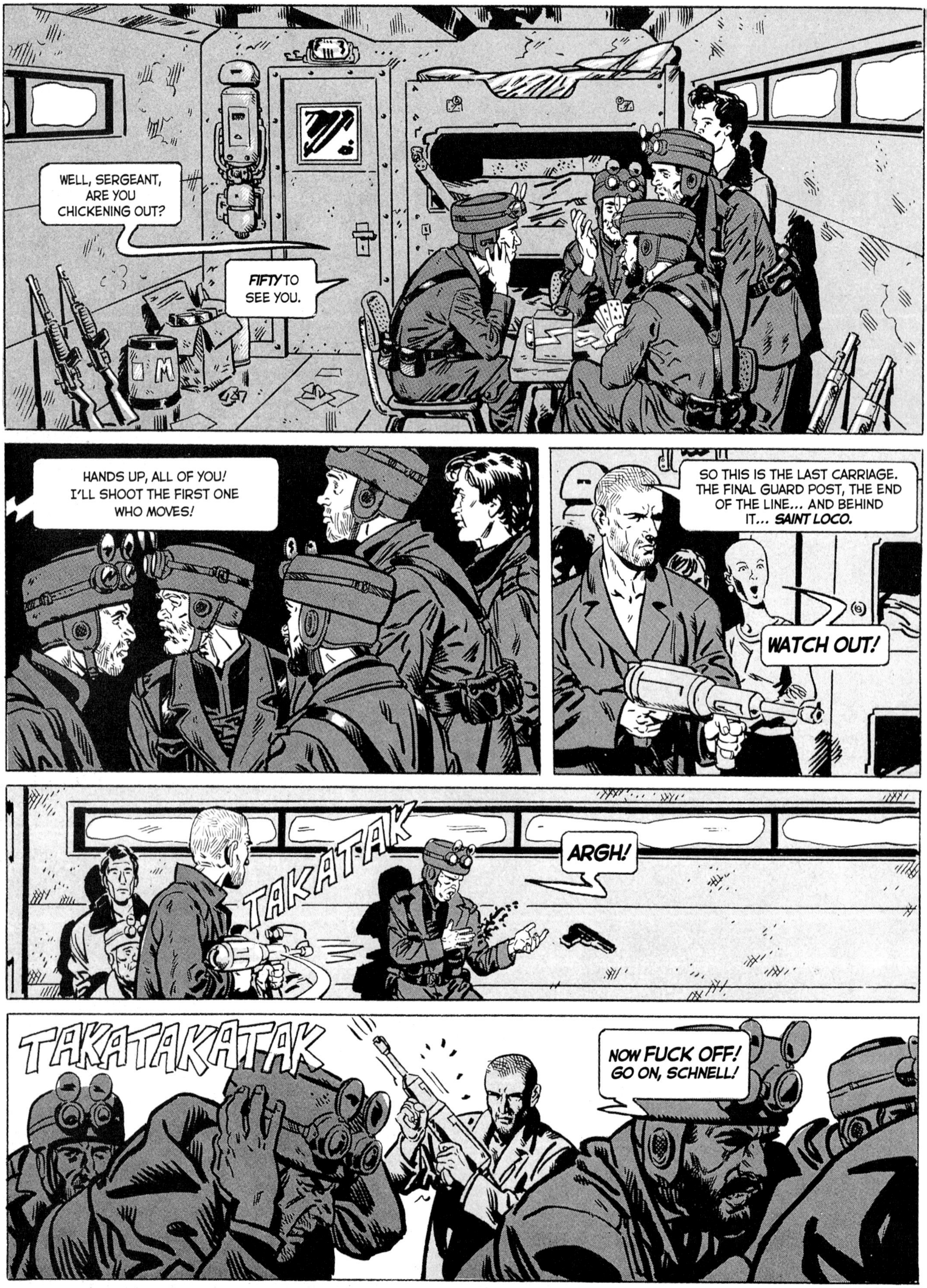
WELL, SERGEANT, ARE YOU CHICKENING OUT?
FIFTY TO SEE YOU.
HANDS UP, ALL OF YOU! I'LL SHOOT THE FIRST ONE WHO MOVES!
SO THIS IS THE LAST CARRIAGE. THE FINAL GUARD POST, THE END OF THE LINE... AND BEHIND IT... SAINT LOCO.
WATCH OUT!
TAKATAK
ARGH!
TAKATAKATAK
NOW FUCK OFF! GO ON, SCHNELL!

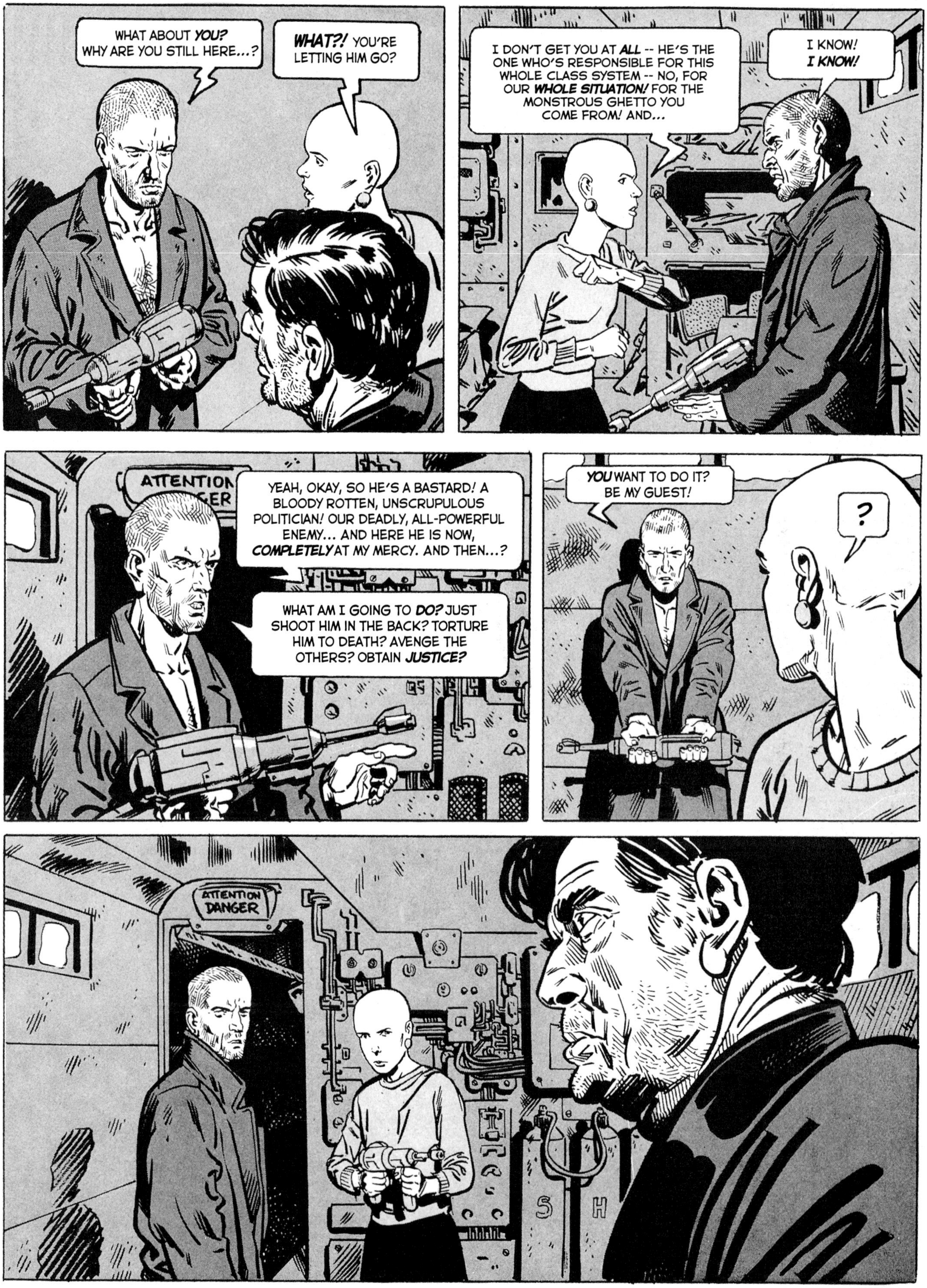
WHAT ABOUT YOU? WHY ARE YOU STILL HERE...?
WHAT?! YOU'RE LETTING HIM GO?
I DON'T GET YOU AT ALL -- HE'S THE ONE WHO'S RESPONSIBLE FOR THIS WHOLE CLASS SYSTEM -- NO, FOR OUR WHOLE SITUATION! FOR THE MONSTROUS GHETTO YOU COME FROM! AND...
I KNOW! I KNOW!
ATTENTION
YEAH, OKAY, SO HE'S A BASTARD! A BLOODY ROTTEN, UNSCRUPULOUS POLITICIAN! OUR DEADLY, ALL-POWERFUL ENEMY... AND HERE HE IS NOW, COMPLETELY AT MY MERCY. AND THEN...?
WHAT AM I GOING TO DO? JUST SHOOT HIM IN THE BACK? TORTURE HIM TO DEATH? AVENGE THE OTHERS? OBTAIN JUSTICE?
YOU WANT TO DO IT? BE MY GUEST!
?
ATTENTION DANGER

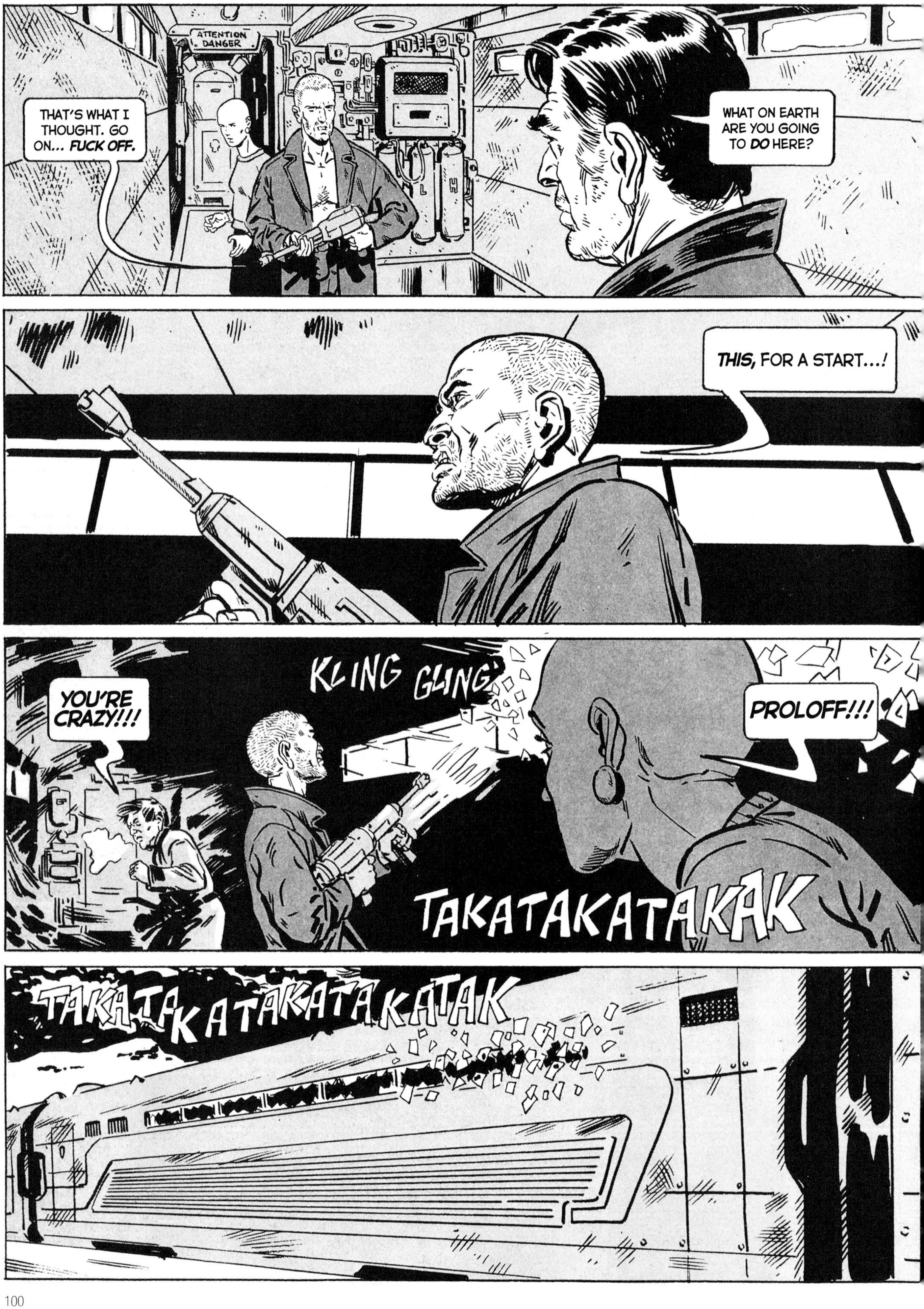

ATTENTION DANGER
THAT'S WHAT I THOUGHT. GO ON... FUCK OFF.
WHAT ON EARTH ARE YOU GOING TO DO HERE?
THIS, FOR A START...!
KLING GLING
YOU'RE CRAZY!!!
PROLOFF!!!
TAKATAKATAKAK
TAKATAKATAKATAKATAK

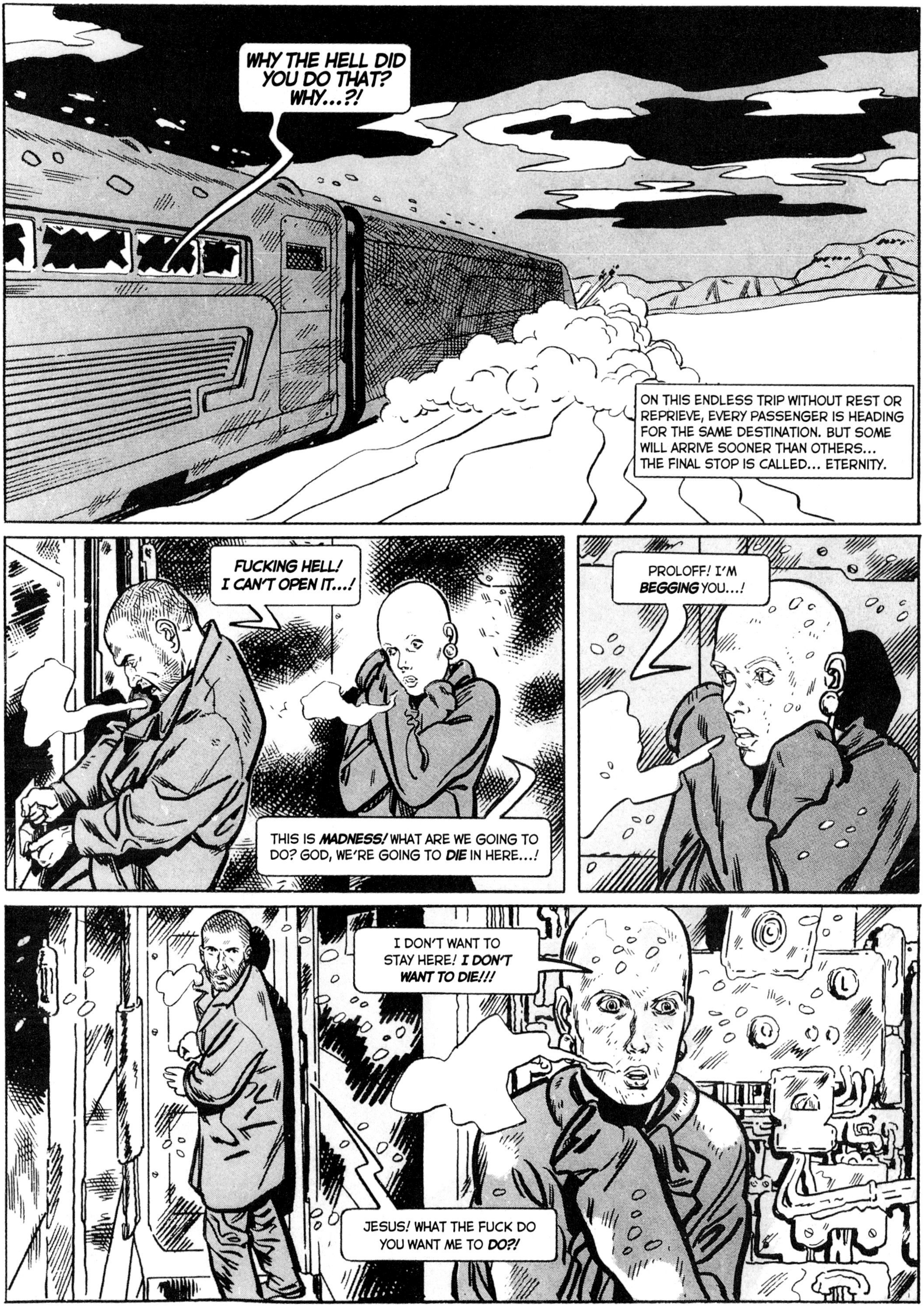
WHY THE HELL DID YOU DO THAT? WHY...?!
ON THIS ENDLESS TRIP WITHOUT REST OR REPRIEVE, EVERY PASSENGER IS HEADING FOR THE SAME DESTINATION. BUT SOME WILL ARRIVE SOONER THAN OTHERS... THE FINAL STOP IS CALLED... ETERNITY.
FUCKING HELL! I CAN'T OPEN IT...!
THIS IS MADNESS! WHAT ARE WE GOING TO DO? GOD, WE'RE GOING TO DIE IN HERE...!
PROLOFF! I'M BEGGING YOU...!
I DON'T WANT TO STAY HERE! I DON'T WANT TO DIE!!!
JESUS! WHAT THE FUCK DO YOU WANT ME TO DO?!

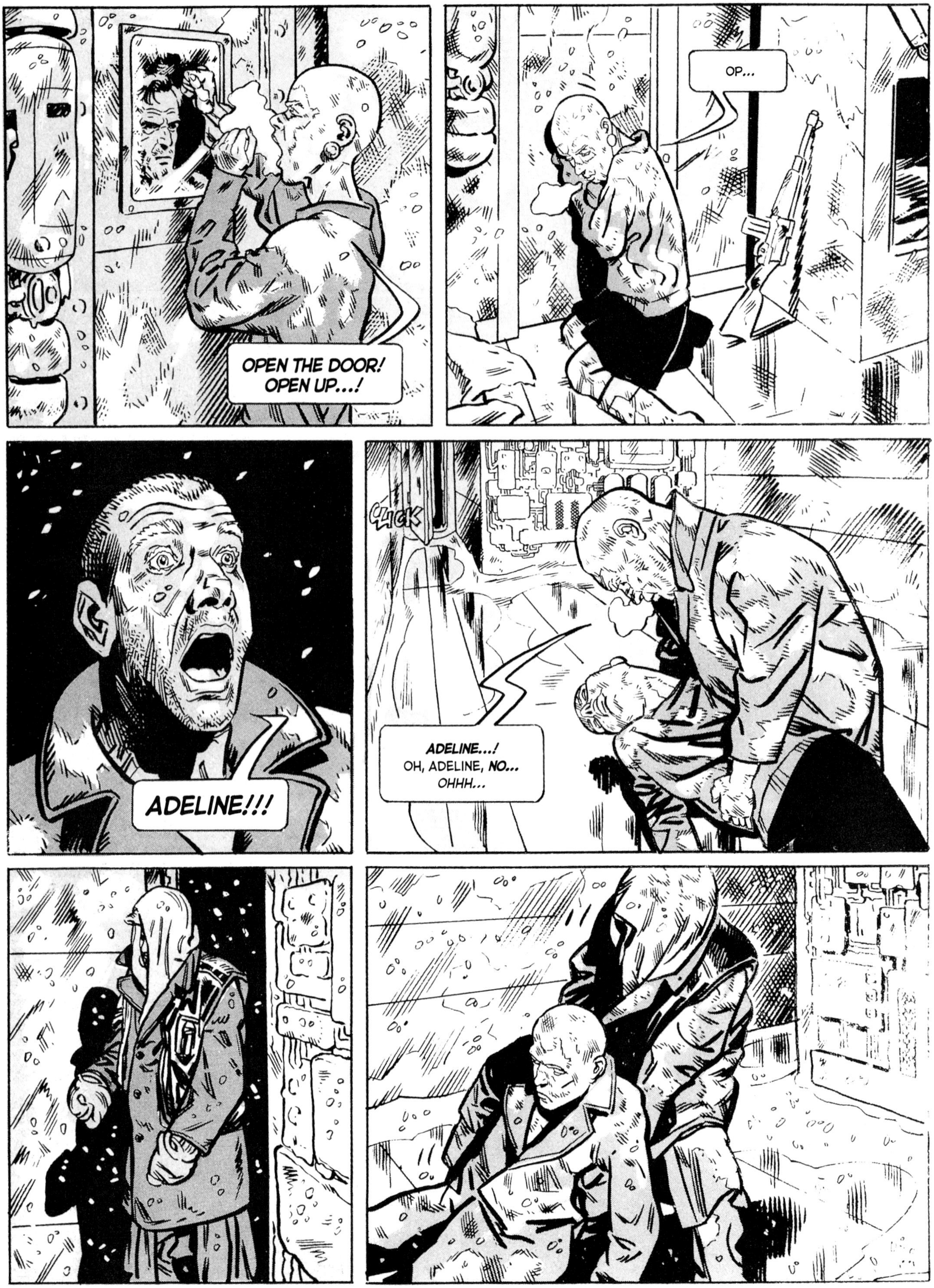
OPEN THE DOOR! OPEN UP...!
OP...
ADELINE!!!
CLICK
ADELINE...! OH, ADELINE, NO... OHHH...

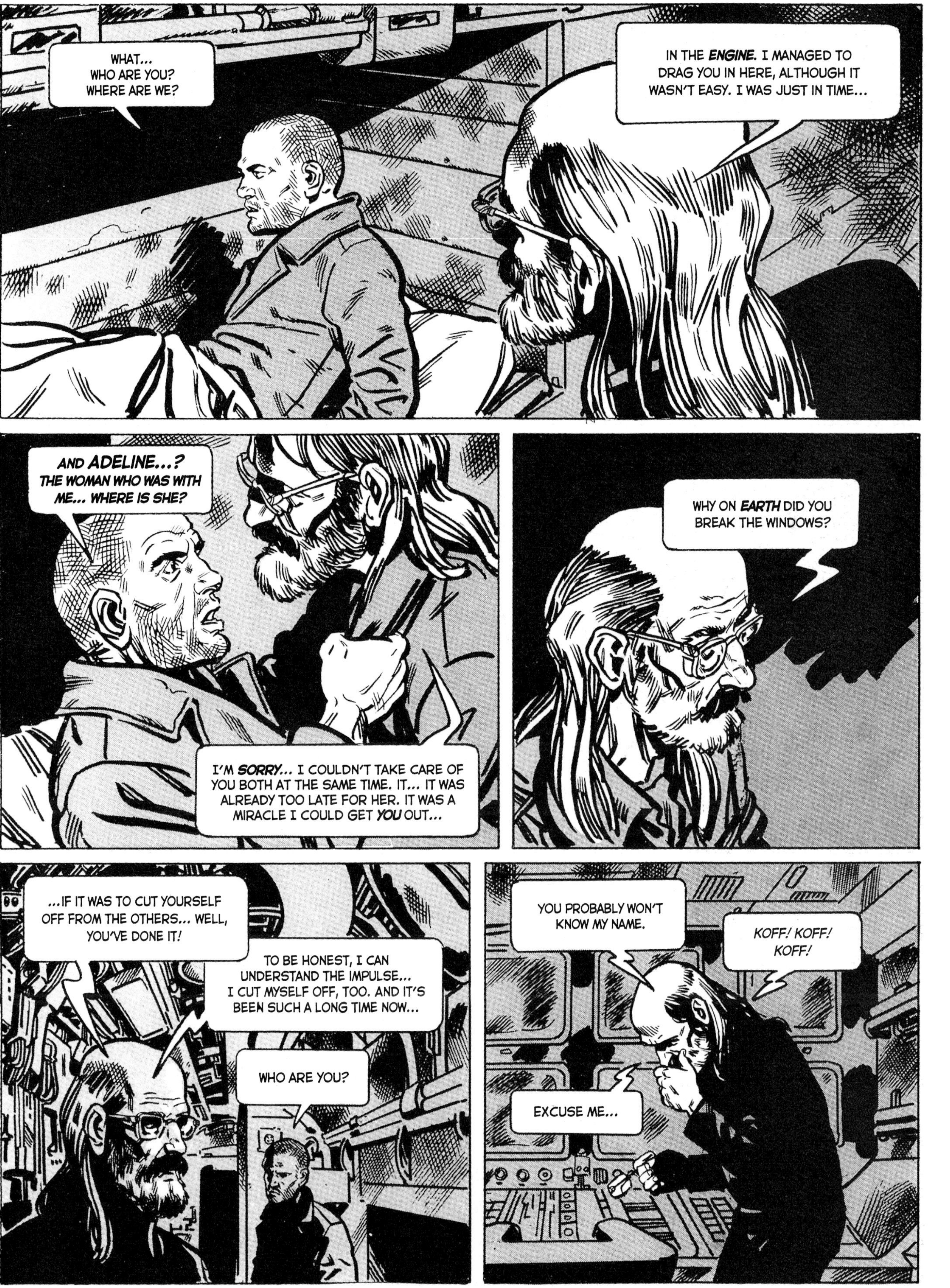
WHAT... WHO ARE YOU? WHERE ARE WE?
IN THE ENGINE. I MANAGED TO DRAG YOU IN HERE, ALTHOUGH IT WASN'T EASY. I WAS JUST IN TIME...
AND ADELINE...? THE WOMAN WHO WAS WITH ME... WHERE IS SHE?
I'M SORRY... I COULDN'T TAKE CARE OF YOU BOTH AT THE SAME TIME. IT... IT WAS ALREADY TOO LATE FOR HER. IT WAS A MIRACLE I COULD GET YOU OUT...
WHY ON EARTH DID YOU BREAK THE WINDOWS?
...IF IT WAS TO CUT YOURSELF OFF FROM THE OTHERS... WELL, YOU'VE DONE IT!
TO BE HONEST, I CAN UNDERSTAND THE IMPULSE... I CUT MYSELF OFF, TOO. AND IT'S BEEN SUCH A LONG TIME NOW...
WHO ARE YOU?
YOU PROBABLY WON'T KNOW MY NAME.
KOFF! KOFF! KOFF!
EXCUSE ME...

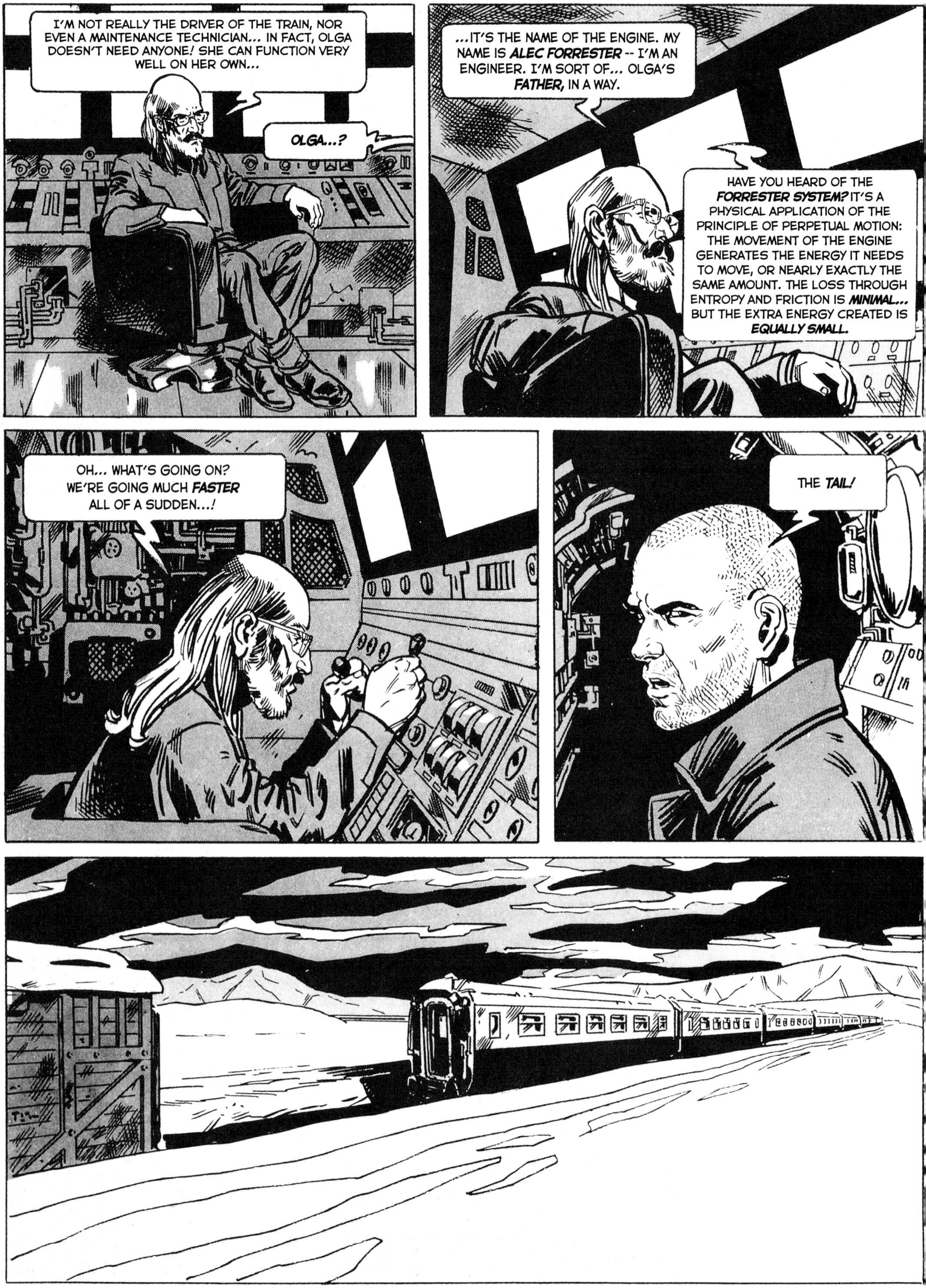
I'M NOT REALLY THE DRIVER OF THE TRAIN, NOR EVEN A MAINTENANCE TECHNICIAN... IN FACT, OLGA DOESN'T NEED ANYONE! SHE CAN FUNCTION VERY WELL ON HER OWN...
OLGA...?
...IT'S THE NAME OF THE ENGINE. MY NAME IS ALEC FORRESTER -- I'M AN ENGINEER. I'M SORT OF... OLGA'S FATHER, IN A WAY.
HAVE YOU HEARD OF THE FORRESTER SYSTEM? IT'S A PHYSICAL APPLICATION OF THE PRINCIPLE OF PERPETUAL MOTION: THE MOVEMENT OF THE ENGINE GENERATES THE ENERGY IT NEEDS TO MOVE, OR NEARLY EXACTLY THE SAME AMOUNT. THE LOSS THROUGH ENTROPY AND FRICTION IS MINIMAL... BUT THE EXTRA ENERGY CREATED IS EQUALLY SMALL.
OH... WHAT'S GOING ON? WE'RE GOING MUCH FASTER ALL OF A SUDDEN...!
THE TAIL!

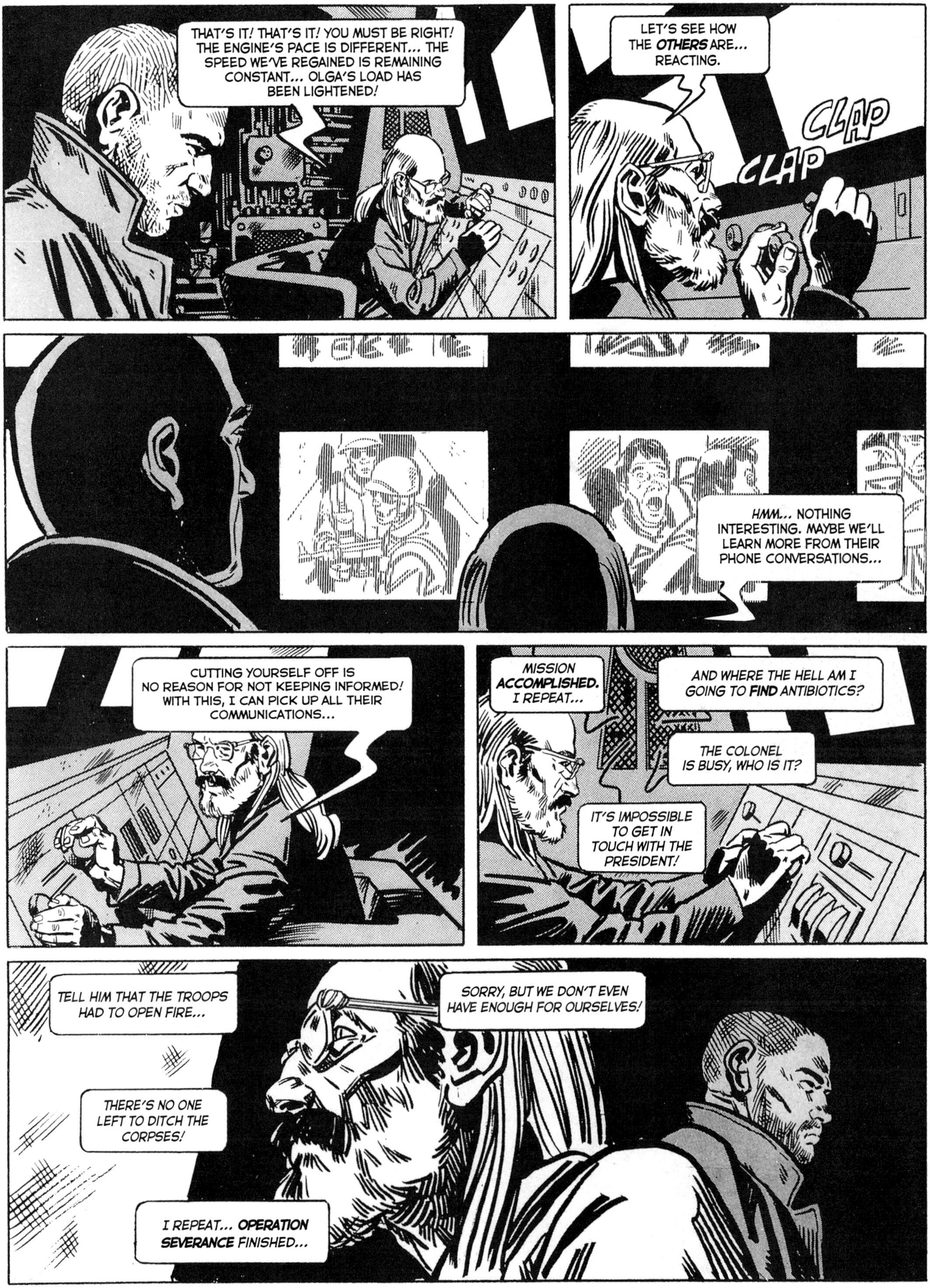
THAT'S IT! THAT'S IT! YOU MUST BE RIGHT! THE ENGINE'S PACE IS DIFFERENT... THE SPEED WE'VE REGAINED IS REMAINING CONSTANT... OLGA'S LOAD HAS BEEN LIGHTENED!
LET'S SEE HOW THE **OTHERS** ARE... REACTING.
CLAP
CLAP
HMM... NOTHING INTERESTING. MAYBE WE'LL LEARN MORE FROM THEIR PHONE CONVERSATIONS...
CUTTING YOURSELF OFF IS NO REASON FOR NOT KEEPING INFORMED! WITH THIS, I CAN PICK UP ALL THEIR COMMUNICATIONS...
MISSION ***ACCOMPLISHED.*** *I REPEAT...*
AND WHERE THE HELL AM I GOING TO ***FIND*** *ANTIBIOTICS?*
THE COLONEL IS BUSY, WHO IS IT?
IT'S IMPOSSIBLE TO GET IN TOUCH WITH THE PRESIDENT!
TELL HIM THAT THE TROOPS HAD TO OPEN FIRE...
SORRY, BUT WE DON'T EVEN HAVE ENOUGH FOR OURSELVES!
THERE'S NO ONE LEFT TO DITCH THE CORPSES!
I REPEAT... ***OPERATION SEVERANCE*** *FINISHED...*

... AT THE BEGINNING, I LIVED IN ONE OF THE CARRIAGES, WAY DOWN AT THE BACK. BUT I WAS HERE MOST DAYS, LOOKING AFTER THE ENGINE...

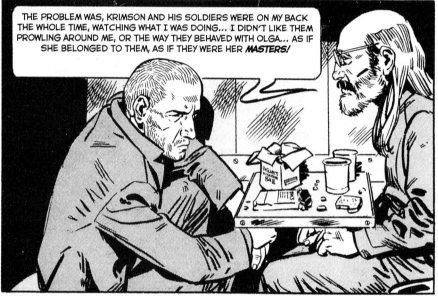

THE PROBLEM WAS, KRIMSON AND HIS SOLDIERS WERE ON MY BACK THE WHOLE TIME, WATCHING WHAT I WAS DOING... I DIDN'T LIKE THEM PROWLING AROUND ME, OR THE WAY THEY BEHAVED WITH OLGA... AS IF SHE BELONGED TO THEM, AS IF THEY WERE HER *MASTERS!*

I COULD SEE, TOO, THAT THEY DIDN'T TRUST ME... THAT THEY WERE PLOTTING BEHIND MY BACK TO REPLACE ME...

BUT THE THING IS, I WAS *SMARTER* THAN THEM! I KNEW WHAT THEY WERE UP TO... I HAD TIME TO GET READY, TO PREPARE! AND ONE DAY...

KOFF! KOFF! KOFF!

KOFF! KOFF!

...YOU'RE NOT *EATING?* YOU HAVEN'T HAD ANYTHING ALL DAY...

IN SHORT, I SLAMMED THE DOOR ON THEM FOR GOOD! THEY CAN'T REACH ME ANYMORE. I TOOK MY PRECAUTIONS, BUILT MY REDOUBTS... THIS IS MY HOME! I'M THE MASTER OF THE TRAIN!

AND I'VE GOT EVERYTHING I NEED TO HOLD OUT... EVEN THOUGH I'M NOT GOING TO LAST VERY LONG...

IT'S BECAUSE OF *HER*, RIGHT? IT'S HER YOU'RE THINKING OF?

YES.

IT'S MY FAULT SHE DIED.... IT'S... IT'S AS IF I'D KILLED HER.

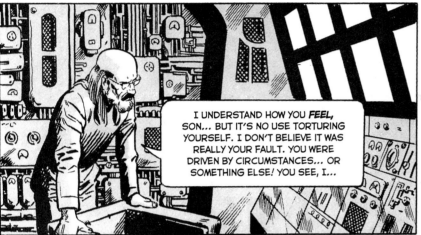

I UNDERSTAND HOW YOU *FEEL*, SON... BUT IT'S NO USE TORTURING YOURSELF. I DON'T BELIEVE IT WAS REALLY YOUR FAULT. YOU WERE DRIVEN BY CIRCUMSTANCES... OR SOMETHING ELSE! YOU SEE, I...

KOFF! KOFF! KOFF! KOFF! KOFF!

THESE COUGHING FITS ARE *EXHAUSTING*... SORRY, WHERE WAS I...?

...YES, YOUR ARRIVAL HERE... FROM THE TAIL... THE FACT THAT YOU MANAGED TO GET THROUGH ALL THE OBSTACLES TO REACH ME... IT'S A *SIGN...!* THAT'S WHY I SAVED YOU. I WAS WAITING FOR YOU, IN A WAY...

?

YOU SEE, FOR ME, THE JOURNEY WILL SOON BE OVER.... I KNOW I DON'T HAVE LONG... AND IT...

...IT WOULD HAVE *BOTHERED* ME TO LEAVE OLGA ALL ALONE...

I THOUGHT THE LOCOMOTIVE DIDN'T *NEED* ANYONE TO FUNCTION...

OH, *ABSOLUTELY!* OLGA IS NOT LIKE OTHER MACHINES!

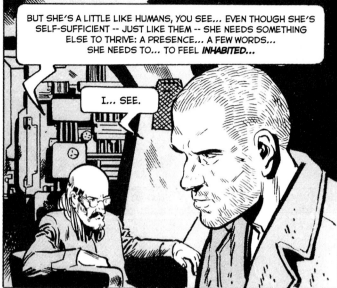

BUT SHE'S A LITTLE LIKE HUMANS, YOU SEE... EVEN THOUGH SHE'S SELF-SUFFICIENT -- JUST LIKE THEM -- SHE NEEDS SOMETHING ELSE TO THRIVE: A PRESENCE... A FEW WORDS... SHE NEEDS TO... TO FEEL *INHABITED*...

I... SEE.

...WITH TIME... YOU, TOO, WILL LEARN TO KNOW AND LOVE HER.

WAIT... IF I UNDERSTAND CORRECTLY, YOU'RE COUNTING ON ME TO -- UH -- *TAKE OVER* LOOKING AFTER HER?

OF COURSE. YOU'LL SEE, IT'S NOT VERY COMPLICATED. WHAT'S IMPORTANT IS YOUR *PRESENCE*... DON'T FORGET --THE SURVIVAL OF THE TRAIN AND ITS THOUSANDS OF INHABITANTS DEPENDS ON OLGA'S UNINTERRUPTED FUNCTION...

SO *WHAT?* I DON'T GIVE A *DAMN* ABOUT THE SURVIVAL OF THE TRAIN!

CALM DOWN, SON. I UNDERSTAND HOW YOU FEEL, BUT... BEYOND INDIVIDUAL FEELINGS, WHAT MATTERS IS THAT WE SAFEGUARD BOTH *CIVILIZATION* AND *HUMANITY*... OR AT LEAST, WHAT'S LEFT OF THEM. THAT'S OUR MISSION: TO PRESERVE WHAT'S LEFT... WHICH IS THE TRAIN.

IN ANY CASE, YOU DON'T REALLY HAVE A *CHOICE.*

AT LEAST *HERE,* YOU'LL BE LEFT IN PEACE... SOON *I* WON'T BE HERE ANYMORE... NO ONE TO BOTHER YOU ⸘KOFF! KOFF!⸘... AND THERE'S OLGA! ...SHE'LL KEEP YOU WARM AND SAFE... I'M SURE THAT--

ENOUGH!!!

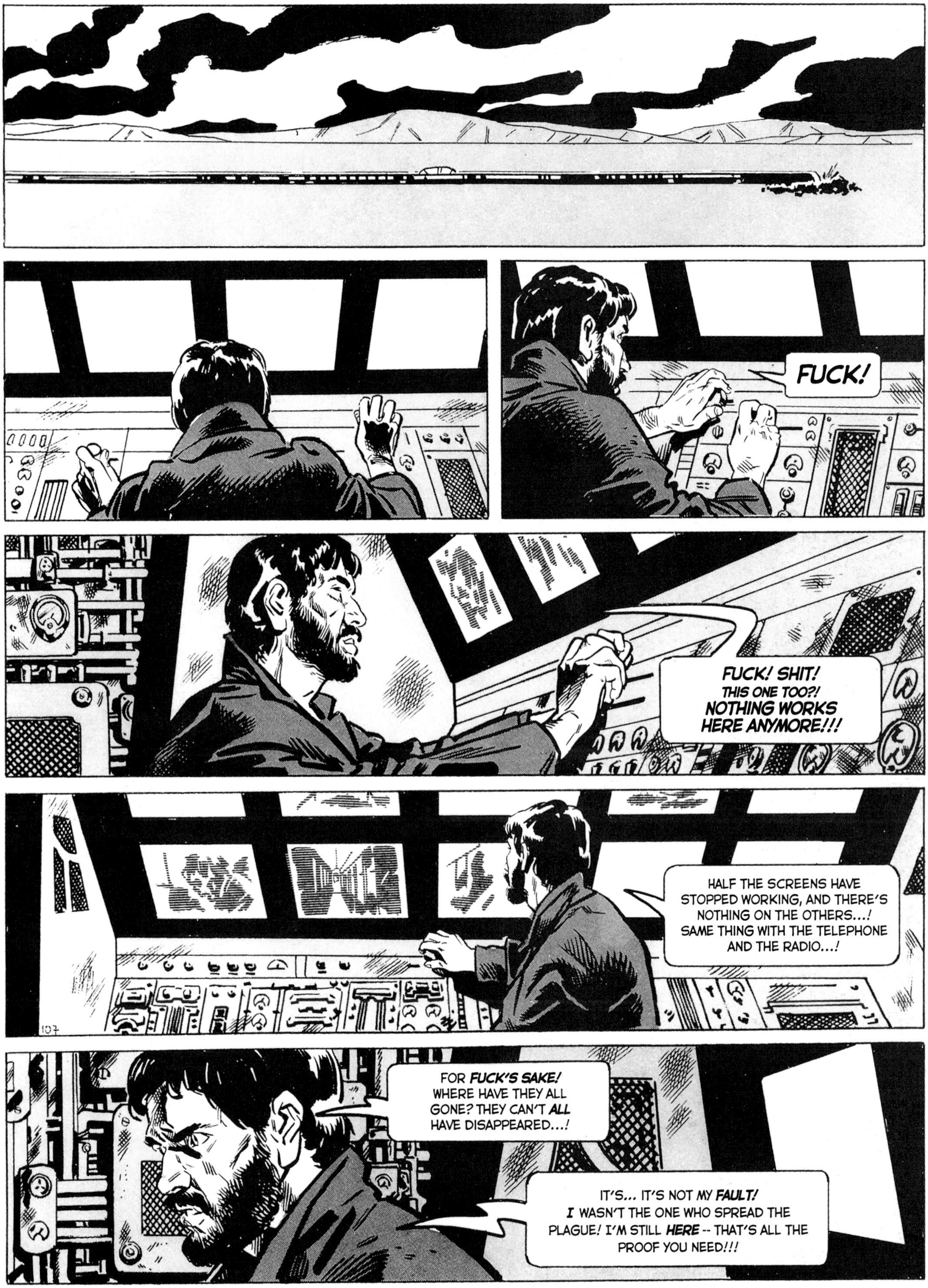
FUCK!
FUCK! SHIT! THIS ONE TOO?! NOTHING WORKS HERE ANYMORE!!!
HALF THE SCREENS HAVE STOPPED WORKING, AND THERE'S NOTHING ON THE OTHERS...! SAME THING WITH THE TELEPHONE AND THE RADIO...!
FOR FUCK'S SAKE! WHERE HAVE THEY ALL GONE? THEY CAN'T ALL HAVE DISAPPEARED...!
IT'S... IT'S NOT MY FAULT! I WASN'T THE ONE WHO SPREAD THE PLAGUE! I'M STILL HERE -- THAT'S ALL THE PROOF YOU NEED!!!

...IN ANY CASE, I DON'T HAVE MUCH LONGER... WE'RE *ALL* CONDEMNED MEN... ME -- JUST LIKE ALL THE OTHERS! SOONER OR LATER -- IT'S JUST A QUESTION OF *TIME.* THE TRAIN MAY USE A PERPETUAL MOTION ENGINE, BUT THAT DOESN'T MEAN SHE'S ETERNAL! SHE'LL HAVE TO STOP ONE DAY...

HEY! BITCH! WILL YOU STOP?

BONK

WHAT...? WHO'S... WHO'S *THERE?* IS THAT YOU, ADELINE...?

I -- I COULD'VE SWORN THERE WAS A KNOCK ON THE DOOR...

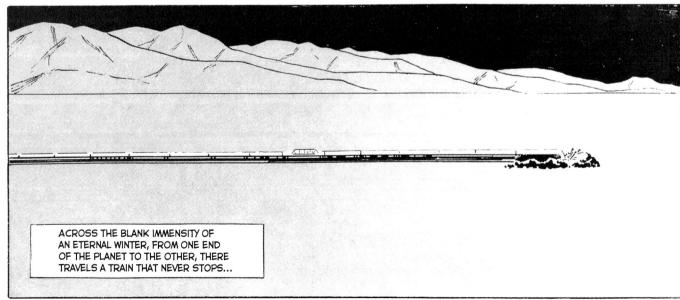

ACROSS THE BLANK IMMENSITY OF AN ETERNAL WINTER, FROM ONE END OF THE PLANET TO THE OTHER, THERE TRAVELS A TRAIN THAT NEVER STOPS...